Heroes in Hard Times

Cop Action Movies in the U.S.

HEROES
IN HARD
TIMES

Cop Action Movies in the U.S.

Neal King

Temple University Press
PHILADELPHIA

Temple University Press, Philadelphia 19122
Copyright © 1999 by Temple University
All rights reserved
Published 1999
Printed in the United States of America

♾ The paper used in this publication meets the requirements of
American National Standard for Information Sciences—Permanence
of Paper for Printed Library Materials, ANSI Z39.48-1984

Library of Congress Cataloging-in-Publication Data

King, Neal, 1963–
        Heroes in hard times : cop action movies in the U.S. / Neal King.
            p.   cm.
        Includes bibliographical references and index.
        ISBN 1-56639-701-4 (cloth : alk. paper). — ISBN 1-56639-702-2
    (paper : alk. paper)
        1. Police films—History and criticism.   I. Title.
    PN 1995.9.P57K56   1999
    791.43'655—dc21   98-56149

Contents

Preface

I saw my first white guy get his head blown off in 1982 during a cable TV showing of *The Border*. The guy runs Latinos over the border in Texas and profits from their deaths, but during a scrap with the hero he falls on his shotgun and . . . blam! Later the hero shoots the tires from under a truck sheltering another bad white guy, who screams as he's crushed. I got a charge from the gruesome violence and did not understand why for another ten years. By then I had begun to think about white male guilt and its punishment in our popular culture. Bad white men abound and die in awful ways in the movies we watch, and I wrote this book both to interpret that bloodshed and to argue with fellow scholars about what it means.

My journey toward this study began with a love of violent movies in which men abuse each other (I shied from slashers, rape-revenge, and westerns in which they rape and murder women). A few years ago, a like-minded colleague and I noticed that manhood seems to drive most Hollywood product: Male heroes abound, young boys mull over their coming-of-age, concerns for potency color many plots and scenes. Then one day I watched *Die Hard*. This engaging movie, in which a cop rescues corporate partygoers from murderous bandits, seemed to work over male privilege and anal sex, of all things.[1] That in mind, and my interest piqued, I reviewed the genre that *Die Hard* represents. This book studies 193 of those movies in some detail and argues that they address economic and moral hard times in the United States.

As I make this argument, I also bicker with an analytic literature about what cop movies mean. Though few people study much cop action, many sociologists, historians, literary and film analysts, and nonacademic researchers have written about a few movies. A list of references would run too long to reproduce here, in part because dozens of analysts with other axes to grind mention cop action movies here and there, devoting a paragraph or a page.[2] Many of them provide little support for their arguments; the writers did not intend close study and simply pass quick judgment. A few manage mini genre studies, analyzing a handful of similar interracial-male-bonding movies.[3] Though some analysts pay more attention to the uniquely cinematic qualities of these stories than do others,[4] virtually all regard the movies in terms of race, class, gender, and sexuality. Many critique the genre as hiding its politics; and most find movies to be in some ways racist, homophobic, individualist, pro-Reagan, capitalist, or misogynist. Some analysts seem to have fun finding loopy subtexts, homoerotic mainly; at least as many seem offended by the movies.

This book adds to that literature a comprehensive definition of the genre, a look at its massive scope, and thus a picture of trends across it. Does *Lethal Weapon* typify cop action? What light do the other movies shed on its horseplay? Do analysts' casual remarks about action movies in general hold water? Assuming that the meaning of a genre movie depends upon patterns in the larger set, I find, for instance, that *Lethal Weapon* looks different to me than to most of the other authors who write about it (see the end of Chapter 5 for more on this).

I especially want to argue with colleagues over the moral complexity and self-awareness of oppressive straight white men. In other words, lots of white guys in cop action turn out to be bad; but do they know it and what do they think about it? Much of the literature imputes both reactionary machismo and political blindness to the genre, accusing it of cynical contradiction, erasure of its historical roots, and vain attempts to make narrative sense as it follows its evil impulses. In such a view oppressors know not what they do; and whiteness, heterosexuality, and manhood remain ignorant charades to be understood mainly by professional class analysts, certainly not by the cops or anyone else in the cop action world. Even when analysts do find "critical" impulses in movies, they argue that forces of "hegemony" or "recuperation" blunt them to the point of uselessness or nonsense.

I will show, however, that cops often spell out the place of racism, misogyny, and capitalist greed in their world. The genre concerns itself directly with political struggle, in a way that anyone who listens to what these characters say can hear. Heroes often describe themselves as spoiled louts who deserve punishment for their collective sins. When others say as much heroes tend not to argue. At the same time, they are these movies' heroes, and they expect a lot of attention paid to their faults and to their dreams of solving their own and their nation's problems. At the very least, I find little reason to think that cops cannot reckon their political situation, their responsibility for it, or the political impulses that drive them into male-bonding and bone-crunching battle. Rather than regard these movies as pernicious, vacuous, illogical, or contradictory, then, I assume that they can make useful sense about the political culture of "losing ground" in which people feel their world going to hell. Rather than compare my own political knowledge and sensibilities to those of the cop action universe, only to find the latter lacking, I approach it as a cracked mirror that we can hold up to ourselves, to see those whom we sometimes blame for our problems. Cop movies can tell us a lot about some of our deepest collective feelings.

In the late-twentieth-century United States, we find many of the privileges long taken for granted now in the forum of public debate and called either unearned perks or natural rights, depending on one's politics. This contest forms the culture of "losing ground" in which I situate these movies. Cop action forms a fictional culture in which we can read some of the fantasies that make up our political scene, the way many of us can imagine dealing with lost ground, class guilt, and the punishment of evil. I like cop movies because they direct our anger with their firepower and speak a collective desire to blame terrible behaviors for our problems. With their grisly violence they stage public abuse of our oppressors; and it matters whom they punish. I'd like to get fans talking about this aspect of these movies and thus tie the pleasures of any movie to the genre's larger politics. I want to see how people speak differently about their society once armed or saddled with the moral baggage carried by these violent characters.

Hence, I use my long experience as a fan to make sense of these movies, and I join that fandom to sociology (steeped in studies of race, class, gender, and sexuality; political contest in general; and the interpretation of film) to render an entire genre sensible in terms of an era of lost ground. The most useful analyses come from those who really love what they study, in a complex, ambivalent "family" way. Even if I remain embarrassed by the defensiveness of cop heroes and the marginal status they accord everyone else, I'm happy to claim ideological kinship. Cops and I share fantastic worlds and address the same problems. I hope that my work benefits from the affection with which I approach this politically charged, wonderfully brutal, and frustratingly straight-white-male-centered genre.

I am pleased to acknowledge that this research bears the marks of patient care from teachers and editors including Janet Francendese, Avery Gordon, Laura Grindstaff, Kent "Aries" Irwin, Michael Kimmel, Wendy Marks, Wayne Mellinger, Frances Montell, Robert Nideffer, Constance Penley, Beth Schneider, Alison Streit, and Joan Weston. This project actually began in conversations with Robin Lloyd, who took me to movies and encouraged me over long years. Most signs of skill or rigor to be found within come of Sarah Fenstermaker's long-term investments in my training and Martha McCaughey's collegial engagement. As far as the good stuff goes, these two have made me the writer I am. Any lack of focus or foundation, however, must stem from exposure to the movie violence to which I enjoy an untreated addiction.

Finally, Toni Calasanti has helped me through the final stages of this project in the nicest possible way, without seeing a single cop movie.

Heroes in Hard Times

Cop Action Movies in the U.S.

1 Losing Ground at the Movies

"**F**uck that, fuck you, fuck that! Look at him. He's nothing. The guy's a piece of shit."

Joe the piece of shit (and the Last Boy Scout) is a private eye, captive of a wealthy criminal, and object of a thug's abuse. Joe asks the latter, "You got a cigarette?"

"Cigarette? Yeah, sure, I got a cigarette."

"You got a light?"

"Yeah, I got a light." But with the light comes a painful crack to Joe's jaw.

The thug chuckles over the bleeding captive, "Hey Baby, I thought you were tough. See, Pablo," he says to the other thug, who toys at a piano, "he's not so bad."

But Joe isn't finished: "I seem to have dropped my cigarette," he says in measured provocation. "May I have another?"

Intrigued, the thug plays along. "Sure. Sure thing, Buddy."

"I'm going to need a light," Joe whispers in warning, "If you touch me again, I'll kill you."

The thug whispers back, "You know I'm going to touch you," and then gives Joe his light and a truly vicious blow to the jaw. Jubilant, he rejoices over his fallen victim: "Bumba! Baby! Haaaa haa ha! Ooooh, Baby! Two for two. We've got two for—" But Joe suddenly comes back with a punch of his own and knocks the thug to the floor dead.

Problem Movies

Cops love their self-abusing vengeance and never more than when they fight rich and perverse white men. *The Last Boy Scout* well represents the cop action genre. Working-class community protectors—cops, for short—blow through racial guilt, sexual hostility, and class resentment with a wise-cracking defiance and a lot of firepower. By pitting themselves against the rich, racist, and woman-hating criminal class, cops stand tall at the centers of their stories. Hard times give them opportunities to retake the center stage they feel they've lost. While on that stage, with all eyes fixed upon them, heroes find privilege, guilt, and dishonor among white men; target the richest with their gunplay; and do their own bloody penance for white male sins. They stake out a white guy turf on which they can star as the most qualified, while they punish the evil around and within them.

In a world that has lost ground to lunacy and greed,[1] cops possess the killing skills they'll need to protect their society from the very corruption that has: (1) given white guys lions' shares of our world's resources, (2) made them look like nasty oppressors to their families and colleagues, and (3) eaten at their status by corrupting their valued blue-collar/professional jobs and turning them into low-status service workers. Cops are not sure what to do about this, and the genre tells stories in which they make some hard decisions. Cop action fixes on arguments over the privileges that so many feel they have lost to moral and economic decline, and it tells a story about workers in a diminishing world. Through close study of the 193 movies that formed the cop action genre from 1980 through 1997, I show how cops mount a morality play about what different people deserve, how they lost it, and what they can do about it.

Cop action mixes the following elements: Whether in law enforcement or civilian work, heroes protect people from harm. They face combinations of three threats to their happiness: alienation from employers, estrangement from loved ones, and violence from criminals. Heroes join forces with fellow employees or bystanders (sidekicks) who give support. Together the heroes and sidekicks argue about class, gender, or race relations and then defeat the criminals with bloody violence. By the conclusions of these stories many heroes have bettered their lives—reconciled with intimates, forged bonds with sidekicks, massacred enemies, or earned respect from communities they have saved. But just as many other heroes have suffered serious losses, most rooted in the guilt they share with the criminals they hunt.

Cop action plays to a wide and hungry audience, and so I train my analysis on the genre's characters and the moral lessons that their heroism offers onlookers. Not all cop action movies hit big, but most make money, and many find huge audiences (the "dirty" Harry, *Die Hard,* and *Lethal Weapon* series, for instance). Some loose and changing combination of the elements of cop action movies must draw our collective interest: the plot structures, the brawny stars, the graphic violence to male bodies, and the good ol' boy humor that keeps murderous movies from becoming too grim. While I cannot describe which qualities in which combinations draw crowds to which movie, I can show what fantasies of sin, guilt, and revenge these movies offer to people losing ground and arguing over privilege. That is, leaving aside the issue of any consumer's interpretation, I treat the genre as a set of stories guided by a common, though complex, moral logic. Assuming that they owe their mass success to more than a big coincidence, I describe how cop action speaks to political struggles and fantasies of rage. Movies can seem "right" if they reflect common assumptions about the world and offer ways to make sense of it. The moral logic of this fictional world merits study because it can offer a version of widespread anger available nowhere else.

Cop action grapples with the frequency of divorce, delinquency among children, sexual deviance among men, sale of drugs to children and the poor, violent crime in general, control of that crime by police, preferential treatment of suspects by race, affirmative action in a meritocracy, segregation and harassment on the job site, deskilling of professional labor, devaluation of blue-collar work, corruption among ruling-class men, and conspiracy theories of economic crisis.[2] The genre weaves these issues into a large story about working-class public servants who feel devoted to and let down by the society they protect. They protest everything mentioned above and prove their worth by killing the men they blame—mostly upper-class, white, male figures of unrestrained greed. The heroes are most often young to middle-aged, working-class, white, and male; and they are usually paired with partners who differ in age, race, class, or gender. The genre thus responds to the sense of "losing ground" felt by so many and maintains a remarkable crossover appeal as it depicts the struggles of the white guy cops with the others around them, be they colleagues, families, or criminals.

Why does Joe talk as he does and beat his captor to death, for instance? What moral logic grounds the horseplay? I assume that it matters that Joe asks the brutal criminal for another light, that he knows that violence will follow, that the thug condescends in a sexual way (his "Ooh Baby" sounds like a lascivious purr), that the scene plays like a ritual of self-invited abuse. As I describe the sense that such details can make to someone mindful of corruption and lost ground, I lay out this world's moral logic and thus one of our collective fantasies of evil and its due.

Joe's masochism tells first of his duty and strength to endure a terrible job serving others, and second of his relegation by others to just that hard labor. The rich white man who holds Joe captive in *The Last Boy Scout* will try to use Joe to make money in a crooked way while he maintains his own upstanding facade. Joe, however, remains pointedly "low-life" (so he calls himself) and unimpressed with the criminal's high-brow status. After he kills the purring thug, Joe meets a more dangerous criminal—a blond, effete, and sadistic man who typifies the threatening, Aryan adversaries of this genre. When Joe rises up in defiance to slaughter them all, he both resembles and wreaks revenge on the scourge of a world losing ground: the greedy, corrupt, brutal, white-male upper class. His attack on the well-off and oppressive, repeated across the cop action genre, suggests deep feelings for the race, gender, and class-based privileges that these doomed criminals, and Joe for that matter, represent. In short, Joe submits to punishment for the sins of the rich white men with whom he shares guilt for a world's ills. He both joins in their spree and moves away from their greed by blowing them all away.

For another example, about two-thirds of the way through *Lethal Weapon 2,* a cop glowers at the criminals he holds at gunpoint.

> I'll make a little deal with you Arjen, or "Aryan," or whatever the fuck your name is. You fold up your tents and get the fuck out of my country, and I won't do anything to you. I'll leave you alone. 'Cause if you stick around here I'm going to fuck your ass. I'm going to send you home with your balls in a sling. You got that?

We might be puzzled to hear such a sodomite threat from a loudly homophobic cop (who refers to the idea of sex between women as "disgusting" and reacts to his male partner's touch with the rhetorical, "What are you, a fag?"). I show that these threats amount to sodomite promises more ordered than random obscenity, that celebrate the most dangerous and deviant play that men can enjoy. With these obscenities, cops voice a popular anxiety over (and interest in) corruption among powerful men, one often portrayed in terms of homoeroticism. Men hold center stage and women join the fray mostly to demand attention, scream, and occasionally die. In the context of fears of losing ground to those corrupted by their privileges, the otherwise senseless details tell a story of our problems and possible solutions to them. That so many of us find sense in cop movies suggests that we can relate to some of these views and fantasies. Indeed, by looking at what real people have to say about lost ground, we can begin to form a framework through which to view this genre and learn from it. I pause here to look at complaints that real people voiced about their country during the time cop movies grew so popular.

That Sinking Feeling

Cops wrestle with contested privileges and ground lost by decent folk, including the white, working-class, male "regular joes" who serve as most of the heroes. Outside these movies debate over political privileges in the United States has grown so widespread that even popular journalists consider it news.[3] Raymond Williams describes large-scale patterns of emotion as "structures of feeling," which he connects to this popular expression of resentment and fears of "losing ground."[4] The structure of feeling provides a way for people to make sense of troubled, diminished lives. It presents sources of and solutions to their problems and gives them a way to throw in their lots with what one critic has called a "culture of complaint."[5] Indeed, demographic and economic shifts have brought what postmodern theorists call a "decentering" of the politically neutral citizen of middle-class American dreams, such that people who might have counted prosperity among their birthrights have a hard time ignoring the disinterest of multinational capitalists in the welfare of their workers.[6] What's more, those who do "succeed" have a hard time chalking up their successes to a rational meritocracy. Finally, people who watch factories, mines, or offices close and must take service jobs in an economy undergoing a "feminization" of labor as heavy-duty blue-collar jobs disappear in favor of lower-status service work, have a hard time holding onto their sense of autonomous, middle-class achievement. This means that promises of prosperity for the bright-eyed among us seem out of reach for many. These recent developments, though hardly unique in world history (famines, wars, and political shifts abound), add up to a pervasive sense of losing ground.

Voices from a report on antihomosexual campaigning tell the story: During a drive to establish an antihomosexual state law in Oregon in 1992, the director of the Western States Center claims that "an enormous number of people feel they have lost something, lost ground, lost jobs, community values."[7] The United Paperworkers local president says he supports the corporate interests behind conservative politics because "we are out here fighting for our jobs and families." "What's a working man to do?" he asks.[8] The Oregon Citizen's Alliance leader observes that "there is a vast number of people out there who want to actively take back lost ground."[9] The director of "No on 9"[10] suggests: "We are not dealing with rational states of mind. It's more like a feeling state. So many people out there are feeling pinched and want to blame it on someone."[11] Working- and middle-class unease grow, bringing feelings of defensiveness against a system that does not work for people, and against groups of others who stand in their way.

People in such straits tend to resent "others": members of the other sex or of another race, nation, religion, or sexuality. Marc Cooper reports that many people in economic straits look for others to blame. He quotes a local political activist: "We don't hate homosexuals. We just hate their behavior. Homosexual power is growing." Another activist in the same community complains: "You know if you give them special status then they got job quotas. My husband already has to face that on the job with minorities."[12] With growing economic unease and discomfort with the increasing attention being given to the voices of "outgroups," comes a sense that something has been taken away from decent folk. Cooper argues that more and more Americans "sense they've been had for the last 15 years, but don't know quite how or by whom."[13]

Dreams of unmarked, liberal democracy abound in our popular culture and form the ideals against which people strain. What I have done with these movies is hold them up to that background, looking for such straining among cops, who seem mindful of the forces described here. Cop heroes fight for some of the privileges built into their personalities at the deepest levels, privileges they believe to be under attack. A list of these would include prestige, autonomy, proud individualism, a working- or professional-class standard of living, the experience of being able to make it if they really try, and the sense of never being accountable as members of minorities. Cops, like many disgruntled members of their audience, find that these dreams do not come true, and that, as Wendy Brown puts it so ominously,

> ever more complex forms of domination by capital and bureaucratic state and social networks . . . create an unparalleled individual powerlessness over the fate and direction of one's own life, intensifying the experiences of impotence, dependence, and gratitude inherent in liberal capitalist orders.[14]

Under such conditions, Brown explains, people are "nakedly individuated, stripped of reprieve from relentless exposure and accountability for themselves," and are thus driven to what Nietzsche called "ressentiment," "the moralizing revenge of the powerless." This moralizing revenge grounds the satisfying hard times that cops pursue.

Straight white men can feel just this lack of potency, a bitterness toward a world that has betrayed them and called them oppressor while moving into their occupational turf, challenging their public authority, and abandoning them at home. Cop action works with these concerns in striking ways. On one hand, white male cops present themselves as unmarked: basically like, and in some sympathy with, oppressed social groups such as African Americans. Within this liberal world view, any tensions between white male cops and their nonwhite male colleagues look like pesky holdovers of an outdated patriarchy that one which can be blown away with some well-aimed firepower. Grumpy old white men need to "catch up," learn to get along with their brothers and sisters in law enforcement, learn to follow some bureaucratic rules and thus earn some attention and support. On the other hand, though, these white male cops also flaunt their white manhood: They crowd the center of the cop action universe, bristle at the entrance of others to their turf, and define their value in opposition to the "less qualified" nonwhite males around them. The fact that whiteness should occupy such a consistently privileged place in the genre probably just feels "right" and "real" in a society in which ideals of race, class, gender, ethnicity, and sexuality mark virtually every activity, not least those of cop heroes.

Cops sound off on such publicly debated matters as racism, misogyny, and homophobia, divorce, crime, and violence. Though all forms of identity suffer crisis perpetually (Who are we? What's happened to us? Have we grown too weak? Will some other group take us over and pollute our heritage?), the accusations of oppression to which so many privileged people must respond give our culture a shape all its own. Against this background, forms of patriarchal authority die hard and make cops wonder which battles to fight. Should they try to restore what Ronald Reagan called "morning in America," in which middle-class white folks live sheltered, free market lives; or should they fight for a different world in which wealth circulates more widely, among those Reagan seemed to regard as undeserving, and in which cops do more than keep the frustrated poor at bay?

A close look at these movies shows more than liberal dreams of corporate freedom, police power, and public conformity driving cops. Why should Joe take more abuse from the thug in *The Last Boy Scout*, after all? What of the torn, blown bodies of wealthy white men and the determination with which heroes pursue their own injuries? The outrageous beating fantasies and sexual/violent penetrations of male bodies present peculiar visions of political order or "morning in America," to say the least. Framed by the similarities and intimacies between the largely white and male cop and criminal ranks, these displays suggest that cop action regards its heroic figures, especially the white guys, as tainted by the corruption that screws up their world.

The hero of *Point Break* (1991), for instance, ends up far from the ideal agent of law enforcement that he aspires to be at the beginning of the movie. Over the course of the story, a white FBI agent named Johnny learns to skydive and surf in order to penetrate a group of male-bonding, free-living bank robbers. As the criminals teach him the joys of physical extremity in the company of men, Johnny becomes obsessed with their charismatic leader, Bodhi. But this criminal kidnaps Johnny's girlfriend, whom Johnny has betrayed with lies and placed in danger in order to get closer to the object of his obsession. Near the end of the movie, Johnny jumps from an airplane without a parachute to take Bodhi from behind in a close, drawn-out embrace. After a hard tumble in the criminal's parachute—all grunts, groping, and intertwined legs for several seconds—Johnny falls lame and must watch his physically intimate quarry escape. Then, abandoning the attentive girlfriend whom he has just saved, Johnny pursues his man to the ends of the earth and wrestles with him some more, finally allowing him to choose, over imprisonment, an ecstatic suicide in an ocean storm. Johnny tosses his FBI badge into the water and stalks off in disgust to surf some more. The credits roll.

This strikes me neither as a straightforward story of chaotic nihilism, male empowerment, heterosexual resolution, and containment of lawlessness by agents of the state, nor as a men's movement-style revelation of wounded idealism behind cynical fronts.[15] The relationships between cops and the crime, domesticity, and figures of authority around them suggest a mix of admission of white male guilt, resentment of privileges such men share, and a desire to send their bodies up in flames (if not down in pounding surf). I find much here at odds with self-empowering backlash. I find men having hard times, caught up in a repudiation of the law and the joys of deadly male bonding. They shuttle women to the side so that the men involved will be men and then take stands against the very law that gives their lives shape. Simultaneously enforcing and breaking the law, these heroes show themselves to be oppressed by and bigger than it. They are better than their jobs and they show it with their hard times.

2 Out in the Cold

Nobody likes you. Everybody hates you. You're going to lose.
—hero to himself in *The Last Boy Scout*

Having lost ground means that real men do work that is both devalued and difficult but vital to a sick world's survival. Cops may be all that stand between their communities and chaos, yet they have a hell of a hard time making their bosses respect them as valuable workers. This chapter first specifies the cop hero's status as "everyman," usually white and male. These heroes' problems begin in the corruption eating their world. Lovers and families, when cops have any, reject them at home for acting like insensitive louts. Bosses deride them for their slapdash approaches to work. Cops just can't get the respect they used to get. Now, those damn families and bosses want them to be nice. Cops regard this pressure as valid in its way; they should be nicer. But they also see it as foolish emasculation of the guards at their community's gates. If cops can't play hardball at work and at home, then the world will fall even further into decline, into the hands of white guys even meaner and more corrupt than cops.

Everyman in Uniform

Cops see their world hurtling into monopoly capitalism and multicultural strife, too busy to defer to working-class joes. The largely white and male ranks of police workers feel that they have lost an esteem they once enjoyed as otherwise un-marked everyman Americans, not simply to declines in discrimination and shifts in industry, but also to the corruption overrunning their world—to evil, in other words. This corruption involves the illicit exchange among men in positions of public trust, men who hoard those resources for themselves rather than circulate them in a rationally meritocratic manner so that all may earn the American Dream if they want. Corruption keeps the rich rich and the poor poorer than ever. Cops see this evil not only in the criminal behavior of corrupt men in positions of authority but also in the constraints cops feel as they try to do their work and maintain their family ties. Workers wish for freedom, authority, high wages, interesting work, and recognition of the value of their labor, and our cop heroes struggle with the managerial class for just those perks. Indeed, cop heroes see management as a foolish assault on the vital work that keep forces of corruption in check.

The genre poses these problems largely as issues of straight, working-class white-male status, and it does this in a number of ways, beginning with the simple demographics of heroism. Fully 80 percent of these heroes are white gentile men, and most of the rest are black men. Heroes also include a very few women, Latinos, and one Jewish man.

Second, 39 percent of sidekicks, cops' helpers, are also white and male. Hence only 12 of the 193 movies do not include a white male in their hero-sidekick "buddy" combinations.[1] That the other 181 movies put a white man front and center or right beside suggests the genre's focus. Cop action further constrains its heroes by forbidding or at least avoiding black-male/white-female miscegenation (most elaborately in *Action Jackson, Bad Boys,* the *Beverly Hills Cop* movies, *Drop Zone, The Long Kiss Goodnight,* and *Virtuosity,* movies in which one cannot help but imagine sex if the black man were white or the woman nonwhite). Male cops so quickly romance female colleagues and friends across the genre and across lines of race in the case of women of color that the absence of romance among these pairs stands out.[2]

Third, the working-class status of the heroes varies little. The exceptions include the few FBI agents and public attorneys. The genre accounts for most of the FBI agents by rendering them refugees from poor families (*Mississippi Burning*), female (*Betrayed* and *The Silence of the Lambs*), or nonwhite (*Shoot to Kill* and *Thunderheart*). The genre then accounts for the lawyers by making them black (*Ricochet*), unhappy with their jobs and destined to quit (*Q & A*), or committed to low-paying forms of legal work with impoverished clients (*Just Cause* and *Shakedown*). Thus do such heroes excuse their rise from the working-class, poorly paid ranks of cops.

While the genre does not suggest that only heterosexual, working-class, white men possess the qualities and suffer the problems of its heroes, it does suggest that they can stand in for an embattled middle-American populace, that most frustrated with recent shifts in American life. Their list of complaints runs long. The collective esteem that heroes believe they have lost—that which becomes a nation's best and brightest—seems ruined by a range of unfortunate trends, including the increasing demands from family members that they turn from bullying to compassion, and from violent work to something safer and more orderly. At work, white cops face the intrusion of black women and men, white women, Latinos, and Asian Americans into their occupational turf, and the deskilling of that very work by managers more interested in control and public relations than in guarding a world from corruption. They stand to lose everything they have enjoyed about their jobs: the exclusive status that white-male-only hiring practices lend, and the authority that freedom to exercise their discretion brings. Affirmative action, bureaucracy, and automation rank high on their list of social screw-ups that threaten not only their personal satisfaction but also the very world they work to protect.

In the face of these trends, cop heroes distrust tightly governed organization life, remain hostile to coworkers who degrade the status of their labor (how elite can it be if anyone can do it?), and duck the demands of families who appear insensitive to the need for their violence. Cops tend to be gruff and self-pitying to the point of social incompetence; and as blue-collar workers in a polarized economy, they're barely making it month to month. After payments to urban landlords, ex-wives, informants, and whomever they pay for the large guns they carry (often pointedly not standard-issue), cops often have a hard time paying their utility bills and complain of their poverty. They're pissed off and not much fun to be around.

There are exceptions. A few heroes have nice though small houses (which they have built themselves, as if to express an old-time masculinity, in *An Eye for an Eye* and *Showdown in Little Tokyo*), and some drive nice cars or pickup trucks (as in *Cobra* and *Lethal Weapon*). Also, a few heroes prove socially graceful in modest ways (as in *The First Deadly Sin* and *The Untouchables*). However, much of what I argue about white men in hard times depends upon the fact that these variations appear most often when heroes are not white men. Black heroes, for instance, are more likely than whites to be socially competent and relatively upscale. *Money Train,* for instance, contrasts a black hero with a white one, the former more conversationally adept, more responsible about commitments, less of a drunk, less likely to initiate crime, and more successful in his romantic life than is his white male companion. Similarly, the black male hero of *Shoot to Kill* is a solid, middle-aged black man who is a sensitive negotiator and apparently a good bureaucrat. He talks of his taste for fine city life and seems to have no problems with his self-esteem. He is mellower and a more rule-bound employee than his rough and ready white coworker, who is as hostile to authority as any other white man. The same is true of the black male heroes of *Action Jackson* and *Ricochet*. Female heroes, black and white, also tend to be personable and more professionally smooth than their male counterparts. They do not regularly pick fights with those around them and are less often criticized for being too disobedient, hostile, or rude.

Thus do white men constitute a distinct brand of heroism, marked by anger over vanishing entitlements, especially to recognition and authority. They wish life were like it used to be and do not understand the demands on their personalities. As subsequent chapters detail, heroes not white and male serve the significant function of showing what happens when outsiders break into cop turf and deal with these white guys. Female-headed movies such as *Blue Steel, Copycat, Impulse, The Long Kiss Goodnight, The Silence of the Lambs,* and *A Stranger Among Us* are largely about the strangeness of a female cop. So are such movies as *Action Jackson, Beverly Hills Cop,* and *Ricochet* largely concerned with the racially marked status of their black heroes. Thus cop action forms a story of a white everyman in uniform, adumbrated with a few tales of others who have also become cops by straying into what everyone marks as white male turf. The fun comes in watching the white guys figure out how to get along in a changing world, and watching everyone else learn how to deal with the buffoons.

Carol Clover, in her analysis of *Falling Down,* notes that the "What do you mean we, white man?" *Lone Ranger* joke "still resonates in American social discourse, haunting, among other things, the concern over the fracturing of the polity into identity-based groups."[3] *Falling Down* tells the story of falling white manhood, "the great unmarked or default category of western culture, the one that never needed to define itself, the standard against which other categories have calculated their difference."[4] One could direct similar remarks toward the vast majority of cop movies. With white men so often their heroes, the movies amount to an extended meditation on the troubling of this unmarked category by forces of corruption from above (which rob white guys of the status that those very forces have established) on one hand, and forces of accusation and rebellion from those other groups so often victimized by that corruption on the other.

As Clover notes, the white man lives "surrounded by people who have claimed themselves as his social victims and clamor for entitlement."[5] The white male cop of *In the Line of Fire* certainly seems aware of his political status. He has been teasing a Secret Service agent about her position as a token among the men, when she asks him, "So if I'm here to court the feminist vote, what demographics do you represent?"

"Let's see—" he reflects, "white piano-playing heterosexuals over the age of fifty. There ain't a whole lot of us, but we do have a powerful lobby."

True enough, few cops play jazz piano, though its bluesy feel lends his story a familiar white-guy soul (cop action most often plays these blues on heavily reverbed electric guitars). These guys see themselves as misunderstood saviors of a society corrupted by bureaucratic incompetence, the deskilling of their protective labor, and a disrespect so pervasive that it saps the strength they need to shield their communities from harm. To repair their broken bonds and stake a claim for the worth of the labor, cops must display both their skills at the protection of communities around them and their limited abilities to work with those not just like themselves. Though many of them may feel that they deserve the displacement they suffer, they never accept it quietly. By confronting their bosses and offering their services to their endangered families, these cops try to regain some of what they have lost. As I show later, the struggle matters more than the outcome. Winners or losers, heroes suffer and strain.

Doom, Despair, and Agony

Martin, the lonely hero of *Lethal Weapon*, does his police work with one eye on suicide, begs a drug dealer to shoot him, and sucks on a pistol after hours as he weeps over a photograph of his murdered wife. A fellow cop asks the hero of *Cop Land*, "What you're feeling . . . friendless, angry, nervous, misunderstood? This is it. This is the life." The hero of *On Deadly Ground*, a corporate security officer with no close friends, responds to being called "a [corporate] whore" by an acquaintance: "You're right about that. You're just wrong when you thought that I was a good man once." For all of their loyal service, these cops face abuse from commanders, alienation from family, and very often some serious ambivalence toward the business of living another day—all because they approach their work with a tendency toward both antisocial, self-punishing violence and a refusal of rational governance.

A flaw in a hero's character is at the center of many genres—the stuff of epic tragedy in Aristotelian dramas of self-awareness and death. The hero must figure out what is fatally wrong with him before he dies. In the more mundane melodrama of so many current genres, weakness simply provides a way for viewers to connect; it makes the hero interesting. The question for cop action is, How do viewers come to see their heroes as human and interesting? What counts as an interesting flaw in these hard times? Neither random stupidity or sexual voracity of low comedy on one hand, nor the craven immorality of soap opera on the other; the weaknesses of cop heroes stem from authority lost and hostilities simmering. Specifically, they have lost respect at work and support at home and it makes them ornery. Derided or abandoned for being too brutal and insensitive, heroes must face the possibility that they really do not deserve the attention they occasionally admit to craving. Says a cop in *Lethal Weapon*, "Guys in the eighties aren't tough. They're sensitive people. They show their emotions with a woman and shit like that. I think I'm an eighties man. . . . Last night, I cried in bed. So how's that?"

Another asks, "Were you with a woman?"

"I was alone. Why do you think I was crying? Merry Christmas."

Cops feel that they have been pushed from the homes they want to protect for too eagerly chasing goons and too seldom loving wives. Divorce, the pressures of alimony and child support, the increasing expectations of emotional competence in men, as well as the murder of women by criminals, all strike cops as developments to be feared. Real men have a hard time maintaining romantic ties, as one in *Dead Bang* seems to realize when he throws a party for cops, "the bachelors, the divorced, and the disenfranchised." Heroes begin single (usually because of previous divorce), do not have romantic partners at all, lose them during the stories, or must overcome rifts to find some affection. As if the odds against sustained commitment and happiness were not high enough, cop action sequels suggest that any domestic resolutions cops do find fall apart before long. In the majority of the genre's sequels (to *Die Hard, Dirty Harry, 48 Hours, Ghostbusters, Speed, Stakeout,* and *Under Siege*) heroes have lost the partners they found in the first movies. In the remaining sequels (to *Beverly Hills Cop* and *Lethal Weapon*) heroes find girlfriends who survive to see the credits roll only in the third installments.

It is not that male heroes dislike romance or cannot relate to women. Some long for the comforts of home and know that their lovers have the same problems in these hard times. Says the hero of *48 Hours* of his estranged girlfriend, "She's got the same problem as half the goddamned population. She can't get the job she's trained for and it pisses her off. She's bitching all the time."

Indeed, cops sometimes approach lovers as kindred souls to some extent. Says the hero of *Ghostbusters:*

> Let me tell you something about myself. I come home from work to my place, and all I have is my work. There's nothing else in my life. I meet you, and I say, "My god, there's someone with the same problem I have."

Sadly, shared economic woes cannot bridge the gaps between women and boorish cops. This woman does not find the cop attractive, and as he leaves he mutters to himself, "And then she threw me out of her life. She thought I was a creep. She thought I was a geek. And she probably wasn't the first." Though attractive women flirt with cops in casual ways, attempts at intimacy have the unfortunate effect of revealing to lovers the shortcomings of cops' personalities. Cops have a vaguely defined hard time communicating with the opposite sex. It's just not what they're good at.

One cop confronts another who has just beaten his wife terribly in *Internal Affairs* (neither man is the hero).

> That's the way it is. That's the way it is, isn't it? How many cops you know, huh? How many cops you know—got nothing? Divorced, alcoholic, kids won't talk to them any more, can't get it up, sitting there in their little apartments, alone, in the dark, playing lollipop with a service revolver. . . . You're on your own.

Cops in such movies as *Lethal Weapon* and *Extreme Justice* come home to pictures of beautiful women who have left them behind, drink heavily, toy with their revolvers, and dive into pools of despair. Most of the heroes live without or at odds with domestic partners. Widowered, divorced, separated, or arguing interminably—dissatisfactions shadow their lives. "Beloved husband of nobody, father of none," the doomed hero of *Dead Heat* supposes his obituary will read.

Domestic troubles appear early on in the form of fights with girlfriends, confrontations with (ex)wives, or spells of mourning murdered loved ones. What domestic bliss most heroes find comes sporadically and toward the movies' conclusions (57 percent of the heroes have secured family or romantic ties by the ends of their stories; the other 43 percent have abandoned their lovers, been abandoned by them, or have never had such contact). The heroes' problems with domestic harmony stem from three unfortunate characteristics of cops' personalities and work lives: Cops neglect their families, bring danger by provoking criminals, and sport the hostile personalities of men skilled at little but murder.

First, heroes pay little attention to their home lives. In *48 Hours*, a hero chides his girlfriend: "I make you feel good; you make me feel good. Now what the hell more do you want from a guy?"

"I wish you'd stop trying to make me mad," she says.

"I don't have time for this. I've got to go to work." And so he does. Later, after blowing her off again, he decides not to apologize. By the time of the sequel, *Another 48 Hours*, she has left him. Usually alone, cops are a shame-ridden bunch, mindful of their incompetence at anything but hunting and gunplay. By the time of the events of *Ghostbusters 2*, the hero's lover has dumped him for neglecting her. He regrets his behavior ("I could have been your dad," he says to her baby) and expresses need, ("You never got it, Dana. I'm a man, I'm sensitive. I need to feel loved, I need to be desired,"), but will not pay attention to her.

Later, Dana explains their breakup. She didn't appreciate being called a "ball and chain" in front of his friends. "I was protecting myself," she says. "I mean, you weren't very good for me, you know. You know that, don't you?"

"Well, heck, I'm not even good for me," he admits.

Neglect of attentive women often results from the lack of self-respect that slipping status brings. The title character of *The Last Boy Scout* was fired from the Secret Service for belting a senator whom he caught torturing a woman for sport. A corrupt world has left him in a low-rent private-eye job, and his wife explains to him why she has cheated on him. "You know what? Fuck you, Joe! Man, you are never around. I was lonely!"

Joe sneers, "Buy a dog."

"I'm not the one who hates you, Joe. You're the one who hates you."

Joe can only maintain his sarcasm: "And I get to live with myself twenty-four hours a day." Most domestic bickering centers on cops' preferences for their jobs over family life. In

Internal Affairs, the hero's wife tells him bluntly that he needs to invest more sexual energy in the marriage. He remains sullen and withdrawn. In *Excessive Force,* the cop has alienated his girlfriend by telling her that he prefers "a good bust over a good fuck anytime."

Lacking the skills to develop friendships and romance, cops pursue their work instead. The responsibility, the hunts, and the violence make them feel like real men, especially when they know they can choose work over domestic comfort and responsibility. "I bet he's a stable guy," sneers a hero of his ex-wife's new fiancé in *Running Scared.*

"He's a nice man," she responds. "And yeah, he's stable . . . at least he's a grown-up." Heroes seem almost happy to leave or be driven from homes for battles with criminals. The cop's neglected wife in *Falling Down* fears that he will die at work and insists that he retire. Emasculated by inaction, he defies her and returns to dangerous duty, even pursuing a murderous criminal unarmed. After shooting a man point blank, he decides to stay on the job, and although he knows that she will hate his decision, he couldn't be happier.

Sadly, this devotion to work brings about the second cause of domestic trouble—the danger to family that cop work stirs up. The hero of *Excessive Force* realizes that the vengeful criminals he hunts have targeted his girlfriend, and that he is "going to get her killed." This danger leaves many cops feeling that they'll have to live their embattled lives estranged from lovers.

Several heroes have been widowered, usually by the action of the criminals with whom they have fought. Martin of *Lethal Weapon* sits on his couch (for fully three and a half minutes of screen time in one scene) drinking, crying, sucking on the barrel of his police revolver, grieving for the wife killed by a criminal gunning for him. The cop in *Hard to Kill* spends the movie revenging himself on the corrupt fellow cops who killed his wife while trying to kill him. "Dirty" Harry must stoically tell people in movie after movie that his wife was murdered.

The wife of *Basic Instinct*'s hero discovered his addictions to murder and drugs and killed herself. The title character of *Cobra* explains his bachelorhood by observing that "not many people could put up with the way I live. And if you found one, I'd say she'd have to be a little crazy."

In short, cops seem to be alone because, as reckless agents of combat, they deserve to be. In *Hard to Kill,* the widowered cop's new lover reassures him that "if people knew how sweet you are, they'd never be scared of you. I'm not scared of you."

But the cop knows better: "Maybe you should be," he answers. Their ensuing sex scene alternates, as many in the genre do, with the approach of murderers to their bedroom. Many women leave cops to shield families from the crises that cops bring. In *The Hard Way* and *Backdraft,* single mothers explain to cops that the chances they take and battles they fight frighten those who raise children. Left behind, the cops scowl and dive deeper into their cynicism and grief.

Third and finally, many woman have trouble with male cops because the latter are ornery. Heroes argue about most anything at the drop of a hat and tend not to see the other sides of disputes. The hero of *Die Hard* spoils a reunion with his affectionate wife by attacking her for pursuing her career. A cop in *Backdraft* asks his girlfriend for evidence that would incriminate her boss, and she complains that she would risk losing her hard-won career in a tough job market. "Four years ago," she says, "I was punching a cash register, okay? . . . I practically run that office now. . . . You're asking me to just throw that all away." The cop is unsympathetic and cuts her off. She does as he asks, ruins her career to help him in his work, and leaves him.

Because of this sort of studied insensitivity, born of absolute commitment to their work, cops suffer a general lack of support from family. Whether they live with others or not, cops do not feel like objects of love. The sidekick in *The Rookie* complains of his parents' neglect while the hero sardonically observes that his own wife just plain hated him. A criminal taunts the title character of *Kindergarten Cop,* "Your [wife] left because she just couldn't stand the sight of you."

So do cops come to understand that their social skills could use some work. Many of them seem to long for a time when women stood by their men anyway.

Year of the Dragon

Year of the Dragon takes abusive neglect of women to the extreme and mixes it with a healthy dose of everything that gets a cop into trouble with his boss. A close look at this movie illustrates the family and work problems. The story begins with friction between white guy hero Stanley and a coworker, whom he replaces in the Chinatown district of New York City. The coworker refuses to admit that some of the prominent businessmen in Chinatown exploit their workers and deal drugs, and Stanley derides him for his dishonesty. As the story progresses, Stanley gets into more and more trouble pressing his case. Bosses hate to offend rich men among them and try to leash the hero: "Stanley you're letting your imagination run away with you. . . . You know what your problem is, Stanley? You move through this department like a piece of heavy machinery. Nobody likes you, Stanley. They all tell you you're a great cop, but nobody likes you."

In fact, Stanley thinks that he is a great cop: "I'm the most decorated cop in the City of New York," he brags to a young Chinese American woman whom he will both romance and recruit into his war against Chinatown's biggest businessmen. "I'm talking action decorated," he continues, "no desk citations." This woman, Tracy, must listen to Stanley's lecture about the oppressive history of working-class Chinese Americans, used and exploited by employers for many decades. He demands that she help him ease their burden now by targeting their ruling class, but she suspects that his racism has as much to do with his desire to clean up Chinatown as with any sympathy for working stiffs. As if on cue, however, thugs storm the restaurant where they argue and shoot it up. Terrorized into cooperation, Tracy agrees to help Stanley.

Later, Stanley will recruit another Chinese American sidekick, a young cop named Herbert. Stanley breaks it to Herbert that he's a slave-driver and a racist and immediately puts him in the line of fire as he moves against the Chinatown gentry.

Meanwhile, as Stanley picks fights with bosses, coworkers, and his new sidekicks, he also fights with his wife, Connie. As if to explain his flirtation with Tracy and hearken back to a world he has lost, Stanley bickers: "Connie, what the hell's wrong with you. I walk in the door, you don't say 'Hello.' You don't smile. All you do is say, 'Stanley, don't break my balls.' "

Connie chews him out for straying from home for a week at a time: "You don't care about our relationship. . . . You have become an arrogant, condescending, self-centered son of a bitch." So indeed should Connie be angry, as she soon catches Stanley in public flirting with Tracy and ignoring her. She kicks Stanley out of the house, and he sleeps with Tracy that night.

Back on the job, Stanley plans to make waves: "Fuck their civil rights!" he boasts to a group of officers. "I want the honchos around here to go ape shit. I want to disrupt the entire congress of Chinatown. Do you understand me? I want chaos!" Soon, Stanley's commissioner and chief call him off his case, and he condemns them for worrying too much about their pensions and not enough about morality. No one will listen to him and he stalks off in a rage. "Nobody wants to win this thing," he complains.

That night, let down by bosses and rejected by both his long-suffering wife and his scornful new lover, Stanley lapses into pure self-pity, telling Tracy as she orders him to leave, "You're the only friend I have left. I just want to be with somebody tonight. I don't know nobody else. Isn't that a real laugh—I don't know anybody? I feel like such an asshole."

After he has begged a while, she relents. After sex, she tells him that she loves him.

Connie is devastated. She has supported Stanley into middle age, been denied children by his neglect, and watches him run to a younger woman's arms. As Stanley moves out for good, Connie sinks into sobs of desolation while he looks on in silence. Alas, poor Connie has not yet known the worst, for Stanley brings home the other sad fact of cops' lives—the danger they stir up by being cops. Even as Connie weeps, a thug working for a Chinatown boss enters the room and slices her throat open. Stanley shoots the killer, buries Connie, and argues some more with his boss about his work.

"We've got an arrangement, a treaty with these Chinese," says Stanley's chief, Louis. "And however tarnished that is, it works. Life is arrangements, Stanley. Life is getting along. That's why this neighborhood is what it is. That's why eight million people every day in this city can function."

Stanley will have none of this: "You know, your 'arrangement' is what killed Connie, Lou."

Stanley's sidekicks, however, disagree, as they begin to feel the heat that killed Connie. Herbert sees it coming and complains, "You don't care nothing for people. You make us all die for you. But I'm not going to kill myself for you, Captain White. No more 'Chinaman Joe.' Those days are over." Alas, Herbert keeps up his work and soon dies in the line of duty.

Tracy also learns what peril Stanley's love brings. A Chinatown boss's thugs gang rape her at knife point. She cries to him afterward,

> Leave me alone! You should take a look at yourself, Stanley. You're selfish, you're callous, you're indifferent to suffering. Your wife was right, and you still don't get the message. How many more people are you going to kill before you do? . . . Just go away!

Finally, Stanley's bosses give up on him and bust him back to an old post, away from Chinatown. "You care too much, Stanley," explains Louis.

"How can anybody care too much?" asks Stanley at the height of his self-importance. He kills one of the crime bosses, and after recuperating from his own wounds for a while, plunges right back into the fray in Chinatown against orders. Louis and Tracy physically restrain him ("He's a great cop but he won't stop. He won't stop," says Louis), and Stanley explains, simply and directly, "I'd like to be a nice guy. I would. I just don't know how to be nice."

Indeed Stanley has pretty much summed up the white guy hero's problem. He lacks the skills that women and bosses want in this new world. He hunts and kills when they want him to consider and be kind. Cops think that women's demands have changed. They seem to want more from husbands than occasional grunts and rough sex on their ways out the door to work. As if this were not problem enough, bosses' demands seem to have shifted as well. They want fewer steamrollers and more peace officers, less shooting and more respect for civil rights and procedure. They want less blue-collar and more service work. Blue-collar work for white guys has often been well-organized, respected, and well-paid. At least that has been our collective mythology about it. Now this fast-growing service labor market features jobs with little pay, security, or dignity. Hence cops regard shifting demands with suspicion and blame them for their slip in status. Heroes refuse to be nice for fear of becoming second-class citizens.

The Workers' Castration

"I may have a lot of personal problems," says a cop in *Ghostbusters 2*, "but I'm a total professional when it comes to my job."

"Every single day I wake up and I think of a reason not to do it, every single day," says *Lethal Weapon*'s cop of his suicidal impulses. "And you know why I don't do it? This is going to make you laugh. You know why I don't do it? The *job*, doing *the job*. Now that's the reason."

The stakes are never small in cop action. Once they have given up on a home life, or at least while they are waiting for their problems to take care of themselves, cops make jobs their lives, and diminishment of their work can destroy their reasons for living. Cops know that few people love them, and they know why. The men among them tend not to be great catches as dates, much less as husbands or fathers. Much of their self-esteem comes from work because at least it involves and pays money for their one skill—they're awfully good at killing people. They need only be pointed in the right directions and set loose to do what they do best. "It's the only thing I was ever good at," says *Lethal Weapon*'s cop in another moment of dejection.

The catch to using work as a refuge appears when the only thing they were ever good at loses its market value. As the cop world turns from tough manly work that strains the heroes' bodies and makes them men to service work that makes them geeks, cops wonder what's gone wrong. Managers, the captains and lieutenants in command, are not so impressed with deadly skills and often wish that cops would rein them in and get with the times: demonstrate skills at obedience, communication, and service rather than at vandalism and combat.[6]

Worker Devotion and White Guy Talent

Let me be more clear about "cop heroes." They work in, or have occasionally retired from, community protection, in police departments (two of three heroes) or any other organs of law enforcement and public safety. I refer to them as "cops" for simplicity's sake. These include FBI agents, private detectives, bounty hunters, noncombat or domestic military officers, security officers for private companies, firefighters, and other private or civil safety employees. All do dangerous work to protect people from harm, and they do it with great skill. In any one cop movie we find many cops. Heroes enjoy top billing as characters and drive the most developed plots with their problems.

Others know heroes as the best at what they do and rely on them for the hardest work, which culminates in the hunting and killing of bad people. Though occasional exceptions present themselves, such as the mountain climber and the skydiver who do not kill for a living (but who learn fast), most cops use lethal force as part of their daily grind and do so with an abandon. Some were trained to kill by specialized military organizations ("Special Forces," "Green Berets," and "the CIA" come up often); others are just unaccountably lethal. They rarely lose fights, even when they take spectacular beatings. The military figures among them have been decorated for skillful combat, and all of those whose histories we know have outstanding records of service. Heroes' problems at work have nothing to do with mediocrity or any lack of qualification, at least when it comes to the killing of others. For instance, "dirty" Harry had won the San Francisco Police Department marksmanship contest many years in a row by the time of 1973's *Magnum Force* (the second of five movies featuring him), and the hero of *Predator 2* has "the best felony arrest record in the history of [the Los Angeles Police Department]." The hero of *Thunderheart* lands a difficult case because of his "impressive record."

Criminals also appreciate cops' deadly skills. Says one in *On Deadly Ground,* "Dive down into the deepest bowels of your soul. Try and imagine the ultimate fucking nightmare, and that won't even come close to this son of a bitch when he gets pissed." So proficient at killing are they that cops are extorted into service by officials desperate for their talents in such movies as *Blade Runner, Demolition Man,* and *Virtuosity.* The boss in *Virtuosity* says it simply: The hero is "the best cop I've ever worked with." No matter what their status at the stories' beginnings, cop heroes finally solve the cases no one else can manage; they kill the criminals whom no other cops can defeat.

Criminals even offer cops jobs in a few movies. "My goodness," says one to a fellow criminal after surveying the hero's destructive work in *Under Siege*, ". . . why didn't you hire this person? I don't know what his price would have been, but it would have been worth it."

Not merely blessed with remarkable skill, cop heroes also show an unshakable devotion to their work. "I'm a New York cop," says one in *Die Hard*, to explain why he would not move to be with his family. "I've got a six-month backlog of New York scumbags I'm still trying to put behind bars: I can't just pick up and go that easy." Engagement with scumbags supersedes life with wife and kids.

In *Dead Heat*, a cop's neglected girlfriend pleads with him to rethink his commitments: "Christ! Haven't you learned anything? You spend ten years out on the street, risking your neck, and it's still not enough."

"Well," responds the happy cop, "I guess I'm just a glutton for punishment." Out of devotion he passes on his one opportunity to save his own life and hunts the criminals instead. As the title suggests, he ends up dead, giving up everything he has for one more day of work.

Cops sneer at the meager rewards their jobs offer but remain devoted nonetheless. While risking his life in *Speed*, one cop banters with another: "Tell me again, Harry, why did I take this job?"

"Ah come on. Thirty more years of this— you get a tiny pension and a cheap gold watch."

"Cool," mutters the sarcastic hero as he puts his life in danger once again.

Some cops look forward to an easy life after hard years in law enforcement; but none takes his eyes off of the vital nature of his role as guardian. "We're not plumbers," one says to the prospect of a strike in *Robocop*, "we're police officers." This sense of responsibility, even in the face of abusive management, brings with it an angst over their importance that inspires some of the most melodramatic moments. The hero of *Running Scared* urges his partner to settle down with him in retirement: "Come on, Ray, let's take a crack at the good life while we can still enjoy it. We've been busting our ass in Chicago and nobody cares." At a stake-out one night, though, the partner isn't so sure.

> I've got to believe we made a difference. I mean, every stiff we put away is someone out of circulation. We must have prevented millions of crimes. Like that garbage truck there. Every night he comes and empties the cans. Every day, the cans fill up again. But if he doesn't show up one day, the city fills up with filth. Know what I'm saying?

At the end of the movie, after a stimulating shoot-out, they find their work too much fun to leave behind. The aging cops in *Falling Down, Fort Apache: The Bronx,* and *Lethal Weapon 3* also stay on the force rather than stroll into the sunsets of their lives.

Although cops demonstrate little religious faith,[7] heroes act as though they see themselves as trash collectors from God. They talk like blue-collar guardians of social justice—oft ignored but all the more proud for it. In *Outbreak,* human life itself depends upon the white male hero's skills. He need only convince his boss to let him do his work: "Billy, why in God's name would you keep me out of there? . . . People are dying! . . . Get your boss on the phone . . . [and] tell him to put me on a plane before the two of you kill a lot of people." Later, the boss relents but warns the hero to keep this top-secret operation quiet: "You were never here."

"No, I was here," says the hero with a reverent tone. "I followed the bug here. I've always been here. And you remember that." Assigning himself a totemic significance to go along with his practical value, he becomes a sort of universal protector.

A boss in *Running Scared* is more critical of the self-importance of his cops. "You know, it's a very bad sign when a cop thinks that Chicago will fall apart without him."

Of his motives, one of these cops notes: "Regular people suck." This might work as a cop hero mantra: Don't suck. Heroes want more than service-worker status. They want jobs that interest them and flatter their sense of self-importance. "This is not some job flipping burgers at the local drive-in," one says in *Point Break,* to remind others to keep up their sense of self-importance. Cops were meant for more than mundane lives. At the same time, they generally avoid promotions to management. That's not the status they want. Sure, they love to tell others what to do and use their posts as a society's guards to claim that authority. But they never align themselves with managers and social workers as a group. Wanting neither to suck nor to hold positions of formal authority, cops regard the role of civilization's guard dogs as the only acceptable alternative. They just want people to see their one lethal skill as the most important skill on earth.

In this regard, *Total Recall* deserves a long look. A blue-collar construction worker, the hero dreams of life as a savior cop. "Lori," he tells his neglected wife, "don't you understand? I feel like I was meant for something more than this. I want to do something with my life. I want to be somebody."

"You are somebody," Lori reassures him. "You're the man I love." Like many cop action lovers, Lori is an indulgent, fawning stunner; but Doug's horror of normality runs too deep. He wanders to a seller of dreams of combat, rescue, and revolutionary change—the stuff of cops' reintegration fantasies. There, a salesman pitches a dream to be electronically implanted into Doug's brain for his enjoyment (the story is set far in the future). The salesman understands Doug's self-loathing well.

> What is the same about every single vacation you've ever taken? . . . You. You're the same. No matter where you go, there you are. It's always the same old you. Let me suggest that you take a vacation from yourself. . . . It's the latest thing in travel. We call it "the ego trip." . . . You are a top operative back under deep cover on your most important mission. People are trying to kill you left

and right. You meet this beautiful, exotic woman. . . . By the time the trip is over, you get the girl, kill the bad guys, and save the entire planet.

Doug is mightily impressed with this scenario and has it implanted into his head. Soon, though, Doug's implanted "mission to Mars" appears to go awry. It takes over his brain and threatens to lobotomize him. Or, at least, so says a doctor claiming to represent the implant company. He appears to Doug in the middle of his "mission" and claims to have been implanted as a character into the dream in order to talk Doug down and thus save his waking, normal self. This elaborate plot device sets up a scene in which the doctor can directly challenge the hero's self-hating narcissism.

> What's bullshit, Mr. Quaid, that you're having a paranoid episode triggered by acute, neurochemical trauma, or that you're really an invincible, secret agent from Mars, who's the victim of an interplanetary conspiracy to make him think he's a lowly construction worker? Stop punishing yourself, Doug. You're a fine, upstanding man. You have a beautiful wife that loves you. Your whole life is ahead of you. But you've got to want to return to reality.

Doug is momentarily deflated by the truth of his desire for godlike significance but then heroically reassures himself of the reality of his newfound manhood, rejects the offer of solace, and blows the doctor's virtual brains out.

Later still, Doug walks through the bowels of the planet, where workers' corpses lie, and listens to revolutionaries discuss his role in the rescue of the proletariat. "The first settlers are buried here. They worked themselves to death; but [the murderous Governor] ended up with all the money. He built cheap domes and watched the kids turn into freaks." Another says, "And if you want to breathe, you have to buy his air." They look at Doug with significance: "Maybe you can change all that." So he does, in an explosive finale in which his enemies die horribly and the oppressed literally find air to breathe through his heroics.

Total Recall fits a larger pattern in which criminals focus on particular cops and so turn them into the linchpins of their communities' survival. A boss orders John, the hero of *Die Hard with a Vengeance,* to bend to the criminal's demands: "If we don't do what this guy says, he's going to blow up another public building."

"Well, why me?" asks John. "What has it got to do with me?"

"I have no idea. He just said it had to be you."

"It's nice to be needed," John mutters.

The hero of *Blue Steel* hunts a murderer who carves her name into his bullets. She is the only one who can identify and kill him. The hero of *Basic Instinct* must hunt a killer who seems to be drawing him slowly in. "What is it you got between you?" asks another cop.

"I don't know," says the hero, confused but excited.

"Something, though," observes the cop. Indeed, only the hero can take the criminals down (though in this odd case he settles for trying to domesticate her; I return to this odd case and its possible import for the genre at the end of Chapter 3). Heroes do what they do best, but managers seldom see it. Cops chafe against management and make these disputes matters of working-class manhood.

Managerial Constraint and White Guy Angst

In *Die Hard with a Vengeance,* the boss sends for the hero. "Well, you better find out what rock he's under and kick it over." The hero, John, suspended for his loutish style, has been drinking too much and has not talked to his wife in the many months since their last fight. He is hung over and in no mood to work. His boss has few kind words for him.

> The jerk . . . stepped on so many toes in this department—by this time next month he's going to be a security guard. His own wife

wants nothing to do with him. And he's about two steps shy of becoming a full-blown alcoholic. . . . McClane is a toilet bug.

Bosses find that manly cops make bad workers.

> Police officers may not be the best candidates for our purposes. They're a physical bunch, they're macho, body proud, finding themselves stripped of all that. It's no wonder they become suicidal."

So says the designer of what is supposed to be the perfectly obedient cop in *Robocop 2*. Rather than obey, white guy cyborgs recall a harmony they're sure they once enjoyed and revenge themselves on those who seem to have taken it away.

The high-volume tirades of cop supervisors against such destructive men are clichés of the genre (the boss in *Red Heat* parodies the character type by installing a goldfish tank and New Age music in his office to lower his blood pressure). Though bad blood between workers and bosses may be nothing new, cops seem to be waking up to a sense of basic worthlessness to the employers of America. In the organizations for which they work, cops are dangerous, expendable, and replaceable.

The cops' biggest problem, in fact, is less the outrageous personality of this or that boss than constraints imposed by a system of bureaucratic management that threatens to turn their jobs into either emasculating, white-collar office work or low-status service labor. Cops fight forces of deskilling, institutionalized decision-making, and public accountability, even if they understand that their own paranoia and lack of social skills makes such constraint necessary. They strain against these systems and so become known to their supervisors as troublemakers.

The dialogue in *Predator 2* evokes the tension between personalized and bureaucratic control, as well as the way in which such control emasculates male cops. Mike walks into his boss's office to say hi and gets a lecture.

> Don't start with me, Mike. Keinemann's already been up my ass
> so far I won't be able to sit down for a week. We're not winning
> this war. As much as it's going to piss you off, you're going to
> have to play the game on this one. Effective immediately, a
> federal task force . . . will be investigating criminal activities
> involving the trafficking and distribution of controlled substances.
> And you *will* extend [them] your full cooperation.

"Which means you're cutting off my dick and shoving it up my ass, complains Mike. In keeping with the allusions to sodomy, characters refer to the activity of the federal agents as "jurisdictional intrusion."

Compromised bosses in *Beverly Hills Cop* and *Blue Thunder* describe the situation with similar metaphors. In the former, the cop's boss yells at him.

> You want to play some fucking bullshit cowboy cop, you go do it
> in somebody else's precinct. . . . The deputy chief just chewed my
> ass off; you see I don't have any bit of it left, don't you? . . .
> You're a good cop, and you got great potential, but you don't
> know every fucking thing. And I'm tired of taking the heat for
> your ass.

In *Blue Thunder*, the boss growls at his subordinate:

> You listen, Frank. That's the way it's got to be from now on: Me
> Captain, you cop; me talk, you listen. If you notice that I don't
> have an ass when I get up out of this chair, that's because the old
> man just chewed it off, just like that.

He snaps his pencil in two in case Frank didn't get the verbal allusion.

Preferring to secure their asses against managerial incursion and protect their genitals from being snapped, cops duck forces of restraint and pursue their jobs with vigor. This performance, however, only gets them into further trouble. The hero of *Another 48 Hours* argues with the supervisor who has busted him for burning a suspect to death. "I'm going to have to recommend to the district attorney that he prosecute you for

manslaughter. . . . I'm sorry, Jack. I'm just doing my job."
Later, concerned that Jack is collecting evidence to clear himself, the boss demands that he give up his gun and badge and
even appears to gloat over Jack's difficulties. Later still, when
asked to characterize the hero's "professional attitude" in the
pretrial hearing, he sums up the problem: "When a police officer takes it upon himself to violate department regulations
and suspects' civil rights, it makes it hard on every good cop
out there trying to do his job."

This supervisor will prosecute Jack for murder if he can.
Cops disobey orders as they wish, destroy property and people
when they feel they must, with little concern for the safety,
much less consent, of the communities they seek to protect. At
the extreme, and in one movie in six, cops get into such trouble that they suffer or face imprisonment if they do not resolve
their cases to the satisfaction of their bosses. By formulating
the tension between worker discretion and managerial control
in terms of murder and all of the ball-busting constraints that
managers can think to place upon it, cop action serves up the
bloodiest form of this tension. All the while, the genre alludes
to a world gone wrong because of ground lost to controlling
employers by working-class heroes.

Worker Discretion and White Guy Destruction

"Dirty" Harry sneers at those who shy from blowing psychotic
killers away on sight. A boss tells him in *Sudden Impact:* "Sixth
sense doesn't count anymore. You can't bust them because
you think they're dirty. 'Psychic' don't cut it."

Nobody listens to the hero of *In the Line of Fire* when he
forms a hunch about an assassin, so he pisses off his bosses by accusing White House officials of endangering the President's life.
Like this hero, many of the cops scorn the credulity of the com-
rades, courts, and easily shocked citizenry who reject their paranoid and brutal methods (this hero's vigilance leads him

mistakenly to rough up a civilian for resembling a criminal, before just barely stopping the real one on the basis of yet another hunch). Though sometimes errant, heroes trust their instincts and regard those who do not as useless or worse. *K-9*'s hero mocks his boss's ignorance about criminal actions: "High-tuned cop sense," he boasts of his hunch. "You remember that, Rog? That's something you used to have, before you became a paper-pushing pansy . . . lips locked to the commissioner's butt."

With their discretion cops choose to drive too fast, hit too hard, shoot too often, kick down doors, and cause legal trouble for their employers, who strike back by yelling at them, suspending them from service, and sometimes just firing them. "I'm sick of your goddamned antics," says the boss in *Excessive Force*. ". . . You're out of control, Terry. This isn't the first conviction we've lost because of your short fuse."

Arrestees sue the cops of *Running Scared* for violation of civil rights ("What about the rights of the woman he killed?" retorts one cop to the bearer of a summons) and fear needing "malpractice insurance." "Our grateful public can't thank us enough," sneers one. Their boss gives some unwanted advice after putting the cops on suspension for wading into battle too quickly. Pressing on their basic lack of skills and value, he reminds them that, "When you've been cops this long, you are not fit for anything else. . . . Show me another career where they let you shoot people."

"We're tired of that—never did any good anyway," they reply. "We've been on the force a long time, and crime keeps getting worse. Maybe we're the problem."

Their boss cannot disagree: "You damn well ain't the solution."

The young hero of *Lethal Weapon* defends himself: "I got the job done! What the hell do you want?" What his senior partner wants is safety, and for the rest of the *Lethal Weapon* series he chides the hero for his violent approach to his job but relents when other approaches fail.

"Pretty fucking unappreciated," complains the hero of *Die Hard*, usually jovial but now angry after a managerial dressing down. When not accused of error or insanity, cops face charges of being reckless and unfit to decide when to work or how. A police chief is disgusted with the cop's unusual approach in *Ricochet*: "Idiot rookie, nine months on the force, endangering civilians, he should have waited for backup."[8]

But the district attorney tells him, "Stop bitching, Eliot. The city is screaming for law enforcement, and what have you given us? Toys like battering ram tanks, day-glow body armor." Though such defense from on high is unusual, the chief's derision is not. He cares for law and the safety of the civilians around him, distrusts the judgment of cops, and prefers mechanical means to enforcement. Supervisors use such technology to wrest discretion from the cops who jump to escalate conflicts into conflagrations. Cops, though they sometimes use such tools to their own advantage, regard the impositions of them as assaults on the value of their labor power—foolish attempts by their bosses to take their canny hunches, sensitive guts, and hair-trigger reflexes out of the loop and demote them from skilled tradesmen to peons. In *Code of Silence*, for instance, the police department has purchased a robot officer designed to shoot criminals who will not go quietly. "Even semi-skilled employees can operate the unit," boasts the factory representative.

The boss warns the hero, "He's talking about you, Cusack, so pay attention. . . . You're looking at the perfect cop. The damned thing follows orders."

Cusack mutters back, "Another gun without a brain," and then outwits the machine in a test, to the anger of his boss.

The hero of *Blue Thunder* uses a heavily armed, computer-linked surveillance helicopter to bring its creators to justice and then destroys the machine and opts for his own wits over the new frontier of high-tech law enforcement. The *Robocop* movies feature failed attempts to synthesize an obedient cop.

Cyborg officers break down or inherit the psychoses of their human parts in the first two movies. In *Robocop 3*, a company lawyer complains about the hero's disobedience of an order, and an employee defends him: "The only reason he'd disobey an order is if he disagreed with it. . . . He made a judgment. Cops do that."

Aside from the connection that heroes draw between their own discretion and the survival of their society, deskilling bodes ill for workers who draw sustenance and pride from their ability to accomplish difficult work. "It's the only thing I was ever good at," says the hero of *Lethal Weapon*. Cops have just a few talents to share; they know how to identify, catch, and kill evil men. They believe these talents to be in unaccountably low demand, and of course they would rather find a market for their labor than let it slip into disuse. Hence, they must argue that their trade shields law-abiding folk from forces of corruption. In the classic military-industrial logic, destruction seems to guard the prosperity of all. It both protects a community and opens it up once again to disenfranchised cops, who stand to regain the esteem of employers, security in their interesting jobs, and a place in the bosom of a society that needs them.

Cops pine for (imagined) times when "AMERICAN" dreams of individualism came true, at least for white men.[9] They long for demands for their limited skills and love from their families. I next show that a minority of the cop heroes manage to recreate some bloody version of that American dream, as wives and children, bosses and coworkers, terrorized by the trouble that cops and criminals stir up, greet them as saviors once more.

3 Back Home Again

I just don't know how to be nice.
—hero to lover in *Year of the Dragon*

I've got you, partner. I've got you.
—sidekick to hero in *Lethal Weapon*

"**W**elcome to the party, Pal!" yells the hero, John, of *Die Hard*, as he sprays a coworker's cruiser with machine gunfire. The black cop has not been doing what John wants him to do and apparently must earn John's respect. Though John has already fired off a "Stevie Wonder" joke about the man's driving, and plays fast and loose with his physical safety, the two will get along nicely and grow close because the partner, or sidekick, devotes himself to John's cause and does not question his tactics. Their boss proves less indulgent and calls John an "asshole" (the worst insult in cop action) when John begins to blow things up. Sidekicks often play supporter to the hero who begins by abusing them.

Sidekicks on White Guy Turf

Demands that they work with others hit cops below the belt and look a lot like matters of affirmative action when you consider that sidekicks tend disproportionately to be black, female, Latino, Asian American, and upper or professional class. Heroes are not terribly sure that these people belong on the job doing this highly skilled, destructive, and prideful work. Managers ask heroes to submit to their judgments about what to

41

destroy, to sacrifice their potency to slow "teamwork," and to cede the turf that made working-class white manhood something special. "You might be a little more of a team player and a little less of a hot dog on this one," yells a boss in *48 Hours*. "You got to do things your own way? Fine! You nail this guy, and make us all look good. But you better watch your ass, because everybody's watching on this one. If you screw up, I can promise you: You're going down."

Says another, in *Predator 2,* "There's no room for showboats, anyone looking to prove themselves. I won't stand for it. Now don't get me wrong, we need good cops down here, and they say you're good at what you do. But the team comes first."[1] Despite their desire for support in other forms, cops can only feel hamstrung and disgusted by new sidekicks.

Sidekicks tend to come up short as macho blue-collar workers, having less in the way of destructive skills, hunches, devotion to work, and time on screen. They do, however, possess social skills in abundance and so make great service workers. They know how to get along with others and make people feel good. The modal buddy relation binds a hero who is working class, white, male, and thirty to forty years of age, to a sidekick who is, in some way, not. For instance, sidekicks are three times as likely not to be white guys (60 percent of the sidekicks as opposed to 20 percent of the heroes are not white,) and the white guy sidekicks are more likely to be professional class. In white guy pairings, the hero boasts a proletarian attitude toward rank, pay, and authority; his sidekick either hails from a wealthier background or aspires to climb some ladder of status. In general, sidekicks may be older and mellower, younger and greener, richer and more cultured, but differences affect their work and drive the arguments among these buddy pairs. Heroes tend to be hard-bitten, alienated, and pissed-off at just about everybody, including the sidekick. They generally represent the underappreciated working class of dinosaurs who have lost status. Sidekicks, in contrast, are more likely to enjoy happiness and a stable home life, and to express affection for others. They may be bystanders thrust upon busy heroes or recruited by them in moments of desperation; but most are fellow employees of similar status assigned to work with the heroes. Though cops meeting for the first time bicker and pick at each other, sidekicks inevitably help their partners.

Most important for the immediate discussion, sidekicks far more often are model employees. They consider the safety of others, follow the rules, and attend to the bureaucratic details that the heroes find burdensome. They less often kill or wreak destruction in the service of community protection. By marking most sidekicks as newcomers to a working-class, white guy turf, the genre turns the business of working under supervision or as part of a team into an issue of invasion and ultimately lost ground. Two consequences flow from this sense of incursion.

First (either because they are new to the business of policing or because they are not working-class white men), sidekicks lag behind in their destructive skills, and cop heroes must often pause in their important work to bring the newcomers along and get them to act the way white guys do. In other words, lost ground threatens not only the heroes' wounded pride but also the very world they defend.

In *Lethal Weapon*, the black sidekick nags the white hero to stop shooting people and stumbles through a martial arts lesson in a sequel. *Die Hard*'s black sidekick has gone so far as to put up his gun for good after shooting an innocent child. While the hero shoots his way from one trap to the next, his black sidekick cheers him on and defends him from a scornful boss but can do little to help until the story's end. *The Last Boy Scout*'s black sidekick recoils from the sight of a gun and never does fire one. "Dirty" Harry's various nonwhite sidekicks take less lethal approaches to their work: In the 1971 movie *Dirty Harry*, Chico Gonzalez even quit when the job became dangerous. Female sidekicks, many of whom are not cops at all, can be particularly untalented; in *Cliffhanger, On Deadly*

Ground, and *Under Siege* they cower, scream, and keep safely behind the heroes. Those who wear badges acquit themselves more reasonably in *Demolition Man, Kindergarten Cop,* the *Robocop* movies, and *Striking Distance,* but none of them wades into combat with anything resembling the style of the heroes they accompany.

So far behind the heroes' talents are those of sidekicks, in fact, that many of them do not make it through their movies in one piece. Temporarily debilitating injury affects heroes and sidekicks equally (battle wounds drive one cop in ten from combat). But death strikes selectively. Whereas only five heroes bite the dust (in *Dead Heat, Gang Related, Maniac Cop, Rush,* and *To Live and Die in L.A.*), sidekicks perish in a fifth of the movies. Bosses hold even this against heroes; they take casualties among sidekicks to indicate heroes' carelessness. In *Code of Silence,* the hero is known for operations in which his partners are wounded or killed, and his boss fumes, "You don't need a partner. You need a goddamned keeper." "Dirty" Harry is also known for the mortality of his sidekicks. By the time of *Sudden Impact* (the fourth of the five movies) he has already lost four partners in the line of duty, seen another become injured and resign (*Dirty Harry*), and will lose his new sidekick by the end of this movie. The hero of *Point Break* is humiliated before a crowd by his boss after a fellow cop dies during one of his operations (and, as if to confirm the hero's recklessness, his own sidekick dies in the next scene, in yet another risky operation initiated by the hero).

Thus sidekicks prove to be demi-cops, neither quite so tough nor nearly so skilled as their heroes. They provide foils against which the maligned talents of the mostly working-class, white male heroes stand out in sharp relief. By surmounting the indignities of their working conditions, cops demonstrate their virility in the face of affirmative action, which, though rarely mentioned, seems to form an important backdrop. Even in those movies in which cop heroes work amicably with their sidekicks (the heroes usually in leadership roles), they brook little interference from above. Still touting the importance of his work to a world in crisis, the hero of *Outbreak* chides his boss: "We're already in deep fucking shit, and if you're going to arrest me, arrest me now! . . . Don't threaten me. Don't threaten my crew. Please, leave us to do our work!"

Cop action heroes live in a world piled as deep as their worst nightmares can picture it. The irony, from the white male cop's point of view, is that the trouble he takes learning to get along with his sidekick, for a short time at least, impedes his timely dispatch of the criminal class. Thus, the bureaucratic strictures that compel the heroes to pair with supportive sidekicks also constrain the spirited defense of the communities they represent.

The second consequence of the heroes' sense of incursion appears in their treatment of sidekicks as second-class citizens, at least until the latter prove themselves by killing people. Experienced, skilled, hard-bitten, and underappreciated, heroism shines brightest when cops must work hardest to bring their sidekicks into the fold and get along with them. Complains a Japanese sidekick to his white male hero in *Black Rain*, "I cannot help you. Nick-san, look at me. . . . I am not like you. For a moment, I thought I could be. . . . Nick-san, I belong to a group. They would not have me anymore."

"You're digging a hole for yourself, Mas," warns the hero. "Sometimes, you've got to go for it." But Mas tells him to go away. As often occurs after such arguments, the hero must wade into trouble alone until the sidekick at last moves to help. In this case, he saves the hero from an ambush and then takes a back seat to the main action (this last minute display of violence on the part of a sidekick amounts to a cop action cliché and nearly always involves catching up to a working-class, white male hero).[2] As much as heroes want support in some form, they go out of their way to mark the difference in qualifications between themselves and their new partners (and heroes do meet sidekicks for the first time in 60 percent of the movies). The white male hero of *In the Line of Fire* regards female Secret Service agents as "pure window dressing." The white male hero of *Striking Distance* expresses dismay at the assignment of a white woman to work with him; the white male hero of *Under Siege* treats his white female sidekick with undisguised contempt for most of the story; and so it goes.

Cop action links the degradation of white male status on the labor market to the endangerment of their communities. Heroes cleave to an individualism that can amount to bigotry because they care so much; they dole out racist and sexist abuse because they want to get the job done. "How can anybody care too much?" Stanley asks in *Year of the Dragon*. The superiority of the heroes over their sidekicks when it comes to getting the protective job done speaks of threats to white male labor-market status. Bedeviled by affirmative action and other forms of integration, white male cops make sure that others know from the first fire fight who has the qualifications here. Cops answer their disgrace in the eyes of employers with their skill at blowing the criminal menace away. In the most typical movies, white male heroes prove their extraordinary value with some much needed support from, of all people, members of the very groups whose success in the noncinematic job market lags so far behind that of white men as a group. Certainly this scenario has something to offer to a collective liberal psyche with its dream of a common America where white men get along with these newcomers and enjoy good times at work.

Cops feel like laborers whose status has been diminished by irrational forces of management whose immediate interests focus on command and legitimacy rather than the safety of communities. They regard themselves as workers exploited but rarely heeded. *Terminal Velocity* even gets a quick joke out of the rejected-working-class-hero position. A cop explains that both she and the criminals she hunts are part of the new "Russian mafia." They are all former employees of the disbanded KGB.

Her partner is incredulous: "KGB laid off? Auto workers get laid off!" That cop heroes should be treated in this manner by the managerial class strikes them as an affront to civilization as they know it. Thus do cops connect workplace constraints to a sense of lost ground, the moral and economic diminishment of a society. Suspicions of corruption and conflicts over procedure wreck the peace for which cops fight. They want to enforce the law but feel their hands tied by the structure of their jobs. The invasion of occupational turf by means of affirmative action and the larger degradation of high-status labor by the progress of micromanagement and bureaucratization strike cops as forces of modernization to be fought. For the sake of the safety of their communities and the status of their labor, cops battle these developments as best they can.

But not all heroes strike this bitter pose. Doubtless a reader can think of the many movies that feature a mellow cop, a rookie, or someone nice in the hero role. Movies such as *Blue Steel, Cop Land, Shakedown,* and *Shoot to Kill* feature heroes who are black, female, nonviolent, or professional class. Do these movies work against the pattern described here? Several of them do by focusing attention on a cop whose characteristics are those of sidekicks, making an experienced, skilled, hard-bitten hero-type character more marginal. *Extreme Justice,* for instance, follows a Latino recruited to work with an alienated, older white man who does the violent work. *Shakedown* centers on a social-climbing, white male lawyer and teams him up with an alienated, older, white male cop who does the violent work. *Shoot to Kill* features a cultured, middle-class black man and teams him up with an alienated white man who does most of the hard physical labor and bitterly resents the black man's presence. *Backdraft* centers on a white male, rookie fire fighter and teams him up with an older, alienated white man who heads their investigation. *The Rock* follows suit with an elderly military man and a young FBI agent, the latter a greenhorn pain in the ass to

the former. In each of these movies, the personality characteristics and age, class, or racial markers of hero and sidekick
stay close to the larger pattern. These movies focus on the
sidekick characters simply to see what life looks like from their
side, and they leave the basic contrast between hard-bitten
working-class white guy and mild-mannered newcomer intact. Stories featuring women do this disproportionately. *Betrayed*, *Blue Steel*, and *The Silence of the Lambs* center on white
women unaccustomed to combat and show them learning
the ropes from older, gruff white men.

Thus does cop action feature a variety of plots that mostly
present the same moral logic. Hero types deal with sidekick
types over issues typical of a society losing ground. Disrespected and isolated, loyal to their jobs but abandoned for reasons they deem irrational and cowardly, these heroes lose heart
with their world in ways that leave some flirting with suicide
and all with self-destruction on the job. They feel impotent in
the conditions under which they work. They miss being mas-
ters of their households, as loneliness and conflict dash the
hopes they might have entertained as youths (the youngest
cops often seem naively cheerful about their abilities to do
good and stay married; and movies such as *Se7en* work hard to
destroy these illusions). Simply, these cops lack the satisfac-
tions that they thought would come with hard work and some
measure of self-sufficiency. They've lost ground.

The angry individualism of these movies, then, the obsessive insistence that self-driven heroes can spit derision and lead
in the faces of those who make demands but give little support,
gives an important kick here. By the ends of these movies, as
fireballs light the gloom of working lives and gunfire drowns
out demands, cops find some of the esteem they are looking
for. Mostly, they find comfort in their friendships with sidekicks. They have fought the criminals, defied their bosses, and
reassured themselves of their place in their community. Heroes
also draw some public recognition for their work (official hon-

ors, comfort for their wounds, or at least some break in the stream of contempt) in one movie in six,[3] and boast newfound or recently repaired romances in most others (embraces between young, carefully coifed women and heroes covered in dirt and blood are the most common signs of this). What reintegrations the cops find seem like prizes for the valiant. They demonstrate their worth and so reap the affection and respect of those who had written them off.

Here we see as individualist a fulfillment as cops find. Of the violent heroes who arose in 1970s cinema, Stuart Kaminsky writes, "That one must ultimately act on one's own is not necessarily a rejection of society; it is simply the affirmation of one's ability to be important, to hold social structure together."[4] Though later I modify the part about holding social structure together, for now it is enough that this is what cops want—to be recognized the way they are sure they once were, as the guardians of a society and protectors of nuclear families, even if in the end many of them walk away from all of it.

With the rest of this chapter, I describe the routes that most cops take back into the communities from which they feel estranged. First, by developing friendships with supportive sidekicks, heroes calm their paranoid fears of the degradation of their occupational turf by the forces of affirmative action and any other process by which others come to work with them. Second, by killing the criminals who endanger their communities, cops enhance their value to the lovers and families who have abandoned or scorned them. In the end, a bare majority of cops have either put together some sort of family life (65 percent) or developed a friendship with a colleague on which they can depend (60 percent). These are the ways in which cops regain some of the ground they have lost: By accepting the nurturing and supportive friendships of others, by learning to be less contentious with lovers, and by rescuing loved ones from the criminals whom cops sometimes literally bring home from work.

Free Therapy

Lilly, the sidekick in *In the Line of Fire*, endures a good teasing from the hero, about her gender, her looks, and her education. At a meeting, the hero informs his colleagues that the criminal has "got, uh, 'panache.' "

" 'Panache'?" says Lilly, correcting his pronunciation.

"Yeah, it means 'flamboyance.' "

"I know what it means," she says, defensively.

The hero smiles and teases, "Really? I had to look it up." Caught guarding her educated status before a proudly proletarian cop, Lilly frowns but says nothing. Cops love to appear out-of-date, useless, ignorant, and knowingly so. Cops look proudly to another time, when they imagine that only women needed communication skills and men could get by with principles, brawn, and stiff upper lips. The title character of *The Last Boy Scout* pines for an imagined world of Pat Boone music, crew cuts, and squeaky clean heroes who know no corruption. Joe abuses his black male sidekick for any moral infraction and is proud to be called a bastard ("And then some," he mutters).

Heroes also regret the world they have made. They speak this regret to sidekicks, who assume traditional roles of emotional subordination and moral superiority. They are the good, the judges, often nearly angelic in their wisdom and patience with the struggling hero and the hard time he has behaving himself. Sidekicks are cheerleaders and therapists. They are also more likely to lead contented, middle-class lives with money to spare and the love of families to give them the moral strength that heroes often lack. As if these comforts bestowed on them expansive temperaments, they come to indulge the sullen heroes and offer them support. Thus can cops crawl back a bit from the pits of self-pity into which they have fallen.

In *Die Hard,* the sidekick, Al, reassures the "pretty fucking unappreciated" hero, John: "I love you, and so do a lot of the other guys down here." John realizes that, as unappreciated as he is, he's just as nasty to his loved ones, especially his wife, Holly, who had to move away from him to pursue her career. Late in the movie, as John fears he may die and glows with the sentiment that untimely death brings, he offers Al a soliloquy of white male regret:

> I want you to find my wife . . . I want you to tell her that, um, tell her that it took me a while to figure out, ah, what a jerk I've been. But um, that— that when things started to pan out for her, I should have been more supportive, and uh, I just should have been behind her more. Oh shit. Tell her that, um— that she's the best thing that ever happened to a bum like me. She's heard me say I love you a thousand times. She never heard me say "I'm sorry." And I want you to tell her that, Al. I want you to tell her that, uh, "John said he was sorry." Okay? You got that, man?

"Yeah I got that, John," counsels the sidekick, "but you can tell her that yourself. You just watch your ass and you'll make it out of there. You hear me?" John does this again with another sidekick in *Die Hard with a Vengeance.*

As with the sensitive men genre, white male personality remains the focus: his guilt, his hostility, his grief. In *Another Stakeout,* a cop reviews his misfortunes on the job and comes to ponder his guilt during a conversation with his sidekick. "Sorry," he says. "Sorry I ruined my life. Sorry the suspect got shot by my gun. I'm sorry the Mercedes went into the bay."

"What about me getting hit?" asks his young sidekick.

"Sorry about that too."

"And rolling down the stairs?"

"I'm sorry about that too. . . . All right! What are you going to do, blame the deficit on me?" He pauses and says that he's "just really sorry that she walked out on me."

The young sidekick teases with affection: " 'Dad,' we still have each other."

"Hmm, a reason to live," mutters the hero in sarcasm. His defensiveness arises from having been called to account for himself more than he thinks he should. He has responded by coiling up and has thus driven the woman who loves him away. His hope lies in his sidekick's love.

In *Striking Distance,* the sidekick derides the hero's self-absorption and lack of survival skills with some sarcasm: "That's right. You're going to sit around here and have a few drinks until you really start feeling sorry for yourself? I don't understand. . . . You won't start respecting yourself until some-one else does first? Well *I* respect you." The hero asks the side-kick to leave him to his desolation, but she stays and has sex with him instead.

In a nice summary of the heroes' problems, the black side-kick of *Heart Condition* explains to the white hero, Moony:

> You see, you want to keep everybody in our little boxes, don't you? You want to keep me in the ghetto; you want to keep [your girlfriend] back at home; even that knucklehead [boss]. . . . You want to keep us all right there where you can see us, don't you? . . . Hey, there's nothing to be scared of, Moony. Nobody's out to get you. You don't have to be scared that we're all going to leave you behind.

Over this last line we slowly zoom up on Moony, suggesting his realization of truth. He comes to love his sidekick and wins back his girlfriend with the occasional display of need. Thus do heroes head back into a world they fear has little use for them. By listening to their indulgent sidekicks, white guys mature.

"What does it take to change the essence of a man?" asks the hero of *On Deadly Ground* of a racist white man he has just savagely beaten.

The other guy sobs, "I need time to change; time . . ."

The hero echoes, "I do too. I do too."

The Native American man whom this hero has just de-fended then tells him, "You are about to go on a sacred jour-ney. This journey will be good for all people. But you must be careful." So, indeed, does this white man grow with the aid of caring Native Americans.

Many analysts have noticed this caretaking aspect of cop action male bonding and argue that the genre is insidiously racist in its effect.[5] On the face of them, these encounters certainly evoke master/slave relations: heroes stand in the center of the cop action culture as the most qualified yet aggrieved workers, and they enjoy the support of the partners who help heroes see their tragic flaws. Robyn Wiegman argues that the casting of movies such as *Lethal Weapon* offers a cathartic reversal of racial positions: By contrasting a black man integrated in middle-class bliss with a white man lonely and confused, these movies stage the reintegration of the latter without having to seem racist.[6] They offer "positive" portrayals of happy black characters, while subordinating them to the white guys' humor, interests, and bravery. The reversal of class positions, then, is both an alibi for the white supremacy bubbling under the surface of their relationships and a wish for what Houston Baker calls "AMERICA," the land of liberal tolerance where no racial hostility taints the bonding that men do.[7] Further, the genre turns black threats into sensitive, by-the-books cops willing to risk their lives to work with white male partners. Whatever nobler motives might underlie the push toward the white guys' reforms, then, it appears to be driven by the hope that the fearsome child of a racist past might come to love the white folks around him. What might feel disturbing and alien in the specter of the black man becomes familiar in every sense of the word. At the extreme, the Uncle Remus reference becomes awfully clear as the generous laughter of heavyset black men marks the reintegration of white cops in such movies as *Backdraft, Die Hard, Downtown, Excessive Force, The Hard Way,* and so on.

This analysis points to sentiments we should expect to find among those who are feeling a loss of privilege: self-pity and self-worship, envy of racial others, horror of black rage, a desire to restore an American dream slipped away, and a desire to prove their worth to the society that has neglected them. The white male hero remains the center of the cop action moral universe, just as whites and men have always been the centers of Hollywood cinema. They blow their opponents away, poke fun at interlopers on their occupational turf, and all the while prove themselves more able and ready than their sidekicks to fight the good fights. The hero responds to his job-related woes and proves himself worthy of the respect and admiration of his subordinated sidekick. Indeed, heroes find strong friendship or romance with sidekicks in two-thirds of these movies, thus providing for themselves much of the emotional support they lack. Cops pursue this fantasy of ground regained through the individual excellence of their work. They despise the systems that employ them but put their few skills to use and so demonstrate their value. Of *Die Hard*'s hero, Ann Ardis and Dale Bauer write,

> McClane both is and isn't a part of the system. He can use it, but he isn't a bureaucrat, he isn't a cog in anyone else's machinery; . . . he thus (as the popularity of this film might suggest) represents Every American White Man.[8]

Though employed by organizations of community safety and supported in all but a handful of cases by at least one sidekick, heroes go it alone in some way. They must work against a system or look like automatonic sissies or robots (a nightmarish scenario elaborated in the *Robocop* series). The fantasy, as Ardis and Bauer argue, is "that the individual can, in the end, win out over anything that challenges his ascendancy."

But, these authors read more "ascendancy" in the hero's exploits than I do. What of the broken homes cops mourn (a home broken again at the end of *Die Hard*'s second sequel)? Some of the cops will mend those in other ways. I turn next to a story in which the cop climbs back into a family by way of both the nurturing love of a sidekick and the terrorism that engagement with criminals provides.

The Hard Way

On the tough streets of New York, where real men fight loony killers and women cannot deal with the violence, John, the hero of *The Hard Way* has just begun seeing single mom Susan. He tries hard to fit romance in between his bouts with the serial killer who obsesses him. She is up front about her desire to date him, but he blows it with his nasty personality, challenging drunks to a fight at a local hangout when he should be attending to her and her daughter. Susan likes something about John (even if we never see exactly what) but wonders whether such a violent man could make a good father for her child. Left to his own devices, John would probably crash and burn in the relationship. Fortunately, his second and third problems (the first being his personality) will help him win Susan, at least for a while. One of these problems comes in the form of a sidekick. True to generic form, John plays the hard-bitten experienced hero-type to the rich, pampered, and smooth sidekick, a Hollywood actor who wants to hang around John to study for a role as a cop. John's third problem is that serial killer, who will have at least as much to do with winning Susan as anything else.

The plots kicks into high gear when boss saddles hero with sidekick. Outraged, John heaps abuse on his new buddy, the actor named Nick, taking every opportunity to mock his naiveté, his phony actor's life, and his lack of destructive skills. Criminals rob Nick and humiliate him while John digs in, defies his boss's order to baby-sit Nick, and generally does things "the hard way." Anxious to ingratiate himself, Nick uses what skill he has, advising John to deal with Susan with some finesse and pay more attention to her. After the date that ends in violence (John sets down his dinner to tangle with obnoxious white guys), Nick goes so far as to role play a date with John, encouraging him to "open up" to Susan more. Though thoroughly grossed out by the sidekick's feminine poise, John might be learning a thing or two.

Later, as John publicly taunts the criminal and hounds him all he can, he becomes more desperate than ever to get rid of Nick. In an elaborate scam, John demoralizes the intrusive sidekick by making Nick think that he has killed a man with his foolish mishandling of a firearm. Nick copes as best he can with John's treachery and later saves his life. Though angry with his abusive hero, Nick sees with a sidekick's eyes an opportunity to show John his faults and care for his feelings: "I finally know what it feels like to be you. It sucks. Susan, me—we wanted to like you. But no; nobody gets in, right? It's 'private.' Well that's not what I call it, John. I call it lonely." Nick stomps off, but a lingering look at the hero's expression says that he has made his point. The hero needs a sidekick's personality to counter the absorption in his work that makes him so mean.

This sort of free therapy gets heroes only so far, though. John learns to work with others, but now must deal with Susan's reservations about him. In their major confrontation, Susan lays out the lover's complaint: "I've been thinking a lot about it and we can't have a relationship."

"Sure we can," stammers the hero. "See, I c— I— cause I can change. I'll try harder."

"No, it's not that. It's not you. You're fine. It's what you do." As John begins to sneer, she too begins to stammer: "It's, uh, it's— it's all the violence. I've spent my life trying to run away from that. I cannot put [my daughter] in a position where she doesn't know if her father is going to come home alive every night or not."

"Yeah, uh, yeah, I understand," says the cynical hero. "Sure, yeah, cops are too angry, too violent, too risky to care about, until you need one. Then— then we're the second coming, aren't we? Yeah, uh, I understand that one all right." He glares as Susan with undisguised contempt and she leaves in silence. But then, just as if on cue, the killer strikes, nabbing and trying to kill Susan to annoy John. Together, Nick and John must save her; and after watching her scream as she dangles from various precipices for several minutes, they do just that. Terrorized beyond reason, Susan changes her mind about John and finishes the movie by his side. Thus does John use two of his problems to solve a third. He puts up with his unwanted sidekick, a wealthy interloper on working-stiff turf, by accepting some free therapy and trying to change his ways. On the other hand, John deals with his criminal quarry by publicly taunting him until the criminal targets his lover in revenge. John can then save her from criminal clutches and win her back again. This second move I regard as a sort of protection racket: So you don't like the violence in my life? Well, love me anyway or die from the trouble that it stirs up.

The Protection Racket

The hero of *Die Hard* humbles his career-oriented wife when he rescues her from the corporate raiders among whom she inadvertently placed herself. Nabbed by the thieves because she is John's wife, she can only wait for him to rescue her. The cop has run a protection scam, in which the woman who has abandoned him learns a lesson in dependence from the battle between criminals around her and the husband who saves her life. One of the more interesting patterns in the genre presents a criminal threat just when the hero feels most rejected. As if on cue, criminals terrorize scornful families and so bring them to see protective cops in a whole new light. I conclude this chapter with a look at this method by which cops address their family problems. Together with sidekicks in support, cops find criminals to hunt; fight with them; and then both risk the lives of estranged family members, who become mightily impressed with the heroes' value as protectors, and save them.

If lost ground includes the abandonment of heroic men as unskilled, contentious louts, then the solution involves convincing those who have abandoned them to reattach value to their murderous labor. Cops do this in two ways, one of which involves a display of need, and the other a display of strength. Both advertise to families the importance of cop labor in a world gone wrong. First, cops display grief over murdered friends and family. Perhaps contact with nurturing sidekicks helps heroes to open up a bit in times of need. Perhaps grief works as foreplay because wives hasten to greet any emotion expressed by otherwise unavailable heroes.

Each time one of the hero's partners dies in *Excessive Force*, his ex-girlfriend—one who gave him up when it became clear that he did not love her as much as he did his job—gives him more attention. She consoles him through the deaths that accompany his work and gets closer to him each time. Similarly, a cop in *Backdraft* effects a reunion with his estranged wife by showing up outside her door one night after his aggressive approach to work contributes to the terrible injury of a rookie in his charge. His mixture of guilt, dismay, and grief melts her anger and they have sex.

The second restorative works even better. In 28 percent of the movies cops work their ways (back) into communities, friendships, and families by saving them from the dangers their jobs bring. In *Excessive Force*, the more the cop's girlfriend attends to him, the more likely it is that she will be attacked by criminals seeking to demoralize him. He saves her a few times before the credits roll, at which point she has devoted herself to him. This defeat of the forces of murderous corruption provides for heroes a way to wrest attention and even love from those who might otherwise reject them for their contentious and violent dispositions. They find threats to community or family and then watch sidekicks and family members gather around them demanding help and protection. Says a dejected white man to the woman he desires: "I've got it! I'll prove myself to you. Yeah. I'll solve your little problem, and then you'll say 'Pete Venkman's a guy who can get things done. I wonder what makes him tick." And so does the hero of *Ghostbusters* push himself into this woman's life. In the sequel, they have dated and broken up over his neglect of her. Feeling lonely again, Pete wants her back and gets his way after rescuing her kidnapped baby. In the first movie, he wants this woman's love, watches as she falls into mortal danger, and then saves her. In *Ghostbusters 2,* he wants the baby's love, watches as he falls into mortal danger, and then rescues him.

Tried for unlawful destruction and violation of a court order against his labor, Pete defends himself on the witness stand to a white female prosecutor, whose position he clearly despises: "Kitten, I think what I'm saying is that sometimes shit happens, someone has to deal with it, and who are you going to call?" Onlookers cheer, but the judge sentences the cops to jail and only relents when ghostly criminals threaten his life. As if on cue, as he scolds the cops for being cops, criminals rise from their graves to terrorize him into submission.

Later, the cops discover the woman Pete loves in danger. "That's great!" one says. "I mean, that's terrible. But it's great for what we would—" he trails off as if embarassed by the crass terms of the racket.

In *Bad Boys,* the hero's wife becomes furious when she believes that he has cheated on her and lied about it. She walks out on him when, as if cued by the hero's need, criminals appear and shoot up the place. She screams; he defends her, just as in *The Hard Way.* As the hero leaves his wife in a safe place to go hunt criminals some more, she cries, "I love you," again and again. Cops reintegrate by exercise of the very impulses that alienate them in the first place. Though the heroes' dangerous employment and uneven temperaments make them unattractive mates, their work as protectors of communities can make them attractive if the surrounding threat looms large enough. Thus does the genre deal with women who fear to live with cops.

Speed provides an instructive example of a couple of strangers brought together by the woman's endangerment. Its story seems finished once the cop has foiled a criminal with the help of the expert driving of his female sidekick. As cop and sidekick lie next to each other catching their breaths, he begins tentatively to flirt with her. Then, the criminal takes her hostage one more time and torments her until she whimpers. Again, the cop saves her and this time celebrates their survival with an amorous kiss. *Speed* suggests that the more threatened are the potential romantic partners, the more may cops romance them. As with melodrama of old, the endangerment of women serves both as aphrodisiac and preliminary to the hero's reintegration. Contrast this to *Black Rain,* in which the woman the cop desires never knows danger. With no saving to offer, he ends their relation with a brief kiss good-bye.

The *Kindergarten Cop* is divorced because his wife did not like being married to a violent man. He still grieves over the loss and longs for a family and barters his talent as combatant for a place in a family unit. He finds a woman stalked by her husband, dates and falls in love with her, all the while posing as her son's kindergarten teacher. Later she discovers what he actually does for a living and protests for having been duped into such a relationship. He pleads,

> I didn't mean to hurt you. I wish I was a kindergarten teacher. But I'm not. I'm a cop. That's all I know how to be. I have a son I've hardly seen in the last seven years. I don't mean anything to him. My ex-wife got remarried; she doesn't want me to be part of his life. I lost my family. I should never have let it happen.

"Why are you telling me all this?" she asks, unclear on the protection racket logic.

"I don't want to lose you," he explains. "I don't want to lose [your son]. I swear you will never have to run from [the criminal]." As women tend to do when cops beg, she relents. They kiss passionately as the music swells and are happily involved at the movie's end.

This hero's claim echoes the line from *Lethal Weapon:* "I do it real good, you know. . . . It's the only thing I was ever good at." The cops who find their way back into the family fold do it through the violence they offer, the brutality with which they heal family wounds (though we see little violence in *Kindergarten Cop,* the cop beats an abusive husband in front of his wife and many of the grammar school students, to the approval of the school's principal).

In *Outbreak,* the hero's boss and his ex-wife chastise him for being paranoid and bossy and for entertaining a "morbid desire to face the end of the world," a time during which his services would be in the great demand he so misses. At the end, he has narrowly saved his wife from a terrible death. Their conversation connects the state of danger they have faced with their reasons for reuniting. "It's a pretty unique experience," she says of being in such danger.

"Sort of like living with me," says the hero. "Would you go through it again?"

She agrees to do so as the movie ends, "Maybe, now that I have the antibodies." We cannot separate the hero's desire to face the end of the world from his desire to mend his marriage. This woman dislikes the hero's bossing and whining, but he has no intention of changing. If he will have her back he must lead the fight against the deadly forces of government corruption. His heroism matters, of course, but so does a woman's ability to suffer and in doing so gain strength and patience enough to endure more time married to a neglectful and domineering man.

"Not many people could put up with the way I live," admits the title character of *Cobra,* "and if you found one, I'd say she'd have to be a little crazy."

"I'm not scared of you," says a woman in *Hard to Kill.*

"Maybe you should be," responds the cop. Heroes know full well that they are no catches as mates. Partners must bring nerves and patience to the partnerships, many of them will find only the sullen silence of heroes who would as soon have teeth pulled as share feelings of devotion or esteem. Women often leave in disgust or despair if they are not killed first.

However, by thriving in conditions of peril and by either meeting women there or drawing them in against their will, heroes can seem the lessers of the evils around. Women uninterested in the grime of violence and corruption earn stern, disappointed looks and then either vanish or heel under duress and sob their apologies. *The Last Boy Scout*'s hero and his wife play a striking scene of restoration. The cop abuses her verbally whenever they meet but has also saved their daughter from death. She appears at the scene of his last battle, stands before him and sobs, over and over, "I'm sorry," while he abuses her some more. Other women return with less extravagant rituals of shame but with a silence about their motives that can seem a bit weird. In such movies as *Another Stakeout* and *Year of the Dragon,* they offer no reason for their forgiveness of the heroes' sins against them. Their behaviors seem outrageously subordinated to the heroes to the point where the performances could be said to lapse into illogic. Indeed, this is as close as I come as interpreter to not understanding anymore. The moral point, however, seems to be that violence brings female submission and so attracts cops who want to patch their family lives by force.

Basic Instinct even toys with this cliché by making it the criminal herself who unaccountably returns to the hero in the wake of a storm of violence. Her reasons for having left him are typical enough; she finds his company barely interesting and fears relations doomed to end in bloodshed. Less typically, however, she dislikes children and family life. She prefers her high-living independence to the prospect of domestic life with the sullen hero. But return she does, and the movie appears to be headed for the usual denouement when the sight of a waiting ice pick reassures onlookers that he will join her string of victims before long. Her unexplained attachment, typical of cop action lovers, gives way to the more dignified intent to send a moronic lover screaming to his grave. Thus does cop action offer a comment on the unrewarding nature of the work white women do. The costs to them are steep and the thanks minimal. Cops repair romantic ties in 60 percent of these movies; and one might have to catch one's breath after considering the work women do to bring these heroes back into their homes.

It Ain't Over Yet

Basic Instinct's hero, like many, loses big time. His sidekick dies screaming, his boss's praise rings false, and he fears (rightly) that the killer runs loose (as they do in one movie in five). He manages only the most tenuous reintegration with a woman who happens to be the killer. So, we analysts must wonder how far these protection rackets take cops as a group.

Work lives wrap up nicely in about 68 percent of the movies; bosses offer minimal respect and coworkers offer esteem in similar proportions. However, 15 percent of the cops quit or get sacked in anger. Others receive no credit for their work, either because what they have done is illegal and would get them arrested or because a manager takes the credit. Many more of the bosses are just as mean when the work is done as they were at the start. For each hero who receives grateful public acclaim for a job well done, we find two whose job troubles persist. Further, as I note above, cops finish movies with families and sidekick relationships intact in fewer than two out of three of these movies. Cops attain satisfaction on all fronts at once—friendship with a sidekick at work, acceptance into a family, respect at work, and an end to the immediate criminal threat—by some means, protection racket or not, in only one movie in four.

In other words, no form of success befalls even two out of three of the heroes, and general satisfaction awaits a minority. Contrast the happiest minority to another in which cops suffer mightily: in such movies as *Betrayed, Homicide, Mulholland Falls, Point Break, Rush, Se7en, To Live and Die in L.A.,* and

Wanted Dead or Alive, for instance, heroes betray their lovers if they have any, watch partners die, and lose or quit their jobs in disgust if they still live at the end to do so. Other heroes, as in *Basic Instinct* and *Rising Sun,* wonder if they have bagged the wrong criminals altogether and have perhaps even become intimate with those involved in the crimes.

What sort of fantasy of ground regained includes such casualties? Sure, heroes address their problems by mocking, besting, and then getting to know the new entrants into their prized job turf. They learn a social skill or two and let that salve their wounded pride. Finally, heroes save those around them from the violence that their work stirs up, demonstrating to all the worth of their skills. This is lost ground regained and as close to happiness as heroes come.

Sadly for them, the cop action world is not so simple, nor the problems so easily solved. Heroes bear uncomfortable resemblances to the criminals they hunt and so bear guilt for the ground they have lost. When heroes face the criminals responsible for oppression and moral decline, they usually face richer versions of themselves. There lies the heart of their hard times. While cops enjoy happy endings as much as anyone else, authority and comfort may not be their real prizes. The ressentiment with which they approach their lives seems to demand protracted suffering, for heroes who were too happy would not be heroes anymore; they would have nothing to fight over and thus make themselves men. Crisis sustains their melodramatic claim on the attention of their society, their real reward. Cops may enjoy good standing at work, family love, and free therapy, but a becoming melodrama will require harder times with their jobs, their families, and their guilt.

4 White Male Guilt

We're the same, you and me. We're the same.
—one bitter white male criminal to another, in *Falling Down*

Cops struggle with their anger toward demanding and intruding others, and then turn it back toward the most racist and misogynist of white men. The analytic literature often attributes to these movies a blindness to their own racial dynamics, as if its moral logic were not so logical after all, or at least not very self-aware (and perhaps only available to professional class academics). In a running engagement with that literature, I show, however, that cops lay out their paranoia and contempt for all to see before they turn their firepower on the criminal class, whose tempting company they abjure in favor of some rough justice. Thus do they have their hard times, hip-deep in nostalgia, righteous fury, and self-hatred. The meanness they repudiate tempts them so, and white men become heroes when they torch the nazis in firestorms of conflicted rage.

Criminal evil lures white men among cops and originates mainly in white men among criminals. The genre gives space to those not white and male, to be sure, and sends some of them through some of the same hoops; but in the end it seems more to meditate on white manhood than anything else. The female or nonwhite male sidekicks often serve as foils for the working through of the white heroes' anxieties. They are the ethical actors to whom the other heroes compare themselves and whose ethical ideals they try to reach, so often in vain. Heroes have a good hard time jumping into fights over racism and woman hating, rendered more explicit than cops might have been accustomed to in their pasts. When heroes cannot manage the upstanding citizenship of their partners, they settle for positions as guards at the gates of those communities. Their sense of mission adds an importance to lives otherwise diminished by their guilt and lack of skills. Their sense of betrayal by a corrupted world adds to their moral kinship with nonwhites and white women. This chapter explores the bitterness, the sense of oppression, and the self-cleansing that cops do.

The Criminal Class

To avoid overstating my case, I lead with the exceptions, which include nearly 16 percent of the criminals. Most of those movies that feature those not white and male as principle criminals direct themselves toward inner city milieux: Such gangster epics as *Colors, Deep Cover, Fort Apache: The Bronx, Showdown in Little Tokyo,* and *Year of the Dragon* feature drug dealers operating in Los Angeles and New York City. A very few feature white women or aliens who do not look like white men, and in a couple of unusual cases serial-killing black men (*Just Cause* and *Switchback*) as their criminals. Three of the stories about aliens (*Ghostbusters 2, The Hidden, I Come in Peace*), however, present their criminals in the bodies of white males.[1]

Another third of the movies feature nonwhites as subcriminals—a diminutive for those who appear in a scene or two and attempt some crime, or who support principal criminals and keep to background roles. These subcriminals appear briefly, remain marginal to the action among white men, and work mainly to exercise heroes before their bigger battles. For instance, "dirty" Harry famously shoots black male thieves in *Sudden Impact* and tells one of them to "make my day." Subcriminals disappear after such scenes and heroes go onto bigger things, in this case conflict between a gang of white rapists and a vengeful survivor of one of their attacks. Nonwhite men are usually petty thieves, drug runners, and other low-level functionaries. In only a few movies do such men enjoy authority of their own: in *Rising Sun* and *Robocop 3,* for instance, Japanese corporate executives associate with murderous white criminals; in *Tequila Sunrise,* a Mexican official runs drugs. Further, only four women carry movies as principal criminals (in *A Stranger Among Us, Basic Instinct, Heaven's Prisoners,* and *Murphy's Law*); and over the course of 193 movies, in the company of hundreds of men, the few female adversaries seem exceptional.

Indeed, for all of these appearances of white women and people of color as thugs, drug runners, murderers, and thieves to be threatened, arrested, or shot, one can quickly notice that white men make up the dominant criminal class and the subjects of this genre's moral logic. By this, I do not mean that the movies just reviewed hold no interest or bear ignoring, any more than the nonwhite male heroes can be shrugged off as tokens. In fact, I can think of three important reasons to be interested in these criminals even as I make my case about bad white men.

First, the most salient aspect of cop action evil concerns class, an issue that arises whether the drug dealers are white or not (criminals of color are always drug dealers, with the exceptions of a counterfeiter, the boss of a stolen car ring, and the two serial killers mentioned above). Most important, all nonwhite criminals except those two serial killers are wealthy. Cop rage targets men of wealth or authority—the men in position to poison their society with their unbridled hostilities and undisciplined exchanges.

Second, the criminals' racial identities sometimes blend in ways that play tellingly on an equation of whiteness with evil. In *Demolition Man,* the criminal black man sports blond hair and blue eyes. In *The Rookie,* Latino actors play car thieves in East L.A., supported mainly by Latino henchmen. Their names—Strom and Liesl—however, are Germanic; the cop refers to their ancestry as "Kraut"; and they warn their Latino henchmen to presume no racial solidarity (perhaps the criminals hail from a German-settled region of Argentina or Brazil). Thus even when the criminals appear not to be Aryan, they can gesture toward the identity still. Nonetheless, Latinos, blacks, or Asians number fewer among primary criminals than one might expect were one looking for a reflection of the noncinematic criminal justice system's complex identification of deviance in America.

Third, and counter to the above points, the mostly white criminal class may actually, indirectly, represent racial minorities and poor people. I turn next to this displacement analysis in some detail, even though I propose a supplementary reading in the end. I consider this theory for the light it throws on both the elasticity of the genre's meaning and the ambivalence of cops. The displacement analysis suggests that if the criminals are in some sense "really" nonwhite, then the genre gives a purely white-supremacist fantasy of deviance and decline. Whom do cops really hate? Who has spawned the disorders of a nation? I ultimately argue that, aside from whatever displacement may occur, the genre's villains are white simply because cops can identify with them and so be tempted into corruption. The question of responsibility for corruption can vex anyone, and cops certainly confuse their loyalties. The genre stages a moral battle for their souls.

Displacement Theory: This Is Not a White Man

A displacement hypothesis suggests that nothing is what it seems.[2] Whiteness is not simply whiteness, maleness is often the opposite, and the wealthy may stand in for the poor. Criminals may be largely rich, white, and male; but, the hypothesis goes, the genre actually directs its stigma toward the proletarian, nonwhite and female. Here, I entertain the notion that the genre stigmatizes subordinated groups in part by its depiction of privileged white men.[3]

The displacement begins with the whiter-than-white appearance of the most threatening criminals, who may seem to come from a race all their own. The genre reserves the clean-cut, blond and blue-eyed look almost wholly for the wildest bad guys. These vicious, loony killers are not so much "anglo," or "caucasian," as WHITE. They embody every log-up-the-ass/Germanic Nazi/Aryan upper-class/gentleman-sadist, racist characteristic imaginable. Colonel Stuart from *Die Hard 2* looks like a blond parody of Oliver North, and the villains of *Die Hard* and *Passenger 57* share a mannered, tailored sadism. Mr. Joshua of *Lethal Weapon*, with his baby-blond hair, earns himself a disparaging reference as an "albino." The brown-haired terrorist from *Nighthawks* dyes blond before battling the cops. The suspect women of *Basic Instinct* are evil to the degree that they are Aryan; the most vicious killer among them is the blondest. The vengeful killer of *Murphy's Law* is an older version of the same. The list of Aryan killers goes on to include the smooth-talking aesthete from *The Last Boy Scout*, the "Aryan Brotherhood" drug dealers from *Fatal Beauty*, the cultured smuggler from *Beverly Hills Cop*, the racist biker thugs from the *48 Hours* movies, the "Aryan warrior" from *Ricochet*, the fascist mass murderer in *Cobra*, the right-wing military thug from *Blue Thunder*, the bleach-blond sniper from *The Hard Way*, the surfing bank robbers of *Point Break*, their foolish counterparts in *Extreme Justice*, and many more. The Aryan criminal class certainly stands in stark contrast to the heroes' black, Asian American, and Latino sidekicks. As I point out in Chapter 3, these partners tend to distinguish themselves in their reluctance to do violence.

Nevertheless, the displacement argument suggests that we not be fooled. White men might not always be white men, and patterns that at first seem robust may be trivial or, worse, deceptive. Yvonne Tasker, for instance, argues that references to white racism by South Africans in *Lethal Weapon 2* serve merely to displace racial tensions between the cops.[4] The nature of the criminal class, in other words, is a dodge. Christopher Ames similarly argues that the trend toward Aryan criminals is no more than appeasement on the part of the genre: "No doubt these variations on evil whiteness represent a search for inoffensive villains," as though the movies are settling for Aryans in a compromising feint through which one ought to see.[5] Ames goes on to argue that because the white heroes reaffirm white supremacy, we should ignore the red herring of the fact that they so often destroy white supremacists. Carol Clover, in her study of horror genres, similarly notices that their villains tend to be working-class white guys. She notes that a "displacement of ethnic otherness onto a class of whites—to my mind far and away the most significant 'ethnic' development in popular culture of the last decade—has gone unnoticed."[6] In her argument, these criminal men, victims of "disenfranchisement" all, stand in for American Indians.[7]

Though pertaining to a different genre, with its unique moral logic, Clover's argument about horror is worth pursuing for a moment. Her research offers the intriguing theory that the recurring scenario "urban-woman-raped-by-rural-white-thugs-and-seeking-vengeance" is a reworking of a cowboys-and-Indians fantasy sublimated by a liberal refusal to demonize Native Americans openly. Clover's theory has it that, in liberal times, movies hide the fun of slaughtering the Indians by performing a racial role reversal between "rednecks" and "redskins." The pleasure of the films would lie first in identifying with the injured urban women, who take the narrative places of frontier settlers, and then in watching them wreak bloody havoc on the rural rednecks who stand in for the Indians. Murderous rape survivors function as victimized cowboys out to clean up the American plains, and the viewer gets to lap it up without having to feel like Andrew Jackson.

Perhaps the white wild men of action films substitute in much the same way, standing in for any out-group against whom a vengeful hero or audience might wish revenge as they feel the frustration of a nation gone wrong, but against whom they could not openly take such vengeance without feeling like racists. Here, the Aryans are the one racially other out-group whom most ostensive "antiracists" feel good about blowing away. Indeed, Kaja Silverman suggests that the Aryan killer of *Blade Runner*, with his square military build and bleach-blond hair, bears the burden of racial difference—he is a nonhuman replicant, in addition to being really blond—that might have been taken up by black characters, were there any in the film.[8] The Aryan is the blond racial *other* to the brown-haired cop. If this is true, than the presence of Aryan fascists as criminals may simply deflect white xenophobia onto the more politically acceptable terrain of intrawhite combat. Hence, the white heroes may bond with their conciliatory nonwhite sidekicks while still taking aim at the angriest elements of a suggestively *other* racial group. This story could speak to a fantasy of disenfranchised white men taking comfort in the arms of those by whom they feel threatened while acting out their sublimated rage.

Along the same lines, Susan Jeffords argues that the Aryan criminals of such movies as *Die Hard* and *Lethal Weapon* stand in for "enemies of Reaganism: terrorism, lawlessness, disloyalty, and the deterioration of the family."[9] For instance, with their internal loyalty surpassing their fealty to the state, the drug dealers of *Lethal Weapon*

> stand for any of the increasingly vocal groups whose challenges to the Reagan ideology were being heard across the land, groups whose identifications were increasingly defined not in terms of national loyalty, but in terms of racial, sexual, gender, or ethnic identity . . . communities of color . . . gays and lesbians . . . women . . . the poor . . . refugees . . . the disabled . . . the aging, and so on—what the Reagan and Bush administrations labeled "special interests."[10]

Such people's critiques of our society tend to disrupt the Reagan-era fantasy of morning in America, with its homogenous and consenting polity. In Jeffords's reading, the criminal class, however white, racist, right wing, rich, misogynist, and privileged they may *seem*, stand for just these rebellious and threatening communities of disenfranchised people. Why would such a moral logic appeal? Jeffords suggests that white men fear "a struggle for equal justice in which white men do not figure, and in which they are no longer the active or receiving agents of a legal system."[11] Hence, they serve the threatened state and target lawless criminals who, though white and male, actually stand in for the above-mentioned communities. Again, in the displacement argument, though white men certainly do figure in these movies as the oppressors, this appearance dodges the real point.

We can find some value in such displacement logic to the extent that it helps us to appreciate the ideological strain under which white men operate. Reagan/Bush rhetoric certainly made demons of groups with few resources, and we may well expect to see them pilloried in the popular culture of white male resentment. Nevertheless, displacement arguments attribute this moral strain to the producers of the movies, to the structure of the narratives, or to the subconscious minds of characters, whereas I prefer to regard characters as aware of and able to recognize the patterns in their behavior, in part because they so often comment on it. In other words, I argue that the genre does not so much displace a tension that it cannot handle, as face it and work with it in a straightforward way. We should look for evidence of its moral logic in the self-reports of characters, just as an ethnographer would in conversation with members of any subculture. Displacement theorists seem to have dismissed out of hand the possibility that cop action might be a huge repository for white male guilt as part of rather than instead of white male supremacy. Hence, I next offer another view—one that engages in less second-guessing and takes the details of the criminals' behaviors seriously.

Another Reading: Bad White Men

I resist any desire to find repressed meanings until I have taken seriously the most straightforward reading imaginable to a longtime fan (at least, *this* longtime fan), I will entertain the idea that cop action targets for destruction privileged Aryan manhood itself, rather than as a stand-in for something else. Simply, this well-off white manhood is the pinnacle of xenophobic evil against which cops, with all of their own white male rage, must turn in order to side with lovers and sidekicks. It presents a target for cops as they try to earn the respect and support of the nicest people they know. Criminals have blown away the ground under cops, and cops repudiate them with violence.

Criminals lavish hostility on their worlds. Some pursue neo-Nazi action (e.g., *Betrayed, Dead Bang, Fatal Beauty*). Others simply scorn those darker skinned than themselves (e.g., *Action Jackson, The Rookie, Sea of Love*). Comparison between heroes and the most violently racist criminals are made more tempting by the fact that 75 percent of the latter are dirty cops, those community protection employees whose crimes break the cop code against murder for money or hateful kicks. They cross a line of honor and join the criminal class. Nearly half of the movies feature dirty cops as principal criminals; and these bad guys love to oppress people of color, whether as contra-supporting CIA agents torturing Latinos (e.g., *Above the Law, Die Hard 2, The Last of the Finest*) or as local white cops murdering black men in their midst (e.g., *Fort Apache: The Bronx, Shakedown, Strange Days*). Cop heroes live a hair's breadth from the xenophobic fury of the criminal class and perhaps oppose it all the more when they can feel its pull.

A dirty cop in *Q & A* (that movie's principal criminal, a murderously racist gay-basher) articulates the sense of loss that drives him as he remembers old times and an old-time cop:

> What a cop! I mean, like me, he was the first through the door, the window, the skylight. I mean, he knew there was animals out there. He knew there was a line that the niggers, the spics, the junkies, the faggots had to cross to get into people's throats. He was that line. I am that line! And the fucking judges, the Jew lawyers, the aldermen, the guinea D.A.'s, are raking it in now.

> And we take a fucking hamburger and it's good-bye badge, gun, pension. And all the time it's our life that's on the line, and it's our widows and our orphans!

Bitter, dirty cops attack nonwhites whom they regard as having left their proper places in such movies as *Shakedown,* in which they catch a black man in bed with a white woman and torture him, and *Rising Sun,* in which a Japanese-baiting cop seems to want to do the same when he sees a Japanese man enjoying the company of white sex workers ("plundering our natural resources," he mutters). In *Mississippi Burning,* defensive white cops castrate a black man to terrorize the rebellious community into obedience; and in *Fort Apache: The Bronx,* a white cop hurls a young Latino off a building during a racial uprising, apparently for sport. In *Extreme Justice,* the cops on the informal "death squad" in Los Angeles are especially quick to draw weapons on men of color, to the point where one can ask in sarcasm of a rookie, "He killed his quota of two black men yet?"

The genre links murder of nonwhite community members to villainy among cops. A sixth of the movies feature nonwhite populations as the primary victims of the criminal activity; and in all but three cases, those criminals are, or at least include, racist white cops. Two movies provide an instructive contrast. *Showdown in Little Tokyo* and *Year of the Dragon* both feature Asian American drug lords spreading vice and violence through their communities. *Year of the Dragon* discusses and depicts the suffering of this community and the corruption among white cops who will lift nary a finger to stop it. In contrast, *Showdown in Little Tokyo* has no corrupt cops and depicts as the victims of the drug trade only white kids. In the logic of the genre, people of color are oppressed by whites, and rarely by members of their own group without help from corrupt whites. (The only exceptions to this rule are *Alien Nation* and *New Jack City,* in which members of nonwhite communities are oppressed by criminals among them without obvious white collusion.)

The genre makes these connections in part through the

gingerly manner in which it handles corruption among female and nonwhite cops. Dirty cops abound, and though ten of them are nonwhite men and five are women, the latter number too few, with too much time spent accounting for them and blaming the crimes on white men, for them to count as much more than reverse examples. Their exceptional status reminds us how corruption roots in white manhood.

For instance, the Latino hero of *Extreme Justice* works for a death squad but then decides to expose the racial corruption and draws more sympathy from another Latino on that squad than from anyone else. The twisted plot of *Excessive Force* leads the white hero to suspect a black sidekick of treachery. That innocent black man responds with a stern lecture about white folks making messes and blaming others. The chastened hero learns that another black sidekick really does have his hands in the till; but then, in yet another twist, learns that the *real* problem lies with the white boss, who runs the criminal show and shoots the black sidekick when the latter won't stick with the illicit program.

Such plotting pales in comparison, however, to the complexity of *Timecop*. This movie offers the unprecedented prospect of a black woman corrupted by a white male politician. Twin miracles of cop action moral logic and time travel clear her of her corruption by resurrecting her from the dead to aid in the destruction of that white politician. Finally, *Bad Boys* explains the betrayal of cops by a white female secretary among them in terms of her submission to an abusive man and her protection of her child. Nearly all of the other dirty female cops are obedient lovers of corrupt male cops. Dirty cops are white, male, and racist or misogynist or both; and if not white and male must explain that they did not really mean it when caught doing wrong. White men feel the most anger, the greatest temptation to crime.

Criminals approach white women with the same evil thoughts, and white male cops can just as easily relate to that misogyny as they can to racist rage. Criminals stalk and kill women for sport in an eighth of the movies, a set that amounts to a "serial-killer" subgenre.[12] Again, the criminals are often cops: *Off Limits* features a couple of criminal officers who take pleasure in beating and killing Vietnamese women; crazed cops in *Jennifer 8* and *Striking Distance* do the same with white women; and dirty cops beat their wives in *Internal Affairs* and *Mississippi Burning*. In short, the white men who so dominate the criminal class have a hard time being civil to those who are not white and male.

Where does such white male evil lead? My antidisplacement argument concludes with a thought from the psychoanalytic literature on fantasy and the likenesses that such patterns in villainy make possible. Slavoj Žižek describes the uses to which audiences may put unflattering images of themselves, noting that many people respond as happily to unsympathetic portrayals as to images of themselves as morally pure.[13] For instance, images of kids as brats to be abused might most resemble kids' senses of themselves. Only adults see kids as angels.[14] In similar fashion, black male audiences might respond more readily to views of themselves as cocky toughs in rap music than as the mild-mannered sidekicks.[15] Margaret Cohen suggests, for instance, that an image of a monstrously misogynist and racist man, such as the dirty cop in *Internal Affairs,* probably most entertains the white men who try but fail to be otherwise.[16] In other words, bad white men may be most striking, not as stand-ins for marginalized others, but as outrageous scapegoats for the rank and file mediocre white men who cannot get along with those very others.

The genre's white male evil runs from casual derision to the extravagant torture murders of the serial killer subgenre. This savagery could certainly cover a multitude of cops' other sins. Perhaps, in line with the protection racket logic, the criminal class fools us and merely makes everyday white cops look, well, not so bad after all. On the other hand, the similarities between criminals and cops also tar the latter by association. Cops are also white men and also treat women and nonwhite men with derision. I turn next to those cop heroes' sins. If criminals make heroes look like half decent men, then what shared sins might heroes want to cover, and do they fess up to their guilt?

White Male Guilt

Cop heroes suffer white male paranoia in a time of losing ground. They display their resentments boldly and have become defensive about their aggression. They stay silent when chastised and sometimes even apologize. Where neo-nazi and misogynist serial killers can look like slobbering fools drunk with fury, cops look sort of ornery and stubborn, although at times truly angry. Their white guy hostilities earn them lectures from sidekicks, who work hard to whip cop personalities into shape.

To explore the limits of rage among heroes, I begin with the relations between male and female cops, so rarely analyzed in the literature but just as interesting as the more famous buddy pairs. These pairings display much of the workplace tension one expects in good ol' boy turf. Thousands of men work on each side of the law across the genre; and, barring extras in the background, we find just a few more than a hundred women engaged in law enforcement. Further, of the hundreds of women who appear in these movies, only ten author destruction as heroes (in *Betrayed, Blue Steel, Copycat, Fargo, Fatal Beauty, Impulse, The Long Kiss Goodnight, The Silence of the Lambs, A Stranger Among Us,* and *Vampire in Brooklyn*).

Such women remain new to cop action, as one would expect of an occupation so marked as manly. Though male rookies are seldom heroes, three of these ten heroes have just graduated from their academies. *Blue Steel*'s hero shoots a man on her first day on the job. A superior officer (who will later become her lover) derides her performance, suggests that she will lose her job, and instructs her in the proper use of her weapon.

A number of men wonder why she even wants to be a cop, and each hears a different response: "Ever since I was a kid. . . . I wanted to shoot people"; "I like to slam people's heads up against walls"; and finally, in reference to the serial killer she hunts, "Him."

Male cops affirm the newcomer status of women by expressing endless surprise at their work. "Where'd you learn to fight like that?" asks *Lethal Weapon 3*'s hero.

"Catholic school," answers his sidekick after earlier attributing her skills to "P.M.S."

"I had three brothers," explains another in *Universal Soldier* after coldcocking another cop.

In *Timecop,* the hero turns chivalrous before one of the few "dirty" female cops. He cannot imagine her attacking him and says, "I don't want to fight a woman."

Happily, she says, "Then don't," and knocks him down. Men who can punch their way through a fight rarely draw the admiration of other men; but women's violence never becomes routine.

The reaction of male cops to women's rough work grows even weirder, though, as men quickly disarm female cops and lovers when they get in their licks. The sidekick in *Demolition Man* shoots a criminal but then has her gun taken away and is knocked out by the hero so that he can finish the fighting alone. The sidekick in *Fair Game* shoots a criminal who sneaks up on her as she embraces her hero and then has her gun taken away. The sidekick in *Low Down Dirty Shame* shoots an attacking criminal in a fire fight, has her gun taken away, and is sent off to safety. The cops' lovers in *Excessive Force* and *The Rookie* shoot attacking criminals and then have their guns taken away by the cops they have saved. Even the hero of *Blue Steel,* after shooting an attacking criminal, later has both her badge and her gun taken away by her boss. A few of these women do hold onto their weapons but still distance themselves from the violence. The sidekick in *Under Siege* complains that she will never fire a gun, shoots one man in the hero's defense, and earns only his bemused smirk. The cop's daughter in *Last Action Hero* has a single scene of combat in which she must pretend to be a damsel in distress to avoid calling attention to herself as she beats a man to death.

Female heroes work on tight reins. Male cops prefer them as lovers and draw two-thirds of these colleagues into romance as if to establish themselves as the real cops.[17] Women must explain themselves as gender benders if they do violence and will most likely be treated as women—disarmed, belittled, and romanced. Though, as I show in the next chapter, a few women join the ranks of cops as self-destructive combatants, most stay out because men will not let them in.

Cop manhood depends, however, on more than this exclusion of women. Criminals, one in eight of whom kill women for sport, set a pattern of outrageous misogyny against which one can measure cop morality. Heroes have their own problems with women. Some of these arise in the domestic relations described in Chapter 2, and all point to a pervasive white male guilt for which cops deserve punishment. The more xenophobic and misogynist they are, the more humiliation and injury they will endure. For instance, the rapist heroes of *Basic Instinct* and *Rush* both head for early graves, as does the woman-beating hero of *Gang Related*. Fellow criminals blow the second two away onscreen, and the former has an ice pick awaiting him the day his lover loses patience.[18] Only the guiltiest, almost always white men, deserve the self-abusive combat in which men pay for their sins. Women—morally better in so many ways—have little place there.

Cop and Copycat

You could follow the serial killer subgenre from *Dirty Harry*'s sniper to the baroque sadist of *Copycat,* a movie steeped in the media-friendly FBI "profiling" lore, which benefits in popularity from a mass fetishism of murdered women. Twenty-two cop action movies feature criminals who slaughter women for sport in ugly ways (only three sex-killers concentrate on men, in the Pacino movies *Cruising* and *Sea of Love,* and in the remake of both, *Basic Instinct*). I find myself frightened more by them than by nazi terrorists and high-flying bandits, and I cannot help noticing the warped personalities of the white male cops who hunt them. One of the noncinematic FBI celebrities titled his book *Whoever Fights Monsters,* after Neitzsche's caution that we tend to become what we pursue, and the genre certainly gives us much to think about along those lines. What's wrong with white men, and what makes them so pissed off at white women?

Cop and *Copycat* differ primarily in the distribution of cop functions among characters. *Cop* gives them all to one hero, and *Copycat* splits them among various women and men. Either way, white men turn out to be the problem. To summarize: *Cop*'s white male hero obsesses over the grisly murder of a white woman. He pursues the case until he can identify a serial killer at large; and along the way loses his wife and child to marital conflict, pursues doomed sexual relations with two other women, gets fired over his lawless hunting, and finally blows the killer away. *Copycat* begins with a female officer, who teams with two men and a female expert in serial killers. The two women identify a psychopath at large. Along the way the female hero loses the male cops in different ways (one dead, the other estranged), risks her status at work to continue the hunt, and finally blows the killer away. I'll run through each movie in some detail to show the ways in which they blame a world's problems on jealous and sexually frustrated white guys.

Lloyd, the hero of *Cop* lectures his wife about young women:

> All these little girls have one thing in common. You know what that is? Disillusionment. And it always comes from the same thing: Expectations, the greatest woman-killer of all time, a terminal disease that starts way back when they're all just little

girls, when they're being fed all the bullshit about being entitled
to happiness like it's a birthright. That's what you don't
understand—when to stop perpetrating the myths that ruin their
lives. Innocence kills, Jen. Believe me, it kills. I see it every
fucking day of my life.

Lloyd's dark view of a threatening world teems with pretty
white women, whom he scorns when he feels rejected, and
whom he fears resentful psychos will kill. He clings to hope for
his own daughter though he dislikes most women. "Why can't
they fly, Dutch?" he asks a sidekick. "Why can't they fucking
fly like us, huh?"

Dutch gives an elder cop's advice: "No wings, kid, it's the
way they're made. Nothing they can do on their own is much
fun for them. Without a guy it's all a waste of time. And if you
don't mind a little advice from your dutch uncle, don't try to
change it."

"It's fucking pathetic," says Lloyd. "There's no way [my
daughter's] going to be like that. She's going to fly, Dutch.
The wings are there and they're real big ones."

"You better hope the tits are there and they're real big ones.
In this world she'll get a lot further with a pair of those."

"Jesus, you're as bad as—" It's not clear whom Lloyd could
mean besides himself (we have met no other such characters so
early in the story) when he stops speaking as the car they have
waited for pulls up. The driver tries to flee and Lloyd blows him
away. A voluptuous young woman in a skimpy dress emerges
from the car, and, with a predatory look up and down, Lloyd
offers her a ride home.

Dutch observes, "You see what I mean about big tits?"

Later, Lloyd goes home to find a note from his wife, in
which she announces her departure and intent to keep their
daughter far from him and his assault on her innocence. Lloyd
never does contact them, and in fact demonstrates more concern for finding and blowing away the serial killer than for
restoring his family. Though he never says so, Lloyd seems well

aware of the danger he poses to women whom he dearly loves and wants to protect. His maniacal devotion to the police work of catching killers seems as much an attempt to wrestle private demons as loyalty to his job. Later, Lloyd finds a prostitute murdered, her tortured body bound near the place and position in which he had recently enjoyed sex with her. He finds the grisly scene on a visit for more sex and looks deeply shaken.

The incident echoes the modus operandi of the criminal in *Tightrope,* who torments the cop by killing prostitutes the cop has just bedded, in ways that evoke the cop's own exploits and thus both disturbs the cop and implicates him in the crimes. Similar events occur in *Striking Distance,* in which the cop's former partner kills the cop's former girlfriends, and in *Murphy's Law,* in which a female serial killer revenges herself on a white male cop by framing him for murders. Rejected by his young, cute wife, the cop hero stalks her to her strip club, watches her perform, and then abuses her verbally. The killer dispatches this ex-wife *in flagrante dilecto* with her boyfriend, framing the cop for the murder. Given the cop's behavior, no one doubts that he killed her. Each of these movies plays on the ease with which we can see abusive male heroes moving to violence against the women they desire; and each movie makes its hero face his guilt and then sends him into harrowing conflict with his mirror.

Copycat also compares its bitter white guys, despite its starring a woman as its hero. The fact that white guy characters remain constant suggests that guilt belongs more to them than to heroes. M.J., the hero, works late at night to study crime-scene photos as she hunts a killer who is furious with pretty young white women. Her former boyfriend, Nico, a white male cop, startles her. "You scared me," she says. Nico stews in anger at having been dumped, and the movie cuts back and forth between his resentment and the killer, who also wants nothing more than the attention of women. "He wants what those killers got," says a female sidekick about the young copycat murderer, "—fame, the power to terrify us. . . . We're looking for someone desperate for acceptance. . . . If he wants to be famous he has to be caught."

"So that you can write a book about him," concludes the hero. Both of these white women know the men around them well. What wouldn't such men do to stake their claims on women they find attractive? Soon, the copycat moves in to torture another woman to death, and in the following scene Nico picks a fight in a jealous rage, deriding as he goes young women who enjoy their sexual freedom. The serial killer subgenre, from *Cop* to *The Silence of the Lambs,* concerns white men who hate the white women who spurn or ignore them. Cop or criminal, loose or imprisoned, savage or polite, they are all resentful and they are all scary.

In many ways Lloyd and Nico exemplify the cop-hero type: both grungy in their approach to work with all-nighters and low-rent wardrobes, both unable to maintain affectionate relations, both unable or unwilling to bite back on their hostilities, both callous toward innocent and fun-loving young women. "She's probably so stoned out she never knew what got her, I guess," snorts Nico over a mutilated corpse in *Copycat.* "A lot of little hippie girls—they all want to make love. They all want to be beautiful. That's your type, right, Ruben?" he says to the dapper young sidekick, whom M.J.—perhaps the only woman in Nico's brutish life—does desire. Nico doesn't understand such women and later brings about Ruben's death by carelessness. He tells the grieving hero that he's sorry and later that he loves her. M.J. looks upon him with real compassion but declines to return the endearment and instead walks away to kill a man with feelings very much like Nico's.

Back in *Cop,* Lloyd could relate to Nico's bewildered rage. Meeting an attractive woman who prefers a flowery poet to a rough-edged cop, Lloyd at first becomes disgusted and bored, though hungry for the sex. Later, after he learns that her dreamy poet is his serial killer, Lloyd's boredom turns to real

venom and he castigates this woman for her errant tastes before walking away to kill the man ridden with even more
misogyny.

However similar their white guys, these movies end in very
different ways, each important to cop action moral logic. *Copycat* loses sight of poor Nico, who disappears after failing to
draw a return "I love you" from M.J. With the male cops gone,
the two women fight it out with the criminal, whose never-say-
die taste for blood forces M.J. to drop her womanish dislike for
killing and just blow his head open. Like the bloody finales of
Blue Steel and *The Silence of the Lambs,* this one offers little joy
in the killing. Female heroes in cop action seldom seem pleased
to deliver their coups de grâce. They must kill to make a safer
world, one with fewer white men in it, but they take little pleasure in the ugly chores.

The title character of *Cop,* in contrast, happily wades into
combat with his prey. After spewing rage at the object of his
abortive lust (the one woman who has not left him or been
murdered for having sex with him by this point), Lloyd bar-
gains with the criminal over an exclusive relationship: "Let her
go, Hopkins," says the criminal of this woman, of whom he has
made a fetish. "She's not like all the rest."

"Right," says Lloyd, anxious to get to a relationship more
satisfying than what this woman can offer. "What? Are you
talking a deal?"

"Just let her go."

"Then what?"

"Then we've just got you and me."

"That's the kind of deal I like. You pick the time and the
place, homeboy." Lloyd has tired of angling for women and
turns instead toward a man with whom he can grapple in his
rough-house manner. Serial killers give men like Lloyd the
pleasure of the kind of combat in which they can blow off some
frustrations. Female heroes blow such men away because they
must; but guys like Lloyd do it for fun. *Cop* ends with an eight-

minute-long assignation, the two men slowly cruising each other, each looking forward to the final blows, at last battling to the death. In this way, cop action restores male sexual aggression to what seems to be its rightful place: between the bad white men upon whom this genre centers its story of lost ground.

The movie ends just as Lloyd blows the killer away with a shotgun at close range. As the shot rings out, the screen cuts to black, and after a moment the credits roll, as if the criminal's end closed Lloyd's story as well. The male cops know the criminals they hunt because they share so many of their symptoms. Lloyd begins to understand his criminal prey by arranging photographs of murdered women on his desk. One look at a row of "innocent" young, pretty, white women tells Lloyd how the criminal feels. The "innocence" of women refers to their dreams of men more fun to be around, more caring and concerned with a lover's happiness than a cop hero can be. The implicit demand for skills they do not possess enrages cops, to the point where they can sympathize with killers well enough. The innocence defines womanhood as unfit for the real world of serial killers and the men who must hunt them. By contrast, their rage at those women defines male cops as perfect for it.

Manhunter similarly plays off of the white male cops' eerie ability to descend into the mind of a bizarre killer. The cop has problems as a husband: a history of delving so deep into the minds of misogynist killers that he ends up unable to live with his wife and child, and a devotion to work that leads him to neglect them altogether. He intuits that the criminal stages elaborate sexual rituals with the corpses of the white women because he wants to play at the normal life that his shame-ridden personality denies him. Cops and criminals alike mourn the white nuclear families they might have had were they not so angry with their lovers for wanting more from men. The killer in *Se7en* even visits the hero's wife, tries to play husband to her, and then kills her for spite and thus robs the cop of his marriage—a marriage probably doomed anyway by the cop's disinterest in his wife's aspirations and complaints.

Cops do not all seem so hateful, unattractive, or incompetent. Wives and girlfriends seem happy enough in *The First Deadly Sin, Timecop,* and *The Untouchables;* but they are the only three romantic partners in the genre who do not complain about the shortcomings of their relationships. Sadly for these three, the first woman spends the movie on her deathbed and dies in the final scene, and the second woman dies in an early scene. We have the cops' word that the deceased wife in the background of the *Lethal Weapon* movies was also content. This leaves Elliot Ness's spouse in *The Untouchables* the single cop action wife who makes no complaints and seems truly happy from beginning to end, even when shipped out of harm's way as the criminals move in for the kill (perhaps the setting of the movie in the era of prohibition allows the sentimental view of a happy marriage).

Women in cop action rarely attain heroism—their male colleagues often get in their way when they try. Instead, women serve to define the men around them as true cops— angry enough with demanding women, guilty over victimized women, and ashamed enough of their own misogyny to work at its violent repudiation. This gives cops the hard time and satisfying charge to their gunplay—this mixture of rage and shame befitting white guys in the cop world. They have lost ground as self-satisfied lovers and resent women for making so many demands and leaving them to feel so inadequate. They can be heroes if they limit their expressions of this rage to the occasional argument or manly isolation and avoid the serial killing that they understand so well.

I turn next to the way in which heroes play out a related set of conflicts with their nonwhite sidekicks, who do a great deal of work calling heroes to account for their racial scorn. Nonwhite men see more violent action than women do, since they do not work as figures of sexual innocence against which heroes measure themselves. Instead, men of color follow heroes more closely and confront white guys over their racism. They work as foils for resentment over the diminishment of a white-guy occupational turf. Heroes have a hard time with this incursion. They avoid really bad status by changing their personalities rather than just shooting those who chide them.

Heroes Chastised

Heroes are not as white as the criminals. They are more like no-breed mutts than Aryans and a blond hero is hard to find.[19] Spawn of a middle-American gene pool, these cops are "unhyphenated whites," for whom specific ethnicity (Irish or Italian, for instance) remains more an option than a permanent mark. The genre's few heroic blondes show up in *Flashback, I Come in Peace, Renegades, Showdown in Little Tokyo, Stone Cold, Thunderheart,* and *Wanted Dead or Alive.* When cops engage the Aryan criminal class, they draw battle lines between two kinds of whiteness: the unremarkable-mutt hero versus the blond and often avowedly racist über-men. The mutt-cops tend to have little background dealing with those not white and male and often react badly.

At one end of a continuum of abuse stands the good ol' boy humor. White boys like to poke fun at their sidekicks, perhaps because they can feel better about having their turf trod by women and men of color.[20] Certainly, in a genre that so clearly marks hero and sidekick roles by race, class, and gender, this humor must bear those marks as well. In the *Lethal Weapon* movies, the white hero teases and pulls pranks on the black sidekick, who plays straight man and takes it with good humor. In *Running Scared,* the white cop announces his presence in the black cop's home by blaring a police siren over the bed the latter shares with a date. Perhaps the joking lets heroes vent steam over the workplace frustrations described above. They feel defensive about what they regard as slipping class positions and hit back in little ways when they can at the symbols of that slide.

Another level of abuse involves the recruitment of unwilling men of color in battles between whites, battles in which men of color have little personal interest. For instance, *Die Hard with a Vengeance* features one of the many protection-racket scams that white cops run. A white criminal amuses himself by extorting the white cop John into wearing an "I hate niggers" sign in Harlem one sunny day. A black man, Zeus, sees this and helps John escape with his skin, so to speak. John thanks him and must ask for further assistance; but Zeus says no. Zeus knows perfectly well that a hero/sidekick relation of subordination could develop and prefers to return to Harlem and the black people whose struggles interest him more. He explains to John exactly why he helped him in the first place: "I stopped a white cop from getting killed in Harlem. One white cop gets killed today, tomorrow we got a thousand white cops, all of them with itchy trigger fingers. Got it?"

Like most heroes, John might prefer to keep his distance from such help but follows an order to get Zeus involved. He believes that Zeus won't help white cops out of simple generosity, so John makes up a lie about a bomb planted in Harlem. "Listen," he chides Zeus, "this [bomber] doesn't care about skin color, even if you do." Zeus relents. Later, they argue about racism; and John, feeling unappreciated and perhaps guilty, yells, "Have you got some fucking problem with me 'cause I'm white, Zeus? Is that it, huh? Have I oppressed you? Have I oppressed your people somehow? I'll tell you what your problem is. You don't like me because you're a racist."

Zeus gapes at John's stupidity. "What?"

"You're a racist. You don't like me because I'm white."

"I don't like you because you're going to get me killed!" White people draw blacks into conflicts of white origin as a part of larger pattern of subordination. A separatist out of experience with exploitive white guys like John, Zeus resists this pull.

Self-conscious of the politics of his protection racket, John bickers no more.

Near the end, as death looms, the two men become more friendly, and John indulges in some white male confession. "I'm an asshole. . . . I lied to you, Zeus. . . . Remember I said '[They] found that bomb up in Harlem'? . . . They found it down in Chinatown."

Bemused and disgusted at the same time, Zeus laughs, "Oh, now that's low, even for a white motherfucker like you."

"I told you I was an asshole." So indeed are many of the cops, who usually admit as much. They find many ways to be white and exploit others, and sidekicks chastise them accordingly. These confrontations show us how cops do and do not mirror the criminals they hunt. In the movies in which partners already know each other, racial, ethnic, and gender hostilities seem not to rear their heads in such explicit fashion. Nevertheless, while heroes usually manage minimal respect for their partners, some also move beyond the "just kidding" stage.

The hero of *Thunderheart* refers to residents of the reservation on which he works as "Tonto" and "Chief." Upon meeting a full-blooded Native American cop, he tackles him to the ground and brutally arrests him, with minimal apology when he discovers his error. In *Alien Nation*, a white male hero teams with an Alien sidekick whose species (former slaves stranded on earth) he dislikes. The cop heaps abuse on his comrade ("slag," and other alien-epithets), and the sidekick wonders in response:

> You humans are very curious to us. You invite us to live among you in an atmosphere of equality that we've never known before. You give us ownership of our own lives for the first time, and you ask no more of us than you do of yourselves. I hope you understand how special your world is, how unique a people you humans are. Which is why it is all the more painful and confusing to us that so few of you seem capable of living up to the ideals you set for yourselves.

The cop listens and will eventually learn some respect but cannot account for himself at the moment. "Don't count on me, George," he says. "I never had any ideals."

Heroes learn slowly and dislike to admit their collective guilt, so nonwhite cops must guard against heroes' attempts to demean them. This is not to say that they always do respond, of course. The genre focuses on white men, and sidekicks stay on the sidelines. Nevertheless, they protest the situations here and there. In *48 Hours,* for instance, the white cop assails his captive black sidekick (a convict in his custody) with a slew of abuse ("boy," "spearchucker," "watermelon," "nigger," etc.). Later, after they have developed a bit of mutual respect, the white man excuses his choice of words: "You know, 'nigger,' and 'watermelon'—I didn't mean that stuff. I was just doing my job, keeping you down."

The black man faces him down. "Yeah, well, doing your job don't explain everything, Jack." Jack admits as much and thereafter (and through the sequel) mouths off no more.

In *Rising Sun,* an older and more experienced white cop instructs his black partner to assume a role subordinate to his *sempai* in their dealings with Japanese businessmen. "My *sempai*," the black cop snorts in reply. "That wouldn't happen to be anything like 'massa,' now, would it?" They bicker until the black cop condemns the white man for the ease with which others bribe him and he covers it up as "business." "Well," says the black man of hush money laundered through a country club membership, "That makes everything 'all white' then, doesn't it?" The dirty white cop looks confused and says nothing.

Sometimes, conflict escalates to violence. The Native American sidekick of *Renegades* has to tell his white partner to stop calling him "Chief" and beats him up when pushed past his endurance. In *Off Limits,* a white male cop stationed in Vietnam during the 1960s argues with an A.R.V.N. officer about the identities of the killers of an American soldier. "Yeah," he says in his most intimidating manner, "they were slopes; gooks; little, tiny, slant-eyed V.C. motherfuckers with Hawaiian shirts."

The Vietnamese officer stays cool: "Somehow I find it hard to feel sorry for you losing one friend when hundreds of Vietnamese are dying each day. But then I suppose America is a study in self-possession. [We] should remember that."

The white cop becomes defensive about his self-obsession, and moves to attack in a rage, so that others must pull him off. The A.R.V.N. officer counsels him, "Your passion is misdirected, Sergeant. The man who killed your friend is working for the same people you are." Such indeed turns out to be true—the killer is a white U.S. Army officer, dizzy with xenophobia, who kills Vietnamese women. Learning this, the white cop learns yet another lesson about the supremacy that he represents as a white male cop in a nonwhite community.

I recount these arguments, situations, and character types to give a sense of what racial criticism sounds like in cop action. Cops can be racist, must be told off by members of the groups they despise, and then move on. Surely one would expect no less of a genre that addressed itself to the conflict between liberal harmony and civil discontent. Cops have a hard time with a changing, demanding world. They could hardly be accused of being too passive, receptive, or ingratiating to those around them. They growl and huff before they learn to relax and behave.

Nevertheless, analysts argue about this, for not everyone sees these cops as mindful of their racial conflict. *Rising Sun* draws complaints of racism, not just for its guilty white male cop, but as a racist movie. bell hooks, who must have defined hero and sidekick roles differently than I have, argues that "in his secondary role, the subordinated black man not only happily does as the master orders him, always eager to please, he even falls in love with the Asian woman daddy has cast aside."[21] Similarly, David Ehrenstein notes that the white cop, [John,] "struts across the screen as a preening Mr. Know-it-All, regarding both [the black cop] and his Japanese adversaries as annoyances far beneath his lofty status. . . . Rarely has the white man's burden been given such a[n] overweeningly narcissistic spin."[22] About the specifics of this last critique I am in complete agreement, even if the white guy's status as first-class-prick does more than reaffirm white supremacy. He must learn a thing or two about the guilt he shares with criminals, those who find it so easy to bribe him into complicity.

Paul Cowen, in another example of very different analyses of these movies, regards them as implicitly racist in their depiction of the heroes' hostile joking with their sidekicks: "Such conflict is often presented as harmless, natural, and acceptable, especially if it concerns the relationship between two men."[23] About *48 Hours* in particular, the movie that features as much racist abuse as any other, Cowen worries that the movie "is neither clear about the racist overtones in [the white cop, Jack's] behavior toward [his black sidekick, Reggie], nor those in [Reggie's] attitude either toward himself or toward his companion."[24] In other words, these analysts' argue, by allowing racist remarks to pass between two partners who fast become friends, the movie excuses the hostility, or at least makes it seem a personal, as opposed to a political, matter.

> [Jack] is the "good" guy and hero, saving his partner but effacing the fact that he expressed more prejudice than any other character during the entire film, and that his apparent camaraderie with [Reggie] was actually full of violence, hostility, and mistrust supported by racial differences.[25]

Other analysts fault cop movies for trying to have it both ways. Donald Bogle argues that "*Lethal Weapon* says that there are no significant cultural gaps or distinctions for the two men to bridge. . . . Never is one led to think [that the black sidekick] finds his home a refuge from the white world in which he works."[26] Similarly, depictions of Reggie and Axel, the sidekick and hero of the *48 Hours* and *Beverly Hills Cop* movies, as successfully teaming with white cops "represented a flight from serious confrontation with racial tensions."[27] Specifically, "the fact that . . . Reggie never becomes enraged or truly angry greatly neutralizes the inherent racism" of Jack's baiting in *48 Hours*.[28]

Manthia Diawara and Ed Guerrero support their views of *48 Hours* as a white supremacist movie in part with their assessments of the black and white characters. According to Diawara, the white hero is "tough, persevering and just, whereas [the black man] is exhibitionist, inconsistent (swaying between good and evil) and inauthentic."[29] According to Guerrero, the black man is "an impulsive fool."[30] Neither author elaborates.

I can only observe (in line with the definition of interpretation that I offer in the Appendix) the methodological muddle made by attributions of such disparagement to movies. I mean, *who* finds this black sidekick "inconsistent" and "inauthenic"? Why do such analysts not specify their roles in such derision? There must be a point where a viewer "owns" a hostile characterization and at least takes responsibility for defending it with some specifics rather than simply projecting it onto a movie or its producers. Nevertheless, I read *48 Hours* differently, as yet another movie in which the socially graceful black sidekick teaches the white hero how to attend to his lover, maintain loyalties, earn trust, and rethink his racial paranoia. In the sequel, using metaphors only a cop could love, the sidekick teaches the hero about class and crime: "Jack, you don't get it, do you? You make it sound like everybody went down to the guidance counselor, took a test, and the results came back: 'Crook' was the only job they was qualified for. . . . Let me tell you something, Jack. If shit was worth something, poor people would be born with no assholes." White male cops pick up lessons about the world from those around them. As for the analysts—even taking into account the serious frustration one feels seeing black characters so often stuck with critical/supportive sidekick roles—I cannot guess how one derives from such movies the disparagement of the black sidekick mentioned above.

Cop action makes its racial tensions plain to anyone willing to look. Characters argue about their problems, and those turn out to regard white male morality. Humorous or not, nonwhites do a great deal of work in the genre to direct attention toward racial problems. In *Collision Course,* in which a Japanese cop must team with a white hero in Detroit of all places, working-class joes sound off on their economic woes. The hero complains, "When I was a kid, this whole area [the ghost town of formerly industrial Detroit] was alive; and then you guys came along with your tin can cars and slave wages, —put everybody out of business."

Laughing, Fujitsuka says, "You blame all Japanese for the problem of Detroit."

Teasing, but then more serious, the hero, Tony, says, "No, I don't blame all Japanese. I just blame you—and blame ourselves for getting fat and letting it happen."

Upon his entrance into the working-class haven of a bowling alley, Fujitsuka runs a gauntlet of angry taunts: "Did somebody order sushi?" "We've got a score to settle here, mister," and "I want to know when you guys are going to do something about the balance of trade." A large black man prods Fujitsuka, "How do you expect to improve the relations with other nations if you show them no respect?"

Still, when a white guy threatens violence, another rebukes the goon and spells out cop action's moral punch-line. "You make me laugh. It's guys like you with attitudes like yours that put America in the situation it's in right now." Cop action traces lost ground to bad white men.

As some analysts have argued, the good ol' boy humor may undercut the critical power of the confrontations and leave onlookers with little to think about. Bogle provides a lengthy analysis of such a scene from *Beverly Hills Cop,* a movie, he argues, that "tripped very lightly past the issue of race or racial distinctions. On one level, it turns the very idea of racism into a joke."[31] That joke plays out when the hero, Axel, orders himself a suite in a posh Beverly Hills hotel by denouncing the staff as racist for telling him that they're booked up. Bogle argues that white audiences could find validation in such a scene for their belief that blacks find racism in places where it does not exist.

> The black audience, however, feels that race is probably part of the issue. After all, Axel's ploy does get him the room. Yet because Axel is a bluffer and because the scene is played for quick laughter the idea of racism, in a sense, is suppressed altogether.
>
> Throughout, the film . . . is determined that the audience forget the hero's color.[32]

In such an argument, cop action offers to a society torn by racial strife (or at least to the white people in it) little more than the idea that we can all just get along, that neither racial differences nor discrimination matter as more than butts of humor, and that anyone who worries about them is either paranoid or dishonest. In short, cop action responds to slipping privileges by affirming the acceptability of white racism and denying its consequences.

Indeed, wisecracking cops laugh off most of what they do. The hero of *Lethal Weapon 2* urges a move into action with a quick cheer to his sidekick: "Come on, Rog. Don't be a killjoy. Come on, come on. We're back, we're bad. You're black, I'm mad. Come on!" Does such banter displace or trivialize the racial divide between the men? The liberal dream that we can just get along seems to inspire many in a nation tired of the conflicts that its economic and tribal engines power. The wish that black men would quiet down and leave "us" alone must be popular enough to shape our fantasies in some way.

Nevertheless, I can only wonder how laughter can "erase" or "ignore" anything here in the genre. Some of the humor in cop action seems to celebrate both the ability of men such as *Beverly Hills Cop*'s black hero, Axel, to cope with whites on one hand, and the stupidity of white cops on the other. Humor can air the frustration that racism breeds rather than cover it up

(and maybe give embarrassed white guys a vent for their cha-
grin as they absorb the stinging rebuke). Constance Penley
notes that white trash pornographic humor targets as idiots
white men who cannot please those around them.[33] Why
should humor always torpedo thoughtful debate? Can laughter at stupid white guys subvert nothing? Look for a moment
at one of cop action's highest racial walls, that which forbids
sex between black male heroes and white women (which sort
of fell in 1998's *U.S. Marshalls*). Men breach it in *Heart Condition,* in which a bizarre plot twist puts a dead black lawyer's
heart into the body of racist white cop and then teams the two
men, as cop and ghost. The deceased black man, Stone, begins
the buddy relation by teasing the white cop about his racial
paranoia:

> Personally, I think that this racism, this refusal to acknowledge
> me, stems from feelings of inadequacy. I mean, you look at me—
> what do you see? Someone college-educated, damn good
> looking, hung like a Shetland pony; and you feel threatened. Am
> I hitting a nerve?

The white cop tries to ignore the jokey derision, simmers in
silent shame, and hunkers down to get his white girlfriend and
job back. His pragmatic approach to reclaiming all he has lost
allows for no expressions of grief or shame. His outlet is rage
and rage alone.[34]

Later, as the plot thickens, the cop discovers that his girlfriend has borne a child by Stone (they were involved before
the black man died). The white cop explodes with fury as
everything he loved and for which he labored seems to have
fallen into the hands of this black man and the parasite class he
represents.

> What is this shit? Fucking got to be some kind of curse. . . . Fuck!
> You work your ass off. For what? Fucking what? I'm not good
> enough for [her]. Even my own heart ain't good enough. Shit!
> It's a fucking white curse.

Finally, the cop's fantasies come together: "No it's not. It's a black fucking conspiracy!"

Stone is dumbfounded. "A what?"

"You— you heard me. You fucking people— you creep up around us, you suck up to us, you make us trust you, and then you— all the time, you're robbing us blind!"

"We do that, huh?"

"You, you fucking—"

Stone is on him like lightning: "Yeah, say it, huh: 'niggers,' right? 'Coon,' 'chinks,' 'spics,' 'kike,' 'mook,' 'niggers,' 'niggers,' '*niggers*'!" The two men scream at each other and the cop actually suffers another heart attack from the strain, as if to reject the black organ inside him.

One could say much about such a scene and the fear of black men that it represents. For one thing, *Heart Condition* brushes close to the sensitive men genre, which tell of injuries to well-to-do white men and their subsequent recoveries in the forms of more considerate guys, often black.[35] That genre seems to have been designed to answer the question, What does it take to make a white guy nice? with some abuse and then some therapy. The abuse includes a bullet in the brain (*Regarding Henry*), cancer (*The Doctor*), loss of children (*Hook*), loss of family (*The Prince of Tides*), loss of job (*Doc Hollywood, The Fisher King, Jerry Maguire, Michael*), a nightmare of endless repetition (*Groundhog Day*), and death (*Dave, Ghost*). The therapy includes ministrations from black men, white women, children, and other souls more kindly than the average white man. Similarly, the cop action comedy *Heart Condition* throws at the hero a series of insults and injuries designed to draw his attention, punish him for his crimes, and point up for him his stupidity in the face of a world that will not abide the sense of superiority with which he was raised. The black sidekick Stone must lecture *Heart Condition*'s cop on working and playing well with others in the urban economic milieu. After suffering in shame, the cop comes around.

Certainly cop action has yet to see sex between a black male cop and a white woman on screen. The taboo remains. But it does not go undiscussed, and the blame falls very clearly on the heads of angry white cops, like those in *Shakedown* who catch a black man in bed with a white woman and torture him for it. Bad white men remain the obvious problem.

Why does all of this tension and scrapping seem like a rightful part of heroism? I can imagine a different genre in which white male heroes welcome others into their occupational turf; but it would not give as satisfying a hard time. Cops who got along too well with such newcomers would not retain that gruff exterior for which men are known. The genre occasionally pokes fun at men too anxious to work with others. The nerdy white male sidekicks of movies such as *I Come in Peace* and *Stone Cold* are pleased to meet their new heroes and happy to say so. Those heroes return the enthusiasm with long glares and sullen silence.

Perhaps I am overreaching here, but the hostility to newcomers seems to insure a certain heterosexuality as well, whether the hero confronts women or men (and if I may be a bit arch, something must maintain their straight identity, since the sexual bonding cops do certainly doesn't—see Chapter 7). Years of cop action fandom leaves me imagining a friendly hero baking brownies and making tea for his new sidekick. Maybe they go shopping together after work. To the extent that he is nice to new coworkers, the hero might just seem gay. The non-action cop movie *Partners* (1982) comes to mind, in which a straight cop hero teams with a gay cop to catch a homophobic killer (the movie amounts to a sweet and silly version of the hated 1980 gay-killer movie *Cruising*). *Partners* includes many scenes in which the aproned and fussy gay man cooks and cleans for his new partner and roommate. His friendliness and social competence seem to be a function of the crush he has on the typically awkward and withdrawn hero, who is heterosexual to the degree that he is graceless.

A cop action cliché has a manager introduce the hero to his new sidekick, someone pointedly not white and male. The hero looks at this newcomer, looks at the boss, and walks out in disgust. One could argue that the neo-Nazi and misogynist criminals distract attention from the cop's own xenophobia. Rather than distraction or erasure, though, I find that the genre makes a pointed comparison. It links with humor the frustration of working-class white male heroes who feel their turf shrinking with the hostilities of the criminal class. Many of the cops seem perfectly aware of these connections, and ones who may not be live among those who are. Perhaps they blow the criminals away because they can see the continuum of rage and wish to draw a moralistic line between their paranoia born of lost ground and the murderous license criminals take. Drawing lines is not denial; it is morality.

What most bothers me about this genre is not any "erasure" of inequality or morality with humor or anything else, so much as the obsessive attention that nonwhite lovers and sidekicks must pay to ornery white personalities, as though they had nothing better to do than give free therapy. In Chapter 2 I show what patience wives must bring to their jobs, just to be around the annoying heroes. Sidekicks must also spend as much of their time beating and massaging white personalities into shape as they do hunting criminals. For them, attention to heroes is the job. They pay for the heroes' manly hard times with their energy, as though white manhood were everybody's concern.

Whatever the injustice in their division of therapeutic labor, lovers and sidekicks keep the heat on. In *Colors,* a Latina from the neighborhood the white male hero polices tells him off and dumps him after a brief affair. She protests his abusive treatment of her Latino relatives and neighbors: "That's mean, Danny. You're sadistic. I'm not with you. I'm with them. . . . It's you who threatened me, Danny. You have a mean heart." Thus ends their relationship. Danny slowly sees that his approach to law enforcement alienates the Latinos with whom he might like to get along, and in shame stops trying to reach across the community divide. In the end, he adopts a more compassionate approach to his job and takes on a black male sidekick.

Finally, in *Q & A,* the white hero, similarly dumped by his black-Latina girlfriend over his racist response to her family, moons over the loss. The classless, raceless world of his utopian dreams seems far away. Cops around him, black, white, and Latino, mock him for fearing blacks and yet wallowing in guilt and impotence. A renegade, racist cop, on the other hand, ridicules him for his disloyalty to white men. By the end, after he has failed to stop this murderously bad white man or save anyone, the hero realizes that his corrupt boss, another bad white man, put him on the case only because his confusion about race would keep him from doing anything useful. He quits his job, simmers in shame, and still looks to the woman who rejected him for guidance and support. By this time, he can identify more with the disenfranchised black folks who frighten him than he might ever have imagined he could.

Mulholland Falls

I end this chapter with a slightly closer look at an example of the moral critique of the white guy cop. How bad do these guys get? Everybody tells the hero of *Mulholland Falls* that he's dirty, and he can't deny it. Max, the hero, runs a special squad of Los Angeles cops and lives a guilty life. He cheats on and lies to his wife and tortures and kills suspects on impulse. He beds one young woman and soon after dumps her. Before too long a friend of hers mocks the sullied hero.

> She nearly died when you left. Did you know that? She loved you and you just used her. How does that feel? Come on. You sit there like you're protecting the innocent. All you do is— you beat up on the weak and disregard or destroy anybody or anything that stands in the way of you and your pathetic little

sense of right and wrong or justice and power. You know, if
anybody is responsible for Allison's death, it's you."

This young man, whom Max derides as a fag, kisses Max on
the cheek to bait him, and Max loses his cool, throwing him to
the wall and choking him. Sidekicks must pull the enraged cop
away. A sidekick counsels him: "Max, everybody has weak moments. You've got to get it out. You've got to tell [your wife]."

"Shut up!" shouts the hero. " . . . You carry your own water." The hero sticks with his creed throughout, and tells no
one of his sins. Later, he confronts the criminals, a group of
high-ranking military officers who have infected their men with
cancer in cruel medical tests and killed anyone who might tat-
tle. The criminal general holds forth on morality and existence,
but the slow-witted hero falls behind quickly and finally mutters, "General, I really don't think about these things. Probably I see too much."

"What do you see?"

"People dead before their time."

"Well, that's the history of the world, Lieutenant," explains
the privileged white man. "Some people die before their time so
that others can live. It's the cornerstone of civilization: war, religion, democracy. A hundred die so that a thousand may live."

"Well, General, I take them one at a time. Right now I've
got Allison Pond."

After a thoughtful pause, the general continues at length,
in one of the many speeches in which criminals compare themselves convincingly to cops: "We're not so different you and I,
Lieutenant You see, certain men—a doctor, a national leader,
an officer of the law—give to their society in ways that most
people do not. But in return society gives them certain considerations. Now we don't teach this in school. Uh, we don't
acknowledge it; but those who accept the burden of leadership
understand they have these considerations. And you've accepted the burden of leadership. Haven't you, Lieutenant?"

"What's that, General?"

"Well, you protect society, the ordinary citizen. Now, in doing so, sometimes you may break the law. You may violate the Constitution, the Bill of Rights, 'search and seizure.' In fact, it may even be known that you do so, and yet nothing happens, because it is understood that that is part of the burden of leadership. And you accept it. You accept your sins."

Max declines to pursue this line of thought and returns to the details of his murder case. Later, though, as he asks for support in his hunt, his boss reminds him of his "own water." Max complains about limits on his authority: "Bill, when we set this squad up we answered to nobody but you. . . . Goddamnit Bill, what if they're killing people?"

Bill reminds Max, "Sometimes you guys talk to people and nobody ever sees them again. They become history. Nobody looks too hard into that." Max spends the rest of the movie bouncing between a guilty conscience and the conflicts that give him even more water to carry. He beats up an FBI agent and threatens his criminal quarry but receives payback in the form of his wife's rejection when she learns that Max sleeps around. More furious than ever, Max hunts the criminals down and throws a couple of them from an airplane door to their deaths. At the end his bosses dissolve his entire squad and his wife rejects him again, leaving him to look stupid at the graveside of a fallen sidekick. Max ends up more unhappy than he began, forced to regard himself as yet another bad white man.

If cops, so often guilty of the sins that stain Max, are to rescue any part of their moral status, they will have to figure out how to distance themselves from the really bad white guys who have accepted the burdens of leadership, who abuse their positions of authority. Discovering massive corruption among the leaders who have screwed up their world, cops can often turn resentment over lost ground and guilt over white male evils into alignments with oppressed communities. They join with the victims of white male leadership, those abused by white men in groups lawful and criminal, and so build a better, somewhat less dirty hero.

5 Rage of the Oppressed

You are about to go on a sacred journey. This journey will be good for all people.
—oppressed townsperson to hero in *On Deadly Ground*

We are not the same. I'm an American. You're a sick asshole.
—one bad white man to another in *Falling Down*

Identification with the oppressed grows on heroes as they think about what's screwed up their world. Aligning with the downtrodden can help them make sense of the impotence they feel without propelling them into neo-nazi or misogynist rage. To rebuild the sidekick and family relations from which they draw sustenance, cops often admit to and then always punish the hostile impulses they share with the Aryan criminal class. They harness the rage of their embattled class and turn it against those most guilty of the sins that have both so profited white men as a group and degraded the loving bonds they so badly miss.

Faced with increasing scorn for their few talents, white guys seek enemies to kill in last ditch attempts to impress lovers, sidekicks, and employers with their unique value. But, their problems do not end there. Even were they not such poor citizens and lovers, cops would still have a hard time standing tall because the institutions in which they put their limited faith let them down. Bad white men run those police departments, companies, and other organizations. Cops align themselves with communities oppressed not only by rogue white guys but also by the very organizations for which cops work. Thus do cops dip into the righteous rage of exploited peoples and channel their frustrations in ways that render them a little bit better than the neo-nazis they otherwise resemble.

One movie in six begins by pitting cop heroes against oppressed communities—squatters, terrorized nonwhite peoples, immiserated proletarians, and so on. Heroes come to regard their jobs with suspicion and either take steps to reform police practices or quit their jobs and join the other side in resistance to the police state. Though this set of movies could amount to a subgenre in itself, the plot structure also indicates a more general relation between cop heroes and members of oppressed communities, in which cops turn against their employers not merely to practice their trade but also to break from corrupt institutions and so distance themselves from the corporate and governmental rule. By corrupt, I mean the use of positions of public, rational, and meritocratic responsibility to shirk the formal rules and hoard resources among a few wealthy (and almost always white) men. In these movies, such corruption always turns out to have deprived the cop of love and respect by making it difficult for him to be a proud and well-compensated worker without turning into a dirty cop. He is alienated from his community because he placed too much trust in the men for whom he plied his deadly trade. In either case, he cannot win: unemployed, he has nothing; on the job, he must engage in the very xenophobic abuse that divided the world and robbed him of what nurturance he might have known. The police arm of the government comes to represent, not justice, but the very corruption by which white men prey upon the world in which they enjoy too much authority. As I note above, police corruption underlies the oppression of nonwhite or otherwise oppressed communities. The police cannot be trusted as long as white men run them. Cops become heroes when they identify with the oppressed peoples and so adopt their righteous anger.

A few plot summaries establish the pattern:

In *Total Recall,* the cop works to infiltrate and slaughter a group of rebel workers but turns out to be one himself. In his dreams, he imagines the near-death experience in which he will liberate the workers from the oppressive government. Rebellious workers mock the cop as a government pawn, but finally accept him as a fighter for their cause.

In the *Robocop* movies, the cyborg cop works against striking laborers and cops loyal to their communities but then turns out to have been one himself. In his dreams, he sees the life and family taken from him by the corporation that owns the police force and has programmed him to be their stooge. Rebels stripped of their homes and families mock him as a corporate tool, but finally accept him as a fighter for their cause.

In *Thunderheart,* the cop works to repress nationalist American Indian rebels but then turns out to be one himself. In his dreams, he dies at Wounded Knee, shot by a white soldier. Nationalist Indians mock the cop for working for the "Federal Bureau of Intimidation" but finally accept him as a fighter for their cause.[1]

In *The Running Man,* a cop works to repress rebel laborers and food rioters but turns into one himself. During his flight from the cops who once employed him, he comes to see the wisdom of toppling the faithless government. Rebels mock him as "one of the cops" but finally accept him as a fighter for their cause.

In *Flashback,* the cop works to imprison an antiwar rebel but then turns out to be one himself. In faded home movies he sees himself as a young flower child and comes to view the FBI, which employs him, as part of a larger tool of repression. He battles corrupt law enforcement and quits his job. The elder rebel mocks him as proto-fascist Reagan-youth but finally accepts him as a fighter for the cause.

In *Blade Runner,* the cop works to slaughter runaway slave "replicants" but then appears to be one himself. In his dreams, he sees the implanted memories of a replicant; and he questions the truth of his family memories. Another runaway slave mocks the murderous cop for pretending to be "a good man" but then allows him to live, perhaps in sympathy for their shared losses.

In *Deep Cover*, the (black) cop works to regulate the activity of low-level drug dealers but then turns into one himself. Employed by the wheeling and dealing Bush administration, he becomes disgusted with his role as a killer of black men on the street for a government that advances the political fortunes of drug exporters in Latin America. He turns against his boss and arranges publicly to humiliate the administration in order to protect a fellow criminal. At the end of the story, he wonders which side of the law could possibly be more corrupt.[2]

In *Point Break*, the cop works to put down a group of libertine rebels against labor-market conformity but then turns out to be one himself. He comes to live for antisocial thrill seeking, even participates in a robbery for love, and quits his job with the repressive FBI in disgust.

These cops work for government agencies known more for political repression than for justice or protection. The identity crises suggest links between cops' paranoia at being called "oppressors" on one hand and the immiseration of the victims of a police state on the other. These exploited communities attract cops who blame corruption for their woes. Cops look to survivors of oppression for models of righteous rage, and for alternatives to the old boy networks from which they have inherited so many privileges, perhaps because they also look to those communities and women for nurturance. Thus do cops face their largest moral choices.

Sudden Impact

The movie *Sudden Impact*, which gave us "Make my day," sends "dirty" Harry after a serial killer of men. That killer shoots them in the balls to make a point and then in the head to finish them off. First, Harry undergoes what may be a normal day on the job. Young white thugs he arrested escape punishment on a technicality, he terrorizes a woman-killing mobster into a heart attack, young black thugs hold up his favorite coffee shop, he discovers the corpse with the "thirty-eight caliber vasectomy," and his boss dresses Harry down for "transgression of authority." Harry shrugs at the boss, kills most of the young thugs, delivers the memorable line in his standoff with the last of the coffee shop thieves, and wonders about the serial killer. As usual, he stands for rough justice, against both the greedy/loony thugs and the law-and-order technicians in the city bureaucracy.

Angry about his rough days, Harry threatens to quit, but his black male sidekick reminds him: "You ain't nothing but a cop. That's all you've been; that's all you're ever going to be." His boss has harsher words: "You're a walking frigging combat zone. People have a nasty habit of getting dead around you. I don't want any civilian taking a fall." Sent on the serial killer case to get him out of the city for a while, Harry runs into more violence, and another dressing down by yet another police chief in another town.

Finally, Harry meets the serial killer by accident. She has survived brutal gang rape by a group of white hooligans and is killing them off one by one. She is an attractive woman and he likes her immediately. His dog frightens her off her bike as they meet on a path, and she orders Harry to get control over it. She further orders the dog to shut up, with the kind of immediate result that Harry has been unable to achieve. He admires her command and the anger behind it. Later, after more scuffling with the restrictive police chief who will turn out to be hiding criminal activity, Harry bumps into the serial killer in a bar. He has learned to emulate her mastery of the dog, and she approves. They discuss the constraints on his violent work. "I saw the commotion here the other day," she says. "You're either a cop or 'public enemy number one.' "

"Some people might say both," Harry complains, ". . .

bozos with big, brass nameplates on their desks and asses the shape of the seat of their chairs. . . . It's a question of methods. Everybody wants results, but nobody wants to do what they have to do to get them done. . . . I do what I have to do."

The woman reflects upon this: "I'm glad, Callahan. But, you know, you're an endangered species. This is the age of lapsed responsibilities and defeated justice. Today 'an eye for an eye' means only if you're caught. And even then it's an indefinite postponement and, uh, 'let's settle out of court.' " She stops herself. "Is that profound or just boring? Sorry. I'm sure you get that sort of thing all the time."

"No," says a thoughtful Harry, "I don't hear it enough." Later, the killer finds another of her gang rapists, a local store owner, and shoots him after he begs for his life. He foolishly believes that his status as a small businessman will protect him from her righteous vengeance. Later still, she and Harry become lovers, sympathetic on a deep level.

The gang rapists, realizing that their numbers have dwindled, begin to organize. One catches Harry's sidekick and knifes him: "Kiss your ass good-bye, Sambo." Later they beat Harry miserably, kidnap Jennifer, and stage a final confrontation in which Harry saves her by blowing the most vicious thug off a roller coaster, through a roof, and screaming onto the horn of a carousel unicorn. Harry then lies to the police to cover up her murder spree. He and Jennifer bond over their mutual dislike for the legal system and walk off together as the credits roll, *lex talionis* achieved. This ancient law of revenge, the driving force behind the "rape revenge" horror genre, seems a natural for a white guy cop.[3] He looks to this woman as a model of righteous vengeance, not merely because she validates his own desire to slaughter those who would tear up a happy world, but also because she has a few tricks to teach him about standing up to abuse. He wants her both because she needs him and his few skills and because he needs her sense of political validation as a woman injured by vile white men.

Thus Harry finds a morally comfortable use for his limited skills. Blessed with little of what citizenship demands, Harry looks for people who need him and his gun, in hopes that they might tolerate his personality long enough to give him attention or even take him into their homes. If the pattern among relations across the genre holds, then Harry will spend little time with this latest lover. She will leave him in disgust if she is not killed first (and in fact she has gone by the time of the subsequent sequel, *The Dead Pool*). He will resume his search for something useful to do, something that allows him to vent his rage at the bad men tearing his world apart, something that allows him to stand as tall as a man so contemptuous of himself can. Indelibly marked by public outcry over white male corruption as an undisciplined man, Harry enjoys few unselfconscious moments. Forever on stage before a critical world, forever self-obsessed, Harry lives a life of political theater, the performance of the shame and rage of man who has lost some of the ground beneath his feet. His few rewards include those little moments when he can look criminals in the eye and demand that they require his skills and make his lonely days.

This reading certainly differs from the displacement and contradiction arguments. For instance, Paul Smith notes the coincidence of "dirty" Harry and "rape revenge" moral logic in *Sudden Impact*. Both moral logics bear on vigilante justice. However, Smith also argues that Harry's willingness to lie to protect the identity of a murderer marks "an important shift" from the larger moral logic.

> This alliance between a feminist claim about the law and a right-wing "law and order" agenda is finally unsteady in that the movie has suggested throughout that rapine and violent sexuality is endemic to the very culture that is founded on the law and that Callahan stands for in an extreme way.[4]

Smith's equation of cops with right-wing misogyny leads him to read a protofeminist gesture as unsteadiness rather than coherence in the genre's moral logic, whereas I read it as a typical conclusion.

Rather than measure the distance between my initial assumptions (of right-wing moral logic, for instance) and what cops actually do, I prefer just to observe that Harry's violation of the law fits a pattern worthy of explanation as more than exception or unsteadiness. Many cops cover for criminals they admire. They engage in or countenance lawbreaking across the genre—especially vigilante violence. It takes murder for racist, misogynist, or trivial reasons to spur them to anger: for instance, the sloppiness borne of racial contempt that kills a young Latino in *Code of Silence,* the killing of Latinos for money in *The Border,* the killing of Latinos as part of a cover-up in *Q & A,* or the cold-blooded killing of a white kid out of wounded pride in *Extreme Justice.* Cops hunt such killers down. In *L.A. Confidential,* the hero and sidekick gun down a group of young black men whom they believe guilty of murder. Later, however, they discover the deceased men's innocence. Driven by guilt, they team to kill the white boss responsible for the racist frame-up.

Cops seem content with the vigilante killings of misogynist men by women in such movies as *Innocent Blood, Jennifer 8,* and *The Mighty Quinn.* The difference is that these vigilantes are oppressed by white men. This is the choice cops make. They have a showy hard time standing tall in a world where the tallest men are monsters—serial-killing, cross-burning, gang-raping, drug-dealing, contra-funding maniacs in positions of liberty and authority they do not deserve. Ashamed to associate with such white guys and dependent on those who hold the keys to social grace, cops grasp at codes of honor to justify the skills they can trade for a place in a world they feel has abandoned them.

Fighting the Good Fights

White male cops seem to know that they do not belong to the most exploited groups. White women and people of color have constructed admirable families and communities worth defending and that heroes ought to respect, and they have done this in the face of the very corruption that cops fight. As heroes move through their stories, they cross paths with those fighting their own battles. Sometimes they join in, and other times look on and learn. Though most concluding showdowns star white guys, the genre features a running show of force on the parts of the very people whose embattled status attracts the cops in search of both moral betterment and fitting work.

Several movies, for instance, feature nonwhite nationalists among their communities and criminal elements. They are either gang members who control major aspects of an underworld or communities in conflict with the white world around them. In either case, heroes must negotiate assistance and show their respect to get anywhere.[5] In *Red Heat,* for instance, the white male hero, Ivan, visits a black convict to demand information. The convict heads a large gang with political aspirations, defines himself as a "revolutionary political leader," and stands up to Ivan's attempt at intimidation.

> You can't threaten me, white boy. You want to know what my crime is? My crime was being born. I'm thirty-eight years old and I've been locked up twenty-six of those. I educated myself in here; and I've come to understand that this country was built on exploiting the black man.

He derides the political facade of Ivan's Soviet Union:

> Of course, I don't hear anything about brothers in your country. But your country exploits its own people just the same. So I guess that makes me the only Marxist around here. Right, comrade? You see, this ain't just no drug deal. This is politics, baby. This is economics. This is spiritual. I plan to sell drugs to every white man in the world—and his sister.

The convict leaves Ivan with a threat of his own: "You—you're just another motherfucker we're going to have to deal with."

Similar communities pop up in movies such as *Extreme*

Prejudice, in which the white cop kills the Yankee drug-runner in a Mexican community and then defers to the Latinos sick of subordination by whites and happy to take over the operation for their own benefit. The cop retreats to try to make up with his estranged, neglected Latina girlfriend (with slim chances of saving the relationship in the light of the general pattern).

This nonwhite solidarity fits a larger pattern of retributive justice—the smaller moments in which civilians and cops who are not white and male let loose with vengeful violence. Cop action descends from blaxploitation, after all; and in *Dead Bang,* a department full of black deputies bust up and shoot it out with a community of white supremacists. They appear to take pleasure in their work. In *Die Hard with a Vengeance,* the black sidekick answers the white-guy entitlement of a haughty businessman with a cab ride from hell. In *Passenger 57,* the black hero suffers abuse by good ol' boy cops who take him for a criminal and then goes Mr. Tibbs one better by insulting and beating them as he escapes. *Mississippi Burning* plays a more serious version of the fantasy by setting up a black FBI agent to terrorize another racist white official with a razor blade and the threat of castration. In *Money Train,* a black hero responds to a threatening mobster who calls him "nigger" by thrashing a mob of white men and offering a death threat of his own. Later, a Latina cop answers the racism of her white male boss with a violent, mocking arrest. The *48 Hours* movies feature scenes in which the black sidekick mocks and terrorizes crowds of bigoted rednecks, and in the latter movie shoots a cowboy in the knee, leaving him to scream and thrash on the floor. In each of these movies, the injured white men prove to be trouble no more.[6]

Women play in this same manner when faced with sexual harassment and coercion. Between revenge murders of white men, *Sudden Impact*'s female killer gets off a few one-liners: "Want a lift?" she asks of derisive harassers on the street, "Then shove a jack up your ass." The hero of *Blue Steel* similarly avenges her rape and terrorization by emptying her weapon into the body of the criminal who has abused her. The hero does the same to a killer of women in *The Silence of the Lambs.* Would-be rapists get their throats torn out by a woman with whom they ought not mess in *Innocent Blood;* the hero of *Fatal Beauty* deals with the men who call her "bitch" by blowing them all away; and, on the outer edge of what one might define as a diffuse sort of revenge, a group of privileged or moronic white guys fall prey to an enterprising and vengeful white woman in *Basic Instinct.*

These shows of force redistribute no resources and right few lives. Nor does cop action spend much time with such people overall. Many observers complained that *Mississippi Burning,* for instance, has little room in it for communal black protest.[7] As a cop story, the movie little resembles such historical documents as, say, *Eyes on the Prize* (1987). Nor does the movie link white male anger over lost ground to the long-run struggles of these groups. Instead, these agents of quick revenge pop up in the paths of white men in search of their own identity and offer moral lessons. *Mississippi Burning* documents not the ways in which blacks fought Southern racism but white investments in that struggle. The movie taps into black rage and power and ushers white male heroes into the fray. Similarly, the end of *Thunderheart,* in which a show of Sioux solidarity cows the dirty white cop who oppresses the tribe, leads to the hero's moral positioning but not justice. Cop action fixes too closely on empowered white men as forces to be feared simply to blow them all away for good. Instead, as in *Thunderheart,* such conclusions only point to more political struggle and hard times ahead. The dirty white cop walks free in an FBI "whitewash," and the Sioux Nation must live with the edifice of white political power arrayed against it. In the end, it can only take its stand, the half-Indian white cop front and center in defiance of his white heritage. The Aboriginal Rights Movement provides a moral center, but not the focus of onlookers' attention. It amounts to a stop in a cop's spiritual journey.

Heroes take this business to narcissistic extremes in such movies as *Year of the Dragon* and *On Deadly Ground,* in which they do not so much serve their nonwhite sidekicks as direct the action themselves. They are the heroes, not followers, and others had better listen to them. This relation underlies the entire genre, forming a claim to a (mostly) white male turf. These movies simply hold the white man's exploitation of others in his own struggle up for closer inspection. At the end of *On Deadly Ground,* for instance, the white hero takes a place at the center of a Native American struggle against the exploitation of its environment and gives a speech of his own. Throughout the story, he has made free use of Native American energy and symbolism in his search for an identity. Now he stands before the audience of Native Americans and whites to rail against corporate greed. Of this, Andrew Ross observes:

> What is being alluded to is a long libertarian tradition of reclaiming inalienable rights, freedoms, and controls over the American birthright that are constantly in danger of being pirated and possessed by government and big business. We must take back what is rightfully ours. These days, of course, the white man can only legitimately voice this claim if he speaks in the name of, or in common cause with, the native man. He may still speak with a forked tongue, but the moral power of environmentalism (peppered with white guilt) demands at least that he speak up for, or in cohort with, the native.[8]

Sure enough, white men look for groups in struggle across the genre. Social problems are their stock in trade, and little suits the self-hating hard times better than the overlapping problems of the poor, people of color, and women, those largely blamed on greedy and bigoted white men.

Ross further argues, however, that heroes reclaim their unmarked status as "men whose self-sufficiency positions them beyond class and race." Because they can hold onto such status, he says, "it is such men who are scheduled to speak in such settings, alongside native peoples who alone can grant them salvation for their settler ancestor's sins."[9] Certainly one can read this genre the way Ross does, as a successful reconstruction of the unmarked status of white men, perhaps even as the erasure of race. Viewers could see it this way; I am in no position to know how many do. Nevertheless, such a reading turns away from the show made of white racism and misogyny throughout. It must sidestep the hard times that sidekicks and lovers give white men throughout, perhaps dismissing that therapeutic engagement as a red herring in the real business of celebrating white male power. I disagree with a few analysts of cop action on this point and use a popular trio of movies to illustrate.

Angry white men demonize the most unruly among them, establish their identification with the oppressed, accept criticism from coworkers, and look to them for models of rage. White male cops come to stand upright if not tall in their communities when they repudiate the supremacy and exploitation upon which so much of their privilege rests, while they accept the support of others by their sides. Thus do they find ways simultaneously to express their rage and to regain the care they feel they have lost.

Lethal Weapon

After *Blade Runner* (a staple of the film studies literature for unrelated reasons), *Lethal Weapon* is the most often analyzed movie in cop action, having received more attention than even the "Dirty Harry" movies.[10] Most published analyses look only at the first two movies, and so they often describe this set differently than I do here. One could argue that out of the context of the genre as a larger group, *Lethal Weapon* tells a different story than it does within it. The first movie begins the consideration of what it means to be a white cop in a racist world. The black cop, Roger (whose refrigerator sports a "Free

South Africa/End Apartheid" bumper sticker), interrogates some black kids when one asks him if Los Angeles Police Department (L.A.P.D.) officers "shoot black people." As the kids demand, in chorus, "Is that true?" and Roger stammers, white cop Martin grins at the kids' precocity. Roger suggests, "Maybe we ought to get the kids some ice cream," and they cheerfully drop the subject so that the cops can move on. Toward the end of the movie, Martin saves Roger's daughter from the rampaging white criminals whom they have been hunting and then helps Roger blow them all away.[11]

Lethal Weapon 2 tightens the racial tension. After a slew of jokes about white supremacy, nazis, and South Africa, Martin and Roger mow down the racist staff of a South African consulate. Roger has been threatened for being an unruly "kafir," and Martin has been chastised as a "kafir-lover." The criminal complains to an assistant that the L.A.P.D. "is overrun by blacks, and they hate us." The cops enjoy a final orgy of destruction. Roger's coup de grâce ends the combat, as he defies a diplomat's legal immunity, takes deliberate aim at the imperious white man, and blows him away.

In *Lethal Weapon 3*, after Roger shoots a young black criminal in a fire fight, he becomes furious with the white gunrunners who have spread weapons among black children in Los Angeles, describes this selling of guns by whites as "genocide," and recruits white cops to his war of retribution. By the end of the movie, all of the white criminals, led by a former cop known for police brutality, have been blown away.[12]

As usual, people can read these movies in different ways. Yvonne Tasker and Robyn Wiegman, for instance, both argue *Lethal Weapon* erases and displaces race.[13] bell hooks argues that in such movies as *Lethal Weapon*, "all the black folks follow [the white cop's] patriarchal lead, and worship at the throne of whiteness."[14] Indeed, though I counter these interpretations below, I will note now that the movies do indulge in the same buddy-hostility and good ol' boy humor that mark most cop engagements with its larger concerns. Martin, the white man, remains the hero, his talents as lethal weapon primarily at issue, his domestic troubles given more time on screen, and his role the merry jokester to Roger's straight man. The movie treats the black man as a sidekick throughout. For instance, *Lethal Weapon 2* draws humor out of Roger's pretended plan to emigrate to South Africa to join blacks in their uprising, and *Lethal Weapon 3* wrings a dark laugh out of the ease with which the self-obsessed Martin can distract Roger from his concern with genocide to talk about their relationship (see below). Further, Roger does not wipe out the racial order of Los Angeles or lead any kind of revolution among blacks in his community. One could certainly argue that any movie that channels its rage through the agency of a racist state amounts to an unworthy fantasy of black rage. That a white hero taps into such rage for his own purposes may dilute the fantasy further. All of this makes *Lethal Weapon* a disappointment as a story of black empowerment.

Yet, taken as a group, the movies hardly erase racism or celebrate white supremacy. They are, instead, white male responses to their own guilt, rage, and need. In *Lethal Weapon,* Martin struggles with his losses and feelings of uselessness. He knows that he is good for little else than combat ("the only thing I was ever good at"), and that he needs his friendship with a black man embedded in a community and graced with social competence. Through the movies, Martin seizes every chance to make himself useful in the defense of Roger's community and family. He fights to free blacks of oppression because he has claimed them as his salvation. It is not that he is selfless or verbal about his principles. Far from it; he simply defends the only home he has from the fellow white men who would burn it down: "We're back, we're bad! You're black, I'm mad!"

Once, Martin might have rested in his assurance that good, obedient cops earn white wives and happy homes. When he weeps over the photo of his murdered spouse, he mourns an American dream to which he might have had access. All of that is over now, the world has changed. He is a poor, lonely, suicidal man, ashamed of how little he can offer a world of multicultural corporate management and urban environs, high speed information exchange, and Byzantine legal codes. He looks to his black sidekick for friendship because white manhood now means either his own incompetence and disenfranchisement or racist and misogynist predation. Other people do not much need him, and he does not want to work with the racists who might invite his company. Instead, he steps as far away from these forms of whiteness as he can and assumes the pseudo-patriarchal role of the fighter for the communities of others. Certain forms of whiteness bring dishonor to relations among men (racism in cop action is almost never an issue between men and women, or between women and women). The killing aimed at the "racist" attempts to right that historic wrong or at least lend the cop moral vantage enough to channel his own rage. Of course one finds plenty of subordination between the white cop and the nonwhite sidekick. The point is not the elimination of hierarchy so much as the bonds between different kinds of men and the negotiation of what white male honor means.

Consider *Lethal Weapon*'s final fight. Earlier, Martin and Roger split up to chase and kill the two remaining white criminals. Black sidekick Roger blows his quarry, a U.S. Army general, into the street and roasts him alive in his car. White hero Martin is less effective and loses his target in a street chase (heroes lose their "more qualified" edge over sidekicks toward the ends of many movies). Roger is at first annoyed by Martin's failure but then more alarmed when he realizes that the criminal has gone to kill his family.

The cops chase this Aryan madman, the "albino" Mr. Joshua, and arrest him in Roger's home before he can do more than blow away a television set. Martin, as though well aware of the racial import of the scene and his need to prove his worth, challenges Mr. Joshua to a martial arts duel. While Roger officiates and keeps other cops at bay, Martin eagerly beats the daylights out of his opponent. Then, as the latter lunges for a nearby cop's gun, Martin and Roger together blow him away, Roger firing first, and Martin a heartbeat after as if in slight deference. (The action slows way down and two distinct shots sound so that we can see that Roger takes the lead in this joint effort.)[15]

The fight takes the spectacle of police beatings like that of Rodney King and reverses the races of the beaten criminal and cheering sidekick. Here, a black man looks on in support while a white man vents his fury on the Aryan threat to his dreams. As he grapples with his opponent, the white hero upstages a black man (who has his own taste for vigilante justice and seems happy to deliver the coup de grâce), then delivers the corporal punishment *and* differentiates himself from the ultra-white for his black audience. That the criminal he abuses is white to the point of being albino matters. The hero wishes a reconciliation with what he regards as a black haven of middle-class domesticity, a communal warmth he does not find among whites. He must help purge this community of its ultra-white corruption before he can relax in the black family's home.

Much of this tension between white male angst and black self-defense comes to a head in a stunning scene in *Lethal Weapon 3,* in which the movie explores Martin's relentless self-obsession and most clearly explains his dependence on selling "the only thing I was ever good at." I recount the scene at length because the back-and-forth play between the two men's needs—Roger's defense of his community, and Martin's desire for Roger's love—crystallizes much of the racial struggle. Roger, days from retirement as elder cops tend to be, has shot a black drug-dealing teenager in a shoot out in Martin's defense. Overcome with racial guilt, he cannot face his family and has retreated to his boat to drink himself into oblivion. Martin tells him that he had no choice but to fire and should not blame himself. Shame turns to drunken rage and Roger lashes out at the trigger-happy white cop. "Oh, no, it didn't happen to you, [Martin]. It happened to me. It happened to me! Fucking I— I— I killed that kid. I killed that boy. Oh, yeah— oh, you kill a lot of people. You kill a fucking lot of people."

Martin is so defensive he can hardly speak, "You self— you selfish—"

A member of the notorious L.A.P.D., after all, Roger refines his accusation: "—You ever kill a baby? You've got ice in— ice in your veins. —You ever kill a— *a boy like Nick?*"

In a moment of narcissism pure enough to stop the show, Martin shouts him down: "You selfish bastard! You selfish bastard! You're just thinking about yourself, goddamnit. What about me? Huh? We're partners. We're partners! What happens to you happens to me. After all the shit we've been through, don't you get it? Don't you get it? When you retire, you're not just retiring you. You're retiring us, man. You're retiring us."

"It's not my problem," argues Roger.

"Yes it is."

"It's not my problem."

Martin lays it out: "You're the only family I've got. I've got three beautiful kids. I love them. They're yours. Trish does my laundry. I live in your icebox. I live in your *life!* What am *I* going to do? What am I— what am I supposed to do?"

"I don't care."

"Yes you do."

"I don't care!"

"Yes you do!"

They repeat this exchange several times as Roger takes a swing and Martin hugs him. Roger weeps with frustration and guilt and apologizes to Martin. "I don't know what— I don't know what I'm saying anymore. I don't know what I'm thinking. I'm— three days [to retirement] and now this. I'm sorry."

With Roger where he wants him, Martin relaxes. "That's all right, man."

The scene dips into broad humor as Roger stammers, "No, no, no, no, I'm sorry. I— I don't know what to do. I— I didn't realize that my retirement was going to screw you up."

"Forget it, man. I haven't got any problems. I was out of line saying that shit."

"Look, man. No— Riggs— look— you know— hey— you— you— you know I love you. You know I love you, Riggs, and— and— and your problems are my problems. I mean, it's like— like you said, what happens to you happens to me. So try me. I'm here for you."

"I— I haven't— I haven't got any problems, Roger."

While Martin backpedals from his narcissistic high, Roger encourages him to share his problems. Martin balks at first but then brings up his sex life. In a misunderstanding, Roger punches Martin off the deck of the boat and into the water. Martin pulls him in after; drunken male bonding ensues.

In this long scene, they set aside the issue of the murder of the black boy and allow Martin to fly the flag of white guy need as high as it could go. (Though defensive about the racial subordination forever in the background of their relationship, Martin has not, as far as we know, ever killed a boy like Nick. Instead, Martin needs Roger to stick with a job on the L.A. police force, one that could involve killing a boy like Nick at any time. Later, Roger will describe such killing as "genocide.") Though the cops spend the rest of the movie pursuing Roger's revenge against the white guys who sold the gun to the young black man (after a painful confrontation with the parents of the deceased), this scene reminds us exactly why Martin is along for the ride. He does not directly address the murder of blacks by cops (perhaps for fear of fraying his loving bond). He fears the abandonment that he knows he deserves as a member of a privileged caste and so can only beg for solace. He must beg that Roger stick with him, even if boys like Nick die in the crossfire they stir up plying Martin's one trade. Once they affirm his position in the relationship, he takes a back seat to most of the remaining action until his cues come up for the truly suicidal violence toward bad white men at the end. He is the lethal weapon, a man so worthless that he volunteers to be cannon fodder for Roger to direct, as long as he can keep his place on the edge of Roger's family and his status as the thin blue line between them and a racist white threat. (As a reward for his service, *Lethal Weapon 3* even introduces Martin to a white woman after his own heart—a cop covered with wounds, dismayed by the carnage among boys like Nick, hungry for violence, but more savvy than Martin with the modern world, as women in cop action tend to be.)

Martin exemplifies white cops in hard times. Working class, lonely and dejected, guilty for the predations of fellow whites against the blacks he wants to call family, and unshakably the center of his moral universe, he serves the black community he calls home and uses their oppression, anger, and violent rescue for his own purposes. Martin has made a deal with his partner, offered his one skill as a murderous cop in return for a place in one of the middle-class homes that blacks so often enjoy in this genre. He has made the cop action choice to forsake white brotherhoods of exploitation in favor of warm communities that will shelter him. He has turned from violence-for-money to violence-on-behalf-of-the-oppressed, because there is where he would make his home now that he has lost some of his towering status.

This choice suggests the larger bargain that cops have struck with their society and thus leads to the next chapter and the distinctions cops draw along lines of class. Undisciplined activity among white men can make their economic exchanges look pretty suspect. The fact of unregulated exchange among men seems to stir the homosexual panic among cops for which the genre has become notorious. What kinds of male-male exchange ought cops blow away?

6 The Criminal Class

I could talk about industrialization and men's fashions all day.
— criminal to victim in *Die Hard*

The story thus far presents cops disrespected by a service economy open more to communication skills than to muscle, and by angry lovers who will leave if cops do not shape up. They are out of luck and nearly out of work. Sometimes they take the advice of sidekicks about relationships. Always they prove their value as protectors from deadly evil. Sidekicks, neighbors, lovers, and even some authorities thank them for saving their lives. Heroes patch romantic bonds, strike friendships at work, align with the oppressed, and blow criminals away. They have a hard time repudiating white male rage and accepting moral guidance. Heroic white men find redemption in the defense of those they deride or neglect as coworkers and lovers. They become heroes not despite these paradoxes but because of them. They display but restrain their hateful natures and torch the worst of straight, white manhood.

Good and evil involves more than this, though. What, for instance, should we make of its erotically charged violence? What place do associations between sin, capitalism, greed, and exchanges between men have in their hard times? This chapter spells out a moral logic in the slaughter of men who exchange money. As the terrain in which men trade resources among themselves, male bonding becomes the focus of much of the genre's mayhem. In Chapter 5 I explored the common ground between cop and criminal, their status as white men (mostly) and their strained bonds with everyone else. Here, I describe the differences between heroes and villains, divided by a class-bound code of honor that sorts those who deserve death from those who will live a while longer. Just as scornful bosses make up a managerial class fixed on bending workers to their wills, so do many criminals come from an owner class bent on screwing their society for kicks.

The criminal class includes alongside the loony serial killers and street drug dealers the robber barons, would-be capitalists, and legitimate owners at the helm of so many senates, boards, companies, and committees upon which others depend for their livelihoods. The genre presents these rulers as mysterious, irrational, and whimsically vicious—ideal fodder for fantasies of corruption on high. Sometimes cops join such men in their dealings; and the crimes that doom cops to grief or death include not only xenophobic murders of nonwhites and white women but also robberies that victimize innocents, and murders for financial gain. Cops regard these activities as destructive and seek shelter with white women and nonwhite sidekicks because intimacies between wealthy white men bear evil fruit.

How does one tell a hero from a villain in a genre that associates evil with white manhood generally? One of the more reliable distinctions between the doomed and the saved arises tautologically from my definition of the genre. Cop action movies are those in which heroes are cops. Since, in most stories, the position of the hero as the subjective center allows one to delineate "good" from "bad," I could conclude that the moral logic was just that simple. One begins with the cop around whom the story appears to center, on whom the camera tends to focus, and about whom others often speak, the character from whose vantage we see, and we regard all people who anger him as "criminal" or "bad." For example, near the end of *The Last Boy Scout* the cop Joe fights a criminal named Milo. They pummel each other, Milo stabs Joe in the thigh, and then is blown off a high scaffold by police gunfire. As he falls, a helicopter flies up toward him. We see Milo's falling body first, then the helicopter cockpit, and then the rotors and realize what's coming. Finally Milo hits the spinning blades and explodes in a cloud of red flesh. The fun of Milo's undoing comes partly in his outrageous fate and partly from the fact that he has been cruel to Joe, who has promised him death in return. Milo's dicing is both promise fulfilled and narrative closed; he is but one of many men who die after troubling a movie's hero. Anyone who shoots at a hero, or who threatens, much less harms, a friend or relative of the hero, will probably die by movie's end.

If the moral logic stopped there, then the genre would be as morally blank as its critics take it to be. The cop's code of honor would remain self-referential; whatever the main character did would be good by definition. Indeed, the genre centers on the problems of working-class white men and directs itself to reshaping their personalities. Those who help the hero get his respect, even if they later die by criminal hands. Those who annoy him in legal ways are morally somewhere in between. Some of them die (most women among criminals); others do not (unsupportive bosses). I argue that cop action amounts to an extended meditation on white masculinity and that the genre addresses a sense of embattlement. What better way to depict the oppression of working-class men than to dramatize it with violent assault? Not only are these cops dejected and rejected, they are hunted and fired upon. Such a fantasy could offer much to those bitter over the loss of a certain white-male authority to act.

Cop action evil has some substance, however, and one can see it if one takes cops at their words. I begin my presentation of a distinct criminal class with another popular cop action series.

Robocop

Even the low-rent thugs of *Robocop* talk business as they work: "We steal money to buy coke, then sell the coke to make even more money. Capital investment, man!" says one.

"Yeah, but why bother making the money when we can just steal it?" asks another.

"No better way to steal money than free enterprise!" Thieves of the hard work of others, most capitalists will go down in bullets or flames by the ends of these movies. They kill for profit and will die for their greed in turn.

The criminal plotting begins in the boardroom of the Detroit-based Omni Consumer Products(O.C.P.), where the "old man" CEO gloats over Reagan-era profiteering: "Although shifts in the tax structure have created an economy ideal for corporate growth, community services—in this case law enforcement—have suffered. I think it's time we gave something back." What he means is an automated cop that does not protect anybody. Another executive boasts later of "a guaranteed military sale with [robotic cop] ED-209: renovation program, spare parts for twenty-five years. Who cares if it worked or not?"

Later on this executive confronts our hero, an honest white guy turned Robocop by serious injury and company intervention in search of a salable product. They have made this cop a cyborg and tried to control his behavior electronically (a conflict running through all three movies). As Robocop learns of O.C.P. perfidy, he turns against his employers and tries to arrest the smug executive, who sneers: "Any attempt to arrest a senior officer of O.C.P. results in shutdown. What did you think, that you were an ordinary police officer? You're our product. And we can't very well have our products turning against us, can we?" This callow executive engineers the attempted murder of our hero and tempts street criminals with "virgin territory for the man who knows how to open up new markets." O.C.P.'s motto, that "good business is where you find it," means commiting crime of any sort in the name of profits, buying up the Detroit Police Department to pacify it, and fostering the ultimate deregulation. "We practically are the military," he brags as he arms drug dealers and thieves to take over the city.

Military-industrial capitalism proceeds apace in the sequel, in which O.C.P., still owners of the Detroit Police Department, cuts wages by 40 percent and rescinds pensions. Rival criminals, a bunch of messianic drug runners, operate a sweatshop full of nonwhite women packing narcotics. O.C.P. spots a chance to make "Detroit private" by making it impossible for it to pay back a $37 million loan to them. The company undermines the city's credit and instigates a police strike, creating havoc. The humiliated mayor, a black man, runs a telethon to save his city from bankruptcy and foolishly tries to deal with the drug runners for bailout money. Corruption, crime, and business abound as everyone scrambles for cash. By this time O.C.P. has created another robocop out of a murderous madman and set it loose. In the midst of general crisis, the "old man" CEO derides public ownership of the city: "City Hall is the decaying symbol of mismanagement and corruption," he says, unveiling his psychotic robocop. After our hero kills some of the criminals, the CEO walks away unscathed, and Robocop shrugs to his outraged sidekick, "Patience, Lewis. We're only human."

By the time of *Robocop 3,* of course, things have grown worse. Now O.C.P., with a new CEO, will gentrify some poorer sections of old Detroit by evicting its working class and razing their homes, by whatever means necessary. A special group of eviction-cops called Rehabs engage in "urban pacification," forcing people from homes and shooting them when they like. A local activist decries the "nazi sons of bitches," warning the public that "there is no silver lining, only corporate scumbags who want to line their pockets!"

The Rehab leader counsels the tremulous CEO that "the line between big business and war is a little blurry," kills Robocop's loyal sidekick, and prepares to bomb old Detroit into pacification with the help of the Japanese conglomerate that now controls O.C.P. In the midst of a shake-up, venal white O.C.P. executives commit suicide. The parent company sends a robot of its own to help fight our hero. The Rehabs try to recruit rank-and-file cops, who reject them ("Hey, we don't do that kind of work," the cops object).

In the final confrontation, a surviving activist cheers the crowd of squatters as they go to battle O.C.P.

> O.C.P. is lying to you! They're destroying people's lives for big business. You've got to believe me. I'm speaking for all the homeless and jobless citizens of this city and every city like it run by heartless, capitalist scumbags who want you to think their way, do what they say. . . . There is no silver lining. The only silver is lining their pockets. O.C.P. doesn't care about people."

After killing the various robotic and nazi cops, our hero faces the CEOs. The Japanese boss fires O.C.P.'s head and bows to Robocop in an ambiguous gesture of respect. In all of these movies, the men at the tops of the food chains go unpunished, leaving the hero more to battle next time. Along the way, however, we see the most vicious white guys die screaming for the sins of a military-industrial complex gone berserk. Working-class cops and crowds stand up to this criminal class and blow large chunks of it away. Now, what does all of this suggest about the root of evil in cop action?

Not only do cops disapprove of attacks on them and those on white women and nonwhite communities as detailed in Chapter 5; they also target exchanges among men regarding money. In a pattern familiar from westerns and cop movies of decades past, cops are almost never rich (although sidekicks from well-to-do families show up in *Bad Boys* and *The Rookie*, and both take trouble to account for their upper-class status), while the men they kill often swim in money. Criminals, in constrast, tend to be smooth, well-oiled machines, comfortable in their high-rise haunts, easy in wealth's pursuit. The silver-blond gentlemen of such movies as *Action Jackson, Beverly Hills Cop, Beverly Hills Cop 2, Cliffhanger, Die Hard, Last*

Action Hero, The Last Boy Scout, Lethal Weapon 2, Robocop, Tango and Cash, and *To Live and Die in L.A.,* seem interchangeable after a while. Even those criminals not Aryan are always in it for money—the expensively tailored mobsters of *Black Rain, Kindergarten Cop, Raw Deal, Sharky's Machine, Showdown in Little Tokyo,* and *Year of the Dragon,* and the Japanese businessmen of *Rising Sun* (though in that film, much of the guilt for the principal crime may rest with the Aryan among them). These men revel in outrageous fortunes.

Criminals include many company owners and board members, senators and wealthy foreign politicians. Others are wealthy drug dealers, counterfeiters, and international terrorist/thieves. Most of the dealers and thieves are also respected businessmen in their communities. A sidekick in *Bestseller* takes his hero to a lavish mansion, at which a senator introduces the successful criminal to a crowd of wealthy and approving patrons. The senator notes the criminal's "continuing generosity and compassion." The sidekick boasts, in sarcasm, "There he is. Dennis, what do you think this place is worth? Fifteen, twenty million dollars? He donates it to the city like that," snapping his fingers, "for the common folk to enjoy. The man is the history of America incarnate, a modern robber baron. You know, they built this country. They deserve special treatment."

I Come in Peace finds a knowing gag in the genre's construction of this powerful criminal class. Its criminals include a gang of business-suited snobs called the White Boys. They do business, steal money, live high, and die. When such rich white men go down, even when they are not the main criminals (or criminal at all, in fact), the deaths are likely to be treated as jokes. I show in Chapter 5, criminals tend to pick on oppressed peoples in racist and woman-hating ways. As in *Robocop* they usually abuse those with the fewest resources, the least authority to defend themselves. But, criminals also take aim at a few people in positions of real authority or possession of wealth, and these scenes usually take on a comic tone absent from the other murders. *Falling Down*'s criminal sends a wealthy and snobbish golfer into cardiac arrest and then gloats with populist glee while his victim runs out of breath. *Robocop 3* gets a grim joke out of the suicides of its venal, white male executives. The criminals of *Stone Cold* concoct a plan to murder a zealous and humorless district attorney and an entire state supreme court. In this story the hero arrives too late, and the bad guys actually get to kill one to two dozen senior white politicians before he wades in. The movie even stops to let the criminal boss gloat over his victory; pointing a machine gun at the district attorney who has sworn to bring him to justice, he smiles and says, "You know, at a moment like this I think of my father's last words, which were, 'Don't son! That gun is loaded!'" Happily, the criminal blows the attorney away.

The literature on hostility and losing ground describe people coming to resent the outgroups with whom they compete as jobs disappear, wages go down, and times get tough. Here in the cop action world, we find much of this resentment, as heroes verbally abuse so many others around them. At the same time, though, they reserve their firepower for the criminal class, dominated as it is by profiteering entrepreneurs who murder others for money as well as racist and woman-hating kicks. Cops end up aiming most of their violence at those in positions of corporate and governmental authority, the very groups left untouched by most "hate" campaigns. These upper-class victims are rarely Jewish,[1] and not often Asian American[2] or black. They tend to be European American, often avowedly racist and misogynist, and could easily be seen to die for the sins of those in control over the lives of their proletarian neighbors.

These men die for their fixations on money and official authority that working class cops judge unseemly. The district attorney in *Stone Cold* will do anything to send criminals to their deaths and defend the privilege in the state's charge against the biker thugs who mock it. He dies at the height of his delusions of statist grandeur. The doomed executives in *Die Hard*, though not criminal themselves, foolishly walk into their deaths assuming that the law and their status will protect them. They commit not crime but a more general sin, the boundless consumption to which business and social climbing lead. This vice unites the wealthy civilians with the criminal element, who seem to die in large part because no one respects them as rational, honorable men. Criminals abuse positions of responsibility to hoard resources. They suffer disorders of entitlement and become patriarchal capitalists run amok in a society dependent upon their adherence to rational order.

Disorder is the key. There is something sinister about criminals, something difficult to define, a slipperiness that bespeaks hidden evils. Criminals seem to want more, or less, from the men around them than money. Aside from the unhinged serial killer or racist-nazi types, no one seems very committed to ideologies other than unfettered exchange and profit. A cop action cliché reveals terrorists to be thieves, helpful bosses to be corrupt, and the local government to be a front for deviance. Criminals come disguised by makeup or other identities in *Nighthawks,* the *Die Hard* movies, *Drop Zone, Vampire in Brooklyn,* and others. *In the Line of Fire* presents a computer-generated series of photo alterations to demonstrate the chameleon quality of the criminal. His face shifts subtly from persona to persona, impressing the cops with the difficulty his capture will present. Many groups have served time as objects of paranoid fantasies about the destructive evil they might nurture in secret. Modern moral panics focus on gay men, Jews, aggressive women, and others who might pass in public as plain folks. While suspicions about these groups (especially the women) drive some cop action drama, most of the genre's paranoia attaches to the villains more familiar to traditional melodrama: white male figures of corrupt authority. Fears about the nature of the bonding that powerful people do behind closed doors, and the exchanges those bonds allow, direct the cop violence for which this genre is notorious.

Thus does cop action assume the function of the dema-
gogue. It points out a popular devil and accuses it of all manner of sin. Such fantasies may arise in any society undergoing
rapid shifts in rulership and consequent moral renovation.[3]
The fantasies have worked, in Andrew Delbanco's words,

> to sweep away people's fears that their sufferings were
> meaningless, and to convince them instead that there exists a
> gloating consciousness that has arrayed the world against them.
> The demagogue replaces the sense of life as a series of random
> defeats with the possibility of righteous struggle against a
> huntable enemy.[4]

Cops yearn to begin the righteous slaughter. The terrible violence they rain on the heads of criminals is the genre's payoff;
to this I return below. For now, note that the genre's wealthy
white villains are drawn from among a twentieth-Century "cat-
alogue of demons [which includes] capitalists, industrialists,
prohibitionists, usurers, tax-evading financiers, blacks, Jews,
and other devils innumerable."[5] Though obviously not the
demons of so much current debate on affirmative action, im-
migration, violent crime, and crack use, cop action's rich, white
criminal class are among the central figures in any anxieties
about the errant distribution of resources.

Organizations invested with public trust turn out to be corrupt, mismanaging the resources in their charge and so con-
tributing to the degradation of the world. In *Lethal Weapon 3,*
cops figure out the criminal's gun-running scam after a young
black man is killed in a fire fight for wielding a gun he was not
supposed to have. One cop reports, in tones of outrage and
grief:

> That gun and fifteen thousand others like it were stolen from a
> police department storage facility before they could be destroyed.
> I mean, they should be paper clips right now or— or license
> plates, or— I don't know, anything but a gun. I mean, here we
> are busting our asses on the streets to try and get these weapons

> out of circulation, and now they're headed right back out. . . .
> you stumbled onto something the department's been trying to
> keep a lid on.

The lengthy exposition points up the role of privileged information in the perversion of proper distributions of resources.
Inevitably, oppressed groups are victimized. Of the criminals,
the cop continues,

> They knew police procedures. They knew where the guns were
> stored and how to get in. They even knew the sorting codes on
> the sides of the containers because they took the automatics and
> left the junk behind. It all pointed to a cop.

Thus do criminals use their positions of responsibility, their
ability to circulate information in sinful ways.

Take the criminal leader of *Fair Game,* who gloats of his
work, "You know, when I ran the KGB out of Cuba, I helped
some very politically incorrect characters hide billions of dollars in various free world banks. But, I kept the account numbers. Magic numbers." Later, he sarcastically mocks the very
idea of trust between such men: "I'm a businessman. My word
is my bond." Criminals take pleasure in the use of bureaucratic
knowledge and responsibilities to screw the world as much as
possible.

While corrupt cops distribute dangerous commodities in a
fifth of the movies, civilian criminals are even more likely to be
involved in the exchange of cold hard cash. To say the least,
cops come to see that, as Barbara Ehrenreich observes of
noncinematic America, "capitalists no longer serve as stewards
of social wealth."[6] This corruption among those in positions of
trust is taken for granted by cops and mourned at the same
time, impelling them endlessly into combat on behalf of a society that has been let down. Cops are living or have lived
through a decade of infamous greed, in which "billions were
redistributed upward through tax cuts and other fondly per-
missive policies . . . [and] games of chance . . . whose only

tangible result is a reshuffling of wealth and power among a tiny group of players."[7] Their familiarity with the problem leaves them cynical though still concerned. The hero of *Shakedown* gives a sarcastic rendering of his society: "Hey, bud, the substance of law in America lies in keeping the money in this country out of the hands of the widows and orphans and in the hands of the major insurance companies who know best how to manage it." Though adjusted to this criminal situation, the hero still aims his aggression at figures of racist corruption in the local police department and then marshals help to send them to their graves. Finally, he turns down an opportunity to join a wealthy law firm and stays with the pro bono social service agency Legal Aid instead.

Hostilities to corporate power run across the genre. In *Rising Sun,* the black hero cannot make heads or tails of the exchanges between Japanese and white businessmen. He knows corruption when he sees it, to be sure, and chastises his white partner for dipping into it for personal kicks. Nevertheless, the cloud enveloping corporate bargaining confuses him. Nothing is what it first appears to be, and the "executive fuck chamber" holds secrets that the hero may never uncover.

Indeed, there is something sexual about the way in which many criminals mix male intimacy with their lawlessness and mystery. The criminal of *In the Line of Fire* declines money but accepts the brutality nurtured in him by his government ("Do you have any idea what I've done for god and country? Some pretty fucking horrible things! I don't even remember who I was before they sunk their claws into me!") and pursues idle violence among men "to punctuate the dreariness." His free way with money allows him access to the halls of power, so that he can get close enough to kill the U.S. President for fun. On top of this madness, money, and murder, his interest in the hero as a brother in disillusioned madness verges on the openly erotic. The camera focuses lovingly on his lips as he purrs enticements and intimacies over the phone. Those lips later wrap themselves around the barrel of the hero's gun during one of their clinches and music swells to register the moment's significance.

People have often imputed inscrutable, unexplainable malevolence to the most feared pariahs. Jews were supposed to take the innocent aside and rape them, kidnapping gentile babies and drinking their blood in ritual sacrifice, when they were not engaged in the obsessive accumulation of resources. Much the same has been said of black men, gays, single women responsible for the care of children, and so on.[8] In debates over civil rights, affirmative action, welfare, and so on, others describe such people as grasping, demanding, and sexually threatening to innocents around them. Cop action, however, chooses for its criminals the rich, the lusting greedy empowered by positions of rational authority that they are far too passionate to deserve. During a visit to jail to interview his underprivileged clients, *Shakedown*'s hero passes a business-suited, middle-aged white man in a cell. A guard has nicknamed the prisoner "Ivan Boesky" after a convicted stock trader and happily dispenses condoms to "Ivan's" large, salacious cell mate, who will presumably do to "Ivan" what "Ivan" has done to his world: grab it and screw it. Our hero refuses to chase such dirty money and can take comfort in the rough justice meted to the Boeskys of the world. I turn next to this code of cop virtue. I argue in Chapter 5 that cops closely resemble their criminal opponents. In what ways do they differ? They mark deviance in terms of corruption and class and thereby create a moral logic with which they can blow the bad guys away.

Corruption and Cops' Basest Impulses

Upstanding men do not care about money. Longtime friends, the hero and a criminal in *Tequila Sunrise* train their guns on each other point blank, and the cop says, "You wouldn't shoot me for money." He is right; his noble friend would not.

The hero of *Red Heat* also stands firm as a criminal sneers,

"You are so foolish. I thought you might be more reasonable. Money has a way of doing that to a man. But no, I don't think so, not with you. You are one of those kinds of Soviets that only look forward to death." Cops find honor by choosing blood over money in their exchanges between men. Looking forward to death or spreading it like a disease wherever one goes may not seem so bad to cops; but anyone who plots the murder for profit, bigotry, or kicks, rather than shooting on impulse for self-defense or vengeance, will die by the end of the movie, and most probably by the cop's hand. Though I later throw some doubt on the equation of "bad" with "killed-by-the-hero," I take these patterns as expressions of cop honor.

With rare exceptions (in *Black Rain, Gang Related,* and *Money Train*), cop heroes remain uncorruptible by money, and such fascination with what Karl Marx called pure exchange value provides the standard against which one measures a cop hero. In fact, the hero of *Black Rain* looks pretty chastened when his sidekick criticizes his acceptance of dirty money, and the hero of *Gang Related* dies for his crimes. Only the heroes of *Money Train* get to walk off into a sunset with stolen money in their arms (stolen from a murderous cop). The rest of the cops direct their resentments toward a capitalist system built on greed and stake their claim to working-class pride. They identify the criminal class as not only white and male but enterprising and stand tall by blowing them all away. Cops nickname the hero of *Code of Silence* "Stainless Steel" for remaining "incorruptible" and "untarnished." The title characters of *The Untouchables* gain fame for refusing the bribes of officials. Cops may take money to fund their investigations or achieve other immediate goals; but they may not keep it. The title character of *Beverly Hills Cop 2* only appears to accept a bribe to achieve another goal but then gives the money, in the name of his would-be briber, to charity. In *To Live and Die in L.A.*, the white male hero decides to steal to fund his pursuit of the criminal but has to account for the deviant behavior: "Listen," he says, ". . . I told you that I was going to get [the criminal] and that I didn't give a shit how I did it."

"So now you want to commit a robbery?" asks his shocked sidekick.

"I wouldn't call it that. . . . [I'd call it] taking down a douche bag who's trying to break the law." Law breaking in the service of law enforcement is a normal part of the job, as we see in Chapter 3. Heroes strain against official limits on their tactics; they regard their struggles as the good fights on the behalf of failing communities. Nevertheless, in order to be a hero at all, this cop cannot profit from the dealings.

Though without greed, this cop has crossed another line by instigating a fatal robbery. As if in punishment, a thug blows his face off. Only five heroes die on screen: this thief from *To Live and Die in L.A.*, the thoroughly corrupt cop of *Gang Related*, the rapist of *Rush*, the upstanding hero of *Maniac Cop* (whose death makes no obvious moral point—and is said by the movie's producers to have been scripted for pure shock value), and the zombie hero of *Dead Heat*, whose death only makes him stronger and sillier. Also, two other cops participate in armed robbery under duress, and both end up unhappy. The hero of *Betrayed* wounds a guard to save herself from being shot while working undercover and then finishes the movie a disillusioned wretch over being put in such positions by her employers. She quits the FBI and becomes a vagrant. To save the life of the woman he loves, the hero of *Point Break* takes part in a robbery in which a cop dies. This hero later quits the FBI in disillusionment and stalks off, apparently to a bohemian vagrancy of his own. Thus does the genre draw lines around the deviance of its cops. Heroes maintain both indifference to money and concern for the protection of communities about them, no matter how craven, venal, and worthless those others might seem to cops to be. Participation in crimes aimed at profit lands heroes in trouble. They are white men who can author destruction for private reasons, but they are heroes who resist temptations to murder innocents or enrich themselves.

In *Backdraft,* a cop discovers corruption among his rich, white bosses in city government, becomes enraged, and murders them. When other cops find out what he's up to, he explains himself: "[The alderman] and those assholes were closing firehouses. They were getting our friends killed for money. I had to, Steven. I had to do it for the department." Alas, this vengeful spree accidentally victimizes a fellow worker, and so the murderous cop must die by the movie's end, which he does in spectacular fashion. He represents a number of patterns, including the turn to violence by cops whose faith in their government withers before corruption on high (*In the Line of Fire,* the *Under Siege* movies, etc.), as well as the description of privileged white men in terms of sodomite slang. As with the exchange of resources among criminals, the taint of sexual deviance hovers over business between manly cops, making normal sexuality pointedly tricky.

Overzealous repression of nonwhite communities proves just as wrong as the accumulation of wealth and also presents itself in terms of deviant sex. In *Colors,* two white male cops discuss the policing of Latino and black gang members in the neighborhood in which they work. The elder of the two counsels restraint with the sort of metaphor cops love:

> These two bulls are sitting on a grassy knoll, overlooking a herd of Guernseys, and the baby bull says "Hey, Pop, let's run down and fuck one of those cows." But the papa bull says "No, son, let's walk down and fuck them all."

Later, after it has become clear that the young cop abuses Latinos in the neighborhood, the elder demands:

> Where did you get your fucking hard-on? You know, I used to get jacked up, because I thought I needed that edge. What I remember most from that time is nothing but regrets. Let me tell you something, McGavin: You can't prove anything out on the

streets; it's fucking bozo-land. What you do out there is a job.
You can try to be a professional; that's the best you can fucking
do.

Ultimately, the issue comes back to a cop's place in the world:

> Now in nineteen years I've learned one thing: If you try to fight
> every jerk on the street, you'll be one sad, sorry, son of a bitch at
> the end of every day. You'll never last twenty years; and God
> forbid if you ever get married and take it out on your wife. She
> will walk. She will fucking leave you. So why make it worse all the
> time?

Dishonorable work involves deviant male bonding, which in
turn can destroy cops' families. Corruption warps some with
greed, dazes others with racist rage, hardens most until they
have little idea what to do with women and so lose the presence in their lives of those competent to give them homes.

This tightrope walk seems all the more dramatic for the
transformation of law enforcement into the "getting," "nailing," and "fucking" of other men. If a cop does not watch out,
his obsession with well-heeled men gets the best of his domestic life. The pretzel-logic plot of *Tequila Sunrise,* for instance,
offers a white male hero who longs to "get" a homoerotically
aggressive criminal. He draws in the people around him, including a male friend and a woman whom the two of them are
dating. The woman rebukes the hero for exploiting people in
his obsessive quest for the criminal. Says she: "[The other
man], it seems, has been engaged in his business for purely romantic reasons, while you, it seems, have been engaged in romance for purely business reasons."

"I'm not sure I understand that," says the hero.

"A little vague for you?"

"A little."

"Then let me spell it out: —You want to fuck your friend?
Fuck him and not me." And so do the stakes slowly become
clear, marked as they are by the obsessive concentration on

other men. In *Point Break*, a partner chastises the hero for his fascination with the well-built young criminal, "You're getting too close to this surfing guru buddy of yours."

Indeed, *Point Break*'s hero obsesses over the attractive man he hunts. Near the end, they face off and the criminal gloats, "I know it's hard for you, Johnny. I know you want me so bad it's like acid in your mouth."

This sort of dialogue lines the genre and provides some of its deepest meaning. In *New Jack City,* a cop readies his weapon: "I want to shoot you so bad my dick's hard." Cops voice explicit interests in sex with men in such movies as *Cruising, Cop,* and *Q & A.* In *Cop,* a dirty patrolman has participated in a gang rape and runs a ring of young male hustlers, whose services he enjoys. In *Cruising,* two patrolmen who complain about their demanding wives stop male hustlers on the street and force them to give head. Later, one cruises an S/M club and then Central Park for men. Later still, a bunch of these cruiser-cops beat and terrorize a gay suspect for sport. In *Q & A,* a dirty cop obsesses over drag queens, sodomizes them regularly, and then either beats or kills them out of panicked rage. A hustler informs the cops:

> Let me tell you something. I'm gay, and gay on the street means motherfucking tough; but this [dirty cop] scares the shit out of me. It's his eyes, you know? He's a fag killer. And like all those guys he's gay. He doesn't know it, but the man is gay."

In all of these movies, the dirty cops provide examples of male exchange gone terribly wrong: rape of men, gang rape of women, assassination plots, serial killing, vice rings, queer bashing. None of them call themselves "gay," to be sure. Most of them seem to hate gay men with a passion. Instead, they're just guys.

Cops pursue men and seem perfectly aware of the homoeroticism in their bonds; characters either complain or make fag jokes. Those actions turn cops into criminals. A cop in

Shakedown explains the evocatively faggy phrase "blue jean cop":

> One that's strictly bargain basement—Wranglers and Levis. . . .
> The guys they bust, on the other hand, wear Sergio Valente's. . . .
> Take some cop, some average guy who never had a shot at a big
> bust all his life: He's just going along, grinding out his [$27.5K]
> a year. All of a sudden he ends up on a narc squad, and one
> afternoon he busts some scumbag carrying a bag full of chemicals.
> That bag full of chemicals is worth more than that cop's going to
> make in ten years. The next day, he's off shopping for designer
> jeans. The lure of easy money—-very hard to refuse."

The hero asks this cop about his own ethics, "Straight up, how come no designer jeans?"

"I always figured that they were meant for girls with cute little asses and guys with no balls." Though heroes tend to look good in their jeans, they keep a wary eye on aestheticized consumerism. Sure, cops may shop more than they used to; most of them live alone, after all, and enjoy large handguns and nice wheels when they can get them. Nevertheless, such consumerism can always seem feminine and faggy. Cops who get into money in such fashion will have to explain themselves.

"I could talk about industrialization and men's fashions all day, but work must intrude," says the effete criminal of the aptly titled *Die Hard,* in which he later does just that, sent to his death when the cop breaks the band of an executive's Rolex (his corporate-climbing wife's, as it happens). Industrialization and men's fashions, the paraphernalia of upper-class male desire, lubricate relations among men in which the average cop cozies up not only to Aryan arrogance, wealth unimaginable, and consumerism unchecked but the sexual perversion of privileged men. As I show in Chapter 5, cops often find themselves employed by such deviant men and then must work out their own relationships to the seductive networks of racist male exchange that such jobs represent. *On Deadly Ground*'s hero provides safety for an oil company that poisons the local Native American community. When called "a [corporate] whore," he says, "For $350,000, I'd fuck anything once." The deviance of his work noted, he discovers the scope of his boss's sin, quits his job, and torches the business. Next I examine one of these mixes of capitalism and sex more closely.

Bestseller

Bestseller pairs two unlikely bedfellows: Police Officer Dennis Meechum, a burly, widowered, middle-aged cop hero, and Cleve, the sleek, cultured, mysterious professional killer who wants Dennis to bust his former boss, a prominent businessman. The two white guys work against the rich criminal, and along the way Cleve falls in love, more or less. The movie explores the relations between murder for money and intimacy between men.

Their physical relationship begins when Dennis busts an armed robbery during Cleve's early criminal days. Cleve shoots Dennis and Dennis stabs Cleve, in the belly from below (this sort of suggestive attack occurring often between men in cop action), and Cleve seems impressed with Dennis's manhood: "You've got balls of steel." Cleve shoots him once more and flees.

Fifteen years later Dennis has written a popular book about his years of cop action and finds himself shadowed by Cleve, whom he does not recognize from before. Cleve moves quickly into a caretaking/parenting role, saving Dennis from subcriminal and giving his teen daughter a ride home. Later, as they become acquainted, Cleve begins to nurture his hero: "She's a lovely girl. You've done a good job, especially without a wife to help you out."

Ultimately, Cleve offers Dennis a deal. Cleve wants to nail his former boss, the ruthless tycoon, and he wants Dennis to write a book about it. In return, Dennis gets a great bust and a bestseller. "Come on, Dennis. Since Kate died, you can't get past page fifteen. You can't write, and you're sick of being a cop. You're a burnout. And those unpaid bills—you've got people after you, Dennis. They want their money. I can help you."

"You're crazy," says Dennis of any such close relation between men on opposite sides of the laws regulating male exchange.

"Yeah, well, it's a crazy world," counters Cleve, who shows Dennis how crazy by telling his long story about his life as a corporate hit man.

"Corporations don't have people killed," Dennis objects, with a naiveté always crushed in cop action.

"Oh," counters Cleve, "corporations deal in two things, period: assets and liabilities. I removed the liabilities. I was a corporate executive in charge of just those things, believe me. And you were in on it, Dennis, at the very beginning. We both were." Dennis still does not realize that he and Cleve met before, long ago, and traded wounds during the robbery that set up a robber baron's business. Cleve explains that his tycoon boss hurt his feelings when "he threw me out." Cleve wanted respect from his patron and not just money, since money matters between men almost always involve their feelings for each other: trust, suspicion, desire, resentment. In one of many little visual clues, a stripper dances in the background between them as Cleve talks of money, male bonds, and his wounded pride. For his part, Dennis talks of his general dejection, loss of wife, and bankruptcy. Cleve says caringly, of this upright and heretofore straight man, "You loved her more than you could ever love anyone in your life."

Ever suspicious of Cleve's intentions, Dennis remains hostile. "Just don't talk about her, right?"

"Hey, Dennis, I understand. She's the clean part of your life, I'm the dirty part—the criminal. But you and I know things other people don't, don't we, Dennis, hmm? How it feels to kill a man, for instance. Cop, killer—two sides of the same coin, hmm? We have a natural bond, you and I."

"No," Dennis instists, resisting corrupt bonding as cops often do when lured by aggressive criminals.

"Yes."

"No. We don't have anything in common. I don't have anything in common with you."

"We'll see. We'll see," says Cleve as the throbbing hum of metallic soundtrack grows, swelling as they drive off together. That night, sullied and unsure where his relationship with Cleve is going, Dennis begins to drink. This bond between the men begins to look like that between a homophobe and his gay lover. Dennis likes Cleve and stays with him but makes Cleve do all the affectionate work, always keeping him at arm's length, attraction and repulsion battling in his mind. Cleve represents criminal perversion: sex as death, money to burn, intimacies between men resulting in both death and wealth. The next day, Cleve shows Dennis his old boss, the prominent businessman, introduced at a gala by a senator. Dennis gets the picture and though still unsure about Cleve, explains to his boss, "I've got to play this one out, Monks. I want this guy. I mean, I really want him." Wanting Cleve or Cleve's ex-boss, Dennis sets out across the country with him.

On their tour together, connections between sex, death, and capitalism begin to pile up like the corpses in Cleve's past. Cleve gives Dennis the details of his business affairs by showing him a trail of dead businessmen, including an IRS man killed in his shower and a Securities and Exchange commissioner murdered in his car. Dennis responds to the stories of money and murders, including the financial documents Cleve presents as evidence, as though Cleve were bragging about public sex: "You know something, Cleve, you're full of shit. . . . You could have forged that little beauty yourself. You could have picked it up in a public toilet, for Christ's sake. This isn't evidence, this is bullshit."

"So maybe next time I'll take pictures," teases Cleve. "Is that what you'd like?" Dennis connects financial documents with toilets; Cleve connects murder scene photos with porn.

Dennis's contempt appears to be getting the better of him and he threatens to leave Cleve. As if on cue, however, someone tries to kill them with a bomb. Cleve saves them and gloats, "You're interested again, aren't you?" He catches a man involved in the bombing in a curtained photo booth and for no obvious reason slices his neck open as disco music plays. Cleve's murders tend to take on these trappings of dingy and anonymous public sex, and he later tells Dennis that he once killed a man and wife while they made love. In the cavalcade of these throw-away details, which on their own make no particular sense, *Bestseller* links sex, death, and business. It joins Dennis's dislike of crime to his phobias about male intimacies and his hatred of entreprenurial capitalism. *Bestseller* also connects his earnest approach to his job (he's chasing a major case) to irrational bonding with a deviant men (after all, his new traveling companion once shot him).

The twisted relationship between the upstanding cop and the perverse criminal develops as they talk in a bar. Cleve sings a French song while Dennis talks ballistics with cops on the phone. The conversation slides easily from bullets to sex as Cleve looks around and says, "Never have to leave a bar alone, Dennis. Look at these women. Hmm? We could leave with any one of them." Sliding more between bullets, money, and sex, Cleve talks of his former boss's power to corrupt cops with money into destroying weapons and then flirts with a woman accompanied by a cowboy, who itches for a fight. Dennis calls the cowboy off and explains, "I didn't want you to hurt him."

"I could have," says Cleve with a bit of hunger. "You know that, don't you?"

"Yeah." Such scenes move in what might appear to be haphazard ways from topic to topic, and surely this extended synopsis could confuse anyone who has not seen the movie. In a way, though, that is the point. Talk and imagery really do slip from sex to death to cops to business to murder, to money to men and back again, in, out, and around as men look into each other's eyes and ominous music hums. Cleve turns next to his relationship with Dennis and his habit of mutilating himself.

"May I show you something?" asks Cleve provocatively. He takes another man's cigarette (always a symbol of deadly vice in the genre): "Ugh, filthy habit." He explains as he prepares to burn a hole in his hand: "Will power is what distinguishes the amateur from the professional. Which are you, Dennis? Hmm?" He holds the cigarette to his palm. "Tender part here, nerves close to the surface." He pushes the cigarette into his flesh and it sizzles. "Pain doesn't bother me, Dennis. I don't let it. That's what I mean by willpower. Do you have it, Dennis?" he asks, almost propositioning now, "Will power? Let's hope so." He burns himself again as the synthesized soundtrack music swells. He says carefully, "I like you, Dennis. I really do. I like you a lot, but not enough to sacrifice the book for."

At the sight of his scars Dennis remembers Cleve from the robbery long ago. "How long have you had this little hobby, Cleve?" he asks in a rage.

"Since I was about fifteen," Cleve teases, "I used to use it to impress girls." Understanding that he has been on physically intimate terms with Cleve before, and that this perverse criminal has lied his way into his personal life, Dennis loses his cool in what looks as much like homosexual panic as anything else. He beats Cleve in a fury: "Hurt yet, Cleve? Huh? Tell me when it hurts. Tell me when it hurts, Cleve. I want to know!"

Once other men pull Dennis off, a bloodied but excited Cleve talks Dennis and the bystanders down. Sitting again at the table, he says, "Now you know why I never asked you to take a shower with me," referring to the old knife scar. "You were bound to find out sooner or later, I guess. It didn't hurt. But it did almost kill me."

Dennis gathers himself and finally says, "I'm not going to bust you, Cleve. I'm not going to bust you. I'm going to kill you."

Cleve takes this philosophically. "Fair enough, Dennis. Fair enough."

Bestseller goes on to illustrate its points about sex, money, death, and male exchange in dozens of ways, as Cleve abuses women and stays loyal to Dennis, who remains panicked about their growing intimacy but close to Cleve all the same. Cleve tries to share a woman he picked up in the bar with Dennis while he gloats about the way money flows in America among the corrupt. Later, he takes Dennis back to his boyhood home, a white-bread farm life he once knew. "Dennis," he explains as they lie on a bed together looking at old photographs, "I want people to know what I had to do and why."

"Oh, they'll know, Cleve," says Dennis in disgust. "They'll know. 'Rural America. Growing up on a farm. The American Dream.' "

"Exactly."

"Only this time— this time, something went wrong." Dennis lays out all of his homophobic, antibusiness scorn, his anger at a world gone so wrong. "This time, these nice country people produced a mistake of nature, an aberration, a freak."

"That's all I am to you," complains Cleve: "a freak." Cop action morality laid down, however, Dennis will not budge. He seems to blame Cleve and his whole deviant lifestyle for ruining the world.

Later that night, after sending Cleve away angry, Dennis wakes to find him in his bed, holding a gun to Dennis's head. "A fraction of an inch, the weight of a feather," whispers Cleve, torn between love and the fury of a man scorned. "That's how close you are, Dennis. All I want is a little respect. You don't have to like me, though I suspect you do in spite of yourself."

Dennis laughs, "Yeah, there's no doubt about it, Cleve; you're a real charmer." After a tense standoff together in bed in the dark, they agree to back down and say their good-nights. Such scenes make little sense unless one supposes a growing, conflicted love between the men.

"Am I coming off lovable?" Cleve later asks on a red-eye flight as he gives Dennis a pricey watch, engraved, "To Dennis, from his friend Cleve." Dennis appears unimpressed, and Cleve continues, uncomfortably, "It's a surprise, to celebrate our partnership, so to speak. I mean, we are partners, aren't we, Dennis, in the book, I mean?" Dennis hands the watch back without a word, and Cleve stammers, "It's . . . the best. Did you— did you see the back?"

Eyes closed and lying back in the seat next to him, Dennis explains, "I read it. I'm still a cop."

"And I'm still what I am, is that it, Dennis?" Cleve says, humiliated again.

"Yeah, that's it."

"You don't think I'm capable of doing something decent, something unselfish?" Dennis doesn't respond. "Maybe I'll surprise you."

"I doubt it."

Morality laid out again, they fall asleep together like bickering lovers.

Later, the tycoon's lawyers try to scare Dennis off his case, lauding the connections and corruption of the criminal class: "Try this. We'll tie you up in court for the next ten years. We'll take your house, you car; attach every nickel you earn, even your pension, which you won't be getting anyway, because we have friends in every political office in the city, the state, and the nation. We're a very big business, Mr. Meechum."

"Fuck you," says the hero.

"Friends of yours?" asks Dennis's boss.

"Business associates," he says in disgust.

Later, after Dennis writes most of the book, a colleague asks, "You like him, don't you? Cleve, I mean."

"Yeah"

"And you're going to arrest him." Later still, after a shootout in which Cleve kills a few bad guys and Dennis has to shoot one himself, Cleve gloats: "You let me kill four men."

Dennis scorns him still, "I ought to kill you." Their relationship is coming to a head, Dennis tiring of the swamp of eroticized corruption that has enveloped him and threatens to take him down.

In the final confrontation in his massive mansion, the criminal tycoon explains to Dennis, "Our friend [Cleve] has grown too fond of you. Emotion breeds carelessness in his area of expertise." Cleve manages to get the drop on his old boss, but with Dennis's daughter in some danger, the hero begs Cleve to stand down. In a final gesture of affection, Cleve exposes himself to the criminal, gets shot, and dies in Dennis's arms. Dennis promises to remember him. Indeed, emotion did breed carelessness. Just as greed breeds corruption, affection between men in positions of responsibility leads to death.

In cop action moral logic, murder for money ranks as low as killing women and exploiting nonwhites, and male bonding slides into sexual deviance in all its forms, because it can infect any relationship in which men exchange resources. Cop action therefore rejects male bonding as a route to decent governance but keeps it at the center of its melodramatic world. Just as Dennis loves Cleve, cop action will follow male-bonding anywhere and seems never to tire of it but condemns it without mercy. There, on this terrain of perverse violence on which men grow close to each other, heroes can negotiate a way to do what a man's got to do without actually joining the ranks of the greedy criminals who must die for corrupting their world. Messing around with each other, cops may get too dirty to regain the moral authority they have lost. Their powerful emotions drive violence and breed carelessness. They make for wonderful sport but bad stewardship of a world's resources. Cops merit, they feel, not authority but lots of attention as they wrestle away and slaughter the perverted rich. Straight white men can roll around with the best and spew blood across the screen. Heroes resist temptations to profit.

7 Sodomy and Guts

I want to shoot you so bad my dick's hard.
—hero to criminal in *New Jack City*

I know it's hard for you, Johnny. I know you want me so bad it's like acid in your mouth.
—criminal to hero in *Point Break*

The story to this point generally focuses on men, as though the female cops mattered little. Why and what has that to do with lost ground? Violent bonding remains a boy's game and women, when they intrude, must explain themselves. They fight a fair number of battles, yet stay pointedly female. In the genre white women and girls, like men of color, carry the burden of a heightened moral status. They are the innocents whose suffering drives cops to their heroism and the voices of reason who counsel restraint. What becomes women most in this genre is an absence from the male turf of brutality, an absence vital to the manhood of the heroes (all but ten of whom are men). However skilled they may prove at hand-to-hand combat, for instance, female cops use their weapons less often. *Fatal Beauty*'s hero seems calmer and more humane than the men around her. Rather than snap a knife-wielding youth's neck or blow his head off, she talks him into dropping the weapon and becoming her friend. Later she makes peace and works with another assailant, behavior without precedent among male heroes. *Fargo*'s hero seems almost to parade her life-giving nature with her nine-months-along belly. She discharges her firearm only once, to wound a vicious killer, and

on the way back to the station chides him gently about his errant behavior. When the serious battles loom, women tend either to stay calm or head into the same oblivion as the angriest of black men and nearly all other women and men of color.
As I point out in Chapter 5, they may grab a few vengeful moments in the spotlight, but the moments pass and attention
turns back to white guys who stay center-ring for the real blood
sport.

Where the Men Are Men and the Criminals Are Scared

The culture has changed enough since "dirty" Harry met his
first female partner in 1976 that a few women now run with the
guys; and they draw men to them with their uncharacteristic violence. In *Lethal Weapon 3,* for instance, the hero watches a colleague beat some men and becomes excited. Later they compare battle scars and have sex. Scraped, bruised, and shot, she
seems a perfect match (but disappears at movie's end as the hero
drives off with his male sidekick).[1] In *Tightrope,* the hero pursues his feminist sidekick, a self-defense instructor who knows
how to hurt a man. *Blue Steel,* in contrast, offers a criminal obsessed with the hero because he saw her gun a man down. His
fetishist lust grows as any respect fades. In *Lethal Weapon 3,* the
violent woman may as well be one of the guys; she appreciates
some of the same adolescent Three Stooges humor, packs a rod
in her pants (a quick joke shows the male hero readjusting his
to his crotch after watching her shove hers under her belt above
her ass) and is just as quick to start a fight. *Blue Steel,* however,
represents the more common trend of treating the rage of
wounded women as noble gender deviance.

Only a few women mouth the anal slang of male combat.
The "fuck you"s, "asshole"s and "blow me"s that litter the dialogue of men pop up rarely in women's conversation.[2] They
swear less and spend more time proving that they can take care
of themselves. Their abilities to defend themselves against

personal attack, rarely at issue among men, are women's biggest problems. Finally, women almost never endure the on-screen tortures heaped upon male characters. Whether out of chivalry or disinterest (not that those differ much), men refuse to involve women in the long and hard battles. Certainly, serial killers take a disturbing number of female victims, but the subgenre concentrates on women's fear prior to violence and mutilated bodies post mortem rather than their endurance of pain in the moment (only *Copycat* and *The Long Kiss Goodnight* cross this line). Cop action keeps its suffering gendered and so keeps its male bonding close to its heart. The onscreen torture and pain and the invasive abuse that this chapter documents test honor and measure the hardness of men.

Indeed, the genre's gaze fixes on men's bodies. Film analysts observe that women's bodies make typical objects of the fetishistic gaze. Women's breasts, legs, buttocks, and so on, attired in all matter of cosmetics and other paraphernalia, take up much space in Hollywood product. Viewers glimpse these in cop action, to be sure, but more briefly than one might expect of an exploitation genre. In *Die Hard*, the hero notices a number of women's bodies, but for just a moment each time—a nude woman in another building, a centerfold taped to a crawl space wall, a topless woman pulled from her lover's embrace by laughing thugs. These women pop up but disruptively so from the standpoint of the advancing hero. They do little to move the story forward and work mostly as fleeting signs of a heterosexual world. The hero barely notices. Compare these glimpses to the lingering look at the hero's sweaty chest as he pours his heart out to his partner while waiting to die, or his brave grimace as he digs glass from his bleeding foot. The last half hour of *Die Hard* features the cop's bare-chested body put through a variety of tests: thrashed by an attractive man, blown off the roof of a building, battered by exploding debris, drawn into confrontation with the criminal. Finally, his wife can only look him up and down and whisper, "Jesus."[3] The fetishist gaze fixes on the worked-over male body, proof of sacrifice and suffering in a world gone wrong.

Cop action remains largely an affair among men, in which women fit as media, exceptions, and negative standards against which men measure themselves. In *Terminal Velocity,* a criminal insults a cop when he says that the female sidekick "was more of a man than you could ever be." Women in cop action are rarely "men." When they are, they threaten the authority with which men wade into battle. Fetishized or disarmed, ridiculed or taken to bed, rarely do they run with the boys without their gender front and center as a topic of conversation.

These stories finally center on the bonds between men. Male-female pairs tend to lapse into heterosexual romance unless prevented by competing involvements or interracial taboo. The male-male pairs, however, provide the very different spectacle of cops who love each other but never kiss or make love. These buddy relations, characterized by all of the bigotry, misogyny, and therapeutic sessions of criticism and complaint reviewed above, are also marked by the frequency with which the men refer to romance and homosexuality. Across the genre, even if to deny it, cops joke about dating, kissing, and fucking each other. The hostile hero of *Alien Nation* explains to his sidekick, "I want to get something straight in your head. We are not pals. We're not getting married. We're not going to take long moonlight walks together."

In *48 Hours,* the criminal sidekick complains of wanting sex. "Hey man, I'm in jail, remember that? I'm surrounded by guys wearing blue suits twenty-four hours a day. I ain't built for that shit."

The hero, however, is possessive and regards his sidekick as a man's man, "Yeah, with the clothes you wear, you look like you'd love it."

Later, the sidekick complains some more, "Hey man do you know how close I was to getting some trim just now? You fucked it up."

"Hey, well my ass bleeds for you. I didn't get you out so you could go on a 'trim' hunt." The jealous hero keeps his attractive young sidekick chained to his side, and the two men enjoy the closest relation in the movie, one that leaves no time for women until all of their work is done. At the end, they drive off into the sunrise together, to reteam in the sequel, sans female companions.

In *The Hard Way,* the young sidekick flirts with and hopes to accompany his hero on a date. "I'm staying with you," he earlier insists, worming his way into the hero's home.

"Maybe when my asshole learns to chew gum," responds the hero in his typically anal parlance.

On the eve of the hero's date, sidekick Nick wonders, "You know, it'd be a real education to see what you're like with a woman, you know, in a situation fraught with sexual tension. I don't suppose you want to make it a threesome, huh?"

The hero prefers to work and socialize without his partner and so sends him off to do his homoerotic play elsewhere: "You'll do what you do in Hollywood: rum drinks, fern bars, gerbil racing." And, pointing to Nick's crotch, the hero suggests, "Take that gun out of your pants before you shoot your dick off." He exits, appreciating the wit of his remark about gerbil racing. (Cop fans probably know of the cop action actor famous as the object of rumors of the legendary, homoerotic practice of gerbiling.) Later, however, Nick draws the cop into role playing a romantic spat and expertly assumes a hyperfeminine poise of a drag queen. He gets the hero to play along and seems most content to have established a romantic rapport at last, all to the disgust of the bartender serving them. The next morning, however, in a sort of homosexual panic, the hero handcuffs Nick to the bed and runs off to hunt the butch serial killer alone. Fag jokes abound.

Cops joke about the condomlike function of their bulletproof vests; they tease about dressing in drag for each other or actually do it as they go undercover, as in *Nighthawks* and

Tango and Cash. They kid about the likeness of their relations to the more "sexual" bonds they mock with their fag jokes. Other writers have fleshed out the homoerotic currents in such movies as *Beverly Hills Cop, Deep Cover, Die Hard, Falling Down, Lethal Weapon, Midnight Run, Sea of Love, To Live and Die in L.A.,* and *Total Recall;*[4] and the list of allusions could fill a book of its own. The men never tire of dancing around the topic of the erotic intimacy that their partnerships inspire.

To what end do cops describe their bonds in these ways? The genre earns fame for its violence to property and flesh, and I argue that it speaks to a time when white male authority shrinks as if from attack. How does such common usage as "fuck you, asshole" bear on lost ground? Sensual intimacy, sodomy, and physical torture mediate the white male exchange at the heart of this genre, and all point toward problems with white men and the way in which they respond to shifts in their authority. In the arena of homosocial violence, men who struggle over xenophobia, attention, and greed show what they can do. They exorcise demons that bedevil their society, and come clean, so to speak, as unfit to rule. The terrain of cop action violence stars the men who deserve both the punishment and the distinction it offers. It may amount to a laughable theater of angst (cops joke and smirk at the action), but on its stage cops become stars.

Sodomy and the Fear of Male Intimacy

Historical and literary analysis illuminates the nature of cops' stage and stardom with the observation that people have often used sodomy for public show, as a loose marker for any undisciplined activity by which privileged men threaten social order.[5] By "loose" I mean pointedly undefined. Eve Kosofsky Sedgwick proposes that terror campaigns against sodomites work through denial of the "open secret" that homosocial and homosexual desires look a lot alike.[6] The blurriness of the line between the "straight" and the "queer"—the fact that the butch and rough behaviors that mark male bonding as the most admirable way to rule may at any time stigmatize it as the quickest route to death—drives this terrorist control. That is, one most efficiently disciplines male behavior when all men must worry on some level, all the time, whether they are deviant or not. "In this way, a relatively small exertion of physical or legal compulsion potentially rules great reaches of behavior and filiation."[7] This is why anti-sodomite campaigns in world history have proved such effective means to deal with privileged men. This is also why cop action sexual deviance can never take on the trappings of any well-defined, politicized identity. The "fucking" that deviant male cops do remains fuzzy and allusive, rarely obvious or "gay." It taints all men somewhat, rather than a distinct minority fully.

So male is this ill-defined sodomy that cop action women usually do not get it at all. Like most female cops, the *Demolition Man*'s sidekick remains slow to swear and turns her few attempts into unintentional malapropisms ("[He's] finally matched his meat," and "You really licked his ass"). She misreads the play between the men around her and looks like an ignorant interloper on foreign turf. She cheers her partners with an enthusiastic "Let's go blow this guy," and the hero corrects her: "—Away. Blow this guy *away*."

"Whatever," she says.[8] Aside from suggesting, with the pointedly awkward nature of her attempts to join in, that allusive sodomy is male turf, the scene underscores the importance of the undefinable nature of male sexual deviance. One sees very little "homosexuality" in cop action. Asking "are they or aren't they?" misses the point. Nearly all of them are, for most intents and purposes, straight, which means that they may fuck women but they fuck men. (Although there is always room for doubt. A hustling "gayboy" asks the hero of *Tightrope* if he wants to "try it" and gets in response, "Maybe I have.") Cops sometimes romance women, but they spend nearly all of their physically intimate time, groping and spurting blood and spit, with men. That whatever one might want to call "homosexuality" remains allusive is precisely the point of the demonizing terror that cops wage against the rich and white men generally. In this time of lost ground, in which we must blame the privileged for the corruption blighting our lives, any label related to "sodomy" makes a potent tool, a fuzzy marker with which cops can stamp anyone they wish to fuck over, up, or in the ass. *Demolition Man*'s sidekick tries to cross the line between the allusive and the explicit, and the hero corrects her.

Whatever the specifics involved in its legal definition, "sodomy" in world history has been "part of a universal potential for disorder."[9] More specifically, people have applied the label to deviant bonding among powerful men in societies that, as Jonathan Goldberg observes, "regarded male-male relations as the privileged site not only for political but also for the most valued emotional ties."[10] Sodomy thus marks, among other things, a danger zone in the circulation of resources among the sex most endowed with them. People use it to stigmatize all manner of privileged male bonds. Michael Warner argues of U.S. history that "the Puritan rhetoric of Sodom has begun as a language about polity and discipline."[11] It regarded, in a document he quotes, " 'slackness in rulers and the most horrible and grievous sinne in the subjects.' . . . Sodom was the most prominent example of judgment passed upon a polis."

Sodomy indicates infectious disorder among men, a failure among those invested with authority to discharge their responsibilities. All that male bonding offers—the companionship, brotherhood, mentoring, jobs and advancement, the "complex web of male power over the production, reproduction, and exchange of goods, persons and meanings"—can at any time fall victim to strains of deviance harmful to an entire society.[12] The definition of sodomy, a puzzlement to jurists and clerics for centuries, has vexed so many because male bonding—whatever guys do when they love, admire, and share resources with each other—provides both the very mode of governance and the threat to its legitimacy. For instance, Christopher Newfield observes in nineteenth century discourse a link between " 'unnatural' relations between men and those unnatural (male) relations that lead to the 'vagrance' of the masses, full as they are of ambitious, coming men who upset social hierarchy."[13] Always at risk for going astray as soon as privileged men bend rules on each others' behalves, male bonding matters. It looms large as both import and mystery over those who count on men to work by reason and rule, to pass resources around in a responsible manner and not just keep them to themselves. In our complex society, passion and play among men with responsibilities scare us. Often, we dream of sodomy. Lust corrupts economic relations because, among those with access to wealth, it becomes greed. Intimate and violent male bonding therefore swings in popular perception from the crux of social order to its scourge. We cannot trust men very much when they stick too close to each other, and we certainly cannot trust them with anything of value (other than the job of killing men like themselves, I argue below).

Cop action certainly obsesses over both the unregulated exchange of resources and the guts and glory with which cops flirt, engage, and finally slaughter the criminal class. White men in love and lust with each other serve as potent signs of corruption, and the genre draws countless links between male authority and male-male intimacies. Sexual allusions turn to talk of business, and then back again to intimacies between men. In *Rising Sun*, for instance, cops argue ethics and sex. After a placating game of golf with some corporate types, the white sidekick, John, defends his unseemly hobnobbing: "I was saving face."

The black hero, Web, snorts, "Saving face? Sounds more to me like you were kissing ass."

"Well no, not exactly," says John. "I've done services for those men in the past, and we've shared information." These oblique allusions to business exchanges and perversion come together in a later scene better understood as a collage of images than as a sequence with a linear logic: A fire fight ends when the hero, Web, aims his weapon at fleeing criminals. Two shots ring out as bullets enter him from behind. He falls and opens his eyes. We track toward a blond, female sex worker in a board room looking seductive, half naked in the dress in which she died (murdered by a white male corporate executive out to frame and blackmail a senator for the crime). We cut to Web's view of the man who just shot him in his backside, his sidekick, John, who now fires at fleeing criminals from above Web's prone body. The sex worker moans, "Web, Web"; John leans down, his whispered nickname for Web ("Kohai") overlapping the woman's final moans of "Web." John leans so close to Web's face that he goes out of focus in the point-of-view shot and blots out the light. The shot fades to a slow pan up Web's body in the interrogation room. "And that's all I remember," he says.

"Luckily you were wearing the proper gear," says his boss in one of many allusions in the genre to the prophylactic qualities of bullet-proof vests.

"Yeah, luckily," Web says with a look of anger or disgust.

Talk turns to business as the boss says, "You've read this morning's paper. You were caught in the middle of gang warfare."

Web replies, "Man, I was caught in the middle of a business negotiation." He squirms and laughs cynically at the cover-up of an economically motivated series of erotic exchanges between men, in which sex worker dies a pawn. Sex, business, violence, male aggression and ministration, feminine receptiveness, death, all thrown together in a blur of plot twist and spectacle to illustrate the experience of the cop on the job in a world gone pleasurably nuts. This is the sodomite order in which cops work, at which they laugh in disdain as they wade up to their well-toned thighs.

Ultimately, cops take these images and promises to battle. Men obsess over sodomy during combat, through sexual banter ("asshole," "buttfucker," "blow me," and "bend over buddy"), choreography (combatants often attack from behind and below, aiming for crotch and ass as often as mouth or heart), and the staging of larger violence. (*Die Hard*'s hero, John, drops a bomb into an elevator shaft he has just greeted with a hushed "Fuck me," and then runs from the fireball coming back at him with a frightened "Shit!" A little later a deputy police chief, dismayed by the havoc John wreaks, calls him an asshole. John responds with, "I'm not the one who just got buttfucked!" The deputy walks away in disgust but later warns John's sidekick that he is "really going to nail his ass.") Amid such chatter, criminals die impaled from the rear on assorted objects in such movies as *Cliffhanger* and *Cobra*, *Marked for Death* and *Sudden Impact*. In *Lethal Weapon*, Martin defeats a criminal in a head lock between his thighs (the scene made sexier by the look Martin gives his partner, Roger, while he does it, as though he were a porn performer receiving instructions from his off-screen director). Men kick at each other's genitals and we see their pained expressions close up. Criminals in such movies as *Lethal Weapon 2* and *The Last Boy Scout* thrust large knives into cop's thighs and twist them around in moves suggestive of sexual assaults. The cop in *Striking Distance* has trouble killing the resilient criminal until he jabs a stun gun deep into his mouth and gives him the juice, mocking "Who's the best cop now?" All of the bonding among men, cop and criminal, turns to sadomasochistic rituals of humiliation and death.

Cops draw an old analogy between bodily penetration and dishonor and death. Anthropologists and historians describe cultures that relate male penetration with shame.[14] In such contexts, "to be penetrated is to abdicate power."[15] Besides explaining the popularity of homophobia, this "hygienics of social power" makes sense of the patterns in cop action violence in which penetrators win and those penetrated lose. Characters treat such lines as "Fuck you," "I never forget an asshole," "I'm going to fuck your ass," and "Blow me," as assaults and insults. "Why don't I just fuck you from right here?" says an angry criminal to a cop in a close standoff in *8 Million Ways to Die.* "Assholes" rank lowest and any man fucked by another must seek violent revenge or die. "Fucker," on the other hand, works as a token of at least grudging esteem. Heroes promise abuse (from *Lethal Weapon,* "I never forget an asshole. . . . I'm going to catch them and fuck them"). Criminals savor advantages (from *Robocop,* "Your ass is mine"). Bureaucrats bemoan helplessness (from *Die Hard,* "The mayor's going to have my ass").

Cops love this stuff. In *Showdown in Little Tokyo,* the two male cops grow close and toy with the eroticism of their bond. Just before battle, the sidekick takes a moment (not the first) to admire the hero's weapon: "Kenner, just in case we get killed, I wanted to tell you—you have the biggest dick I've ever seen on a man."

Kenner pauses. "Thanks. I don't know what to say."

"How about 'Don't get killed?' "

A shirtless Kenner holds a short sword erect at his waist and looks at his sidekick: "Don't get killed." He then throws the sword, and several more like it, into the heads of advancing assailants. The sidekick cheers him on.

The hero of *Beverly Hills Cop 2* proves equally lascivious. Cornering his male quarry in the Playboy Mansion, of all places, its yard filled with bouncing, buxom bunnies, he talks as if he were hot only for the man he hunts. "How are we supposed to find him?" asks a sidekick.

"Follow your dick," cheers the hero; and so they do.

Ricochet's hero makes an arrest by taking off his pants and shirt, dropping his revolver, and reassuring a male criminal that "the only weapon I got left is useless unless you're a pretty girl." He lies, it turns out, and whips a little weapon out of his jockstrap to shoot the confused criminal in the thigh—a fa-vorite region for men to penetrate each other. (Of course, the lewd arrest embarrasses the police chief and lands the cop in trouble.)

The title characters of the *Ghostbusters* movies seem mind-ful of the historical status of sodomy as they discuss the danger of crossing the streams of the weapons they carry at waist level—guns that variously fire streams of lightening and vis-cous, white fluid. No less than total destruction of their soci-ety and life as they know it would result, they fear, from such male minglings. Nevertheless, once the female ghost who has flummoxed them turns into the large, doughy Staypuft Marsh-mallow Man, the cops spot the crack in his defenses, consider the deadly crossing, whip out their weapons, and join together in risky homosociality: "There's definitely a very slim chance we'll survive," cheers one.

"I love this plan!" exclaims the hero. "I'm excited to be a part of it. Let's do it!" ("This job is definitely not worth [$11.5 K] a year," mutters the more cautious, black man among them.) The ensuing group spurt yields an ejaculatory explosion of thick, white foamy fluid from the top of the sky-scraper on which they fight. This fluid douses the men, the cityscape around them, and the figure of regulatory authority (an EPA agent) who has constrained their work and play. *Ghostbusters 2* carries the joke and the men spray each other with a viscous, white "mood slime," awaken from their mag-ical slumbers to feelings of physical affection, and enjoy a round of fag jokes. The adventure ends with a portrait of the four male cops, dressed in togas reminiscent of more openly homoerotic times, gathered around the baby boy who be-longs to the woman pointedly not in the picture.

Most cops carry more conventional weapons and so must forego the queeny pleasures of white mood slime. Neverthe-less, they appreciate the significance of their rods. Men shout "Fuck you!" as they point large guns and fire away. *Stone*

Cold's criminal machine guns a cop in the back and says, "This time it's for real, asshole." Men admire each other's weapons: "That's some piece of hardware you got there," says the hero to a young criminal in *Lethal Weapon 2,* a man whose ass he will soon promise to fuck. Cops compare weapon size in such movies as *Lethal Weapon* and *Red Heat.* Criminals do the same in *Robocop* and *Maniac Cop 2.* The criminal in *Blue Steel* worships one of the rare female cop heroes; he's awed and alarmed that a woman should carry one of those massive rods. The buddies of *48 Hours* take the equation more in stride. "Listen," says one man to another, "you owe me a piece of ass. Why don't you give me that gun and we'll call it even?"[16] Cops treat nearly every weapon of death as a valuable tool of intense bonding, free expression, and giddy domination. *Blue Steel* opens with long, extreme-close-up tracking shots over the female cop hero's weapon (her phallic tendencies entrance the men around her). Montages of gun collection and cleaning, rituals shared by affectionate cops and sidekicks, take time in dozens of the movies. Guns amount to a technology of penetration as destruction. To become an object of their use is to endure the most emasculating defeat.

The expression of straight manhood through violence is an old story. I am more interested in the cops' ritual invocation of sodomy. How does this mix with their stance toward affectionate sidekicks, demanding women, xenophobia, and greed? Two readings arise. The first comes from the cop action literature and imputes a reverse-logic displacement, in which appearances fool us. In this view, the slaughter of effete criminals represents a homophobic revulsion at the intimacy of the cops' "buddy" relationships and the projection of their lust onto convenient fag types who just happen to be wealthy. This argument most closely fits the impression we have gained of straight (in many senses of the word) white men lashing out at the others around them in frustration over ground lost to corruption.

I then counter this worthy argument with the idea that the

destruction of rich white men and the glorification of juicy male bonding are precisely the genre's points, and further that these serve as coherent responses to the same feelings of lost ground. Hard economic times produce heroic angst; and heroes escalate the conflicts with the rich to have even harder times. Their roughhousing works as protest and play. White men do male bonding. They do it and do it until someone dies. Criminals do it to keep resources to themselves. Heroes do it for fun and a wage.

Displaced Sex?

I have argued that cops become intimate once they learn to get along. Male-female pairs turn to heterosexual romance, but the male couples enjoy the sodomite bonding so strongly linked to the pursuit of criminals. Just as cops combat the racism and misogyny they understand so well, they also hunt men who engage in the very bonding cops enjoy. The displacement arguments first suppose that intimacies between cops make them nervous so that they want to direct their aggression outward against "fags" in the form of violence, and then that this violence obscures narrative meaning and thus political import. In other words, by beating fags cops stay straight and render the genre all but meaningless. They can cozy up to each other as long as they keep up the violence. Cop action could certainly be seen to apply a double standard to the male-male camaraderie: Some get killed and some do not. In its use of that double standard, cop action can seem both duplicitous and homophobic. According to the displacement argument, what in these movies ennobles the relation between the hero and sidekick seems to be part of the deviance of the queerish criminals, all of whom end up dead.

There are different ways to displace a deviant tendency, of course. Alan Bray and Eve Kosofsky Sedgwick discuss the centuries-old practice of first identifying a group of homophillic men as "sodomites" and then publicly stigmatizing them as "a mechanism for regulating the behavior of the many by the specific oppression of a few."[17] Some men take the rap so that others may do what they do, but all men risk the stigma. Robin Wood argues of male buddy movies in general that, "virtually every Hollywood film that can be read as dramatizing homosexual relations . . . feels the need to cover itself with a homophobic disclaimer."[18]

Sure enough, scapegoating could seem to form a major part of the genre's moral logic. Tania Modleski observes in *48 Hours* and the *Lethal Weapon* movies "an astonishingly open *expression* of male/male desire that nevertheless is accompanied by phobic denial of homosexuality *per se*."[19] Analysts rarely describe the ways in which deviant sex is displaced or denied (much less their evidence that anything *is* displaced or denied). Paul Smith, for instance, asserts that the criminal of *Beverly Hills Cop,* one of the many effete Aryans, "is specifically portrayed as gay." How one recognizes the homosexuality of such a character Smith leaves to our imaginations.[20]

In support of the displacement argument, one could note that, though male criminals never kiss or slip into bed with each other, they are often quite cute and suspiciously male-oriented: the well-coifed terrorist-thieves in *Die Hard;* the buffed-out surfer-thieves in *Point Break;* the attractive young man's adoration of his older criminal mentor in *Ricochet* ("sweetcheeks," a cop tells him, "oh, you're going to look real good in a cell"); the whispery, fashionably dressed thug Milo in *The Last Boy Scout,* who serves the interests of a corrupt white businessman; or the thug in *K-9* who admits to enjoying "gay biker films." Though cops often ogle the women around them, criminals seldom do. When criminals do express attraction to women the patterns include murderous rage (the serial-killer subgenre) or possessive jealousy (usually in a triangle with the cop) but no other attention. In *Point Break,* the women are silent appendages, rarely seen, abandoned without notice or remark. Criminals shoot women to whom they appeared to have been devoted without a second thought in *Cliffhanger* and *Renegades*. In *Die Hard*, the cop John is frequently distracted by the sight of women around him, but his criminal opponents take little notice. Criminals, like cops, prefer brutal engagement with each other to niceties with women. In *48 Hours*, a scorned prostitute tells the cops that the criminal "is going to give you guys a real hard time. . . . I just think he likes shooting cops a lot more than getting laid."

Sometimes the criminals seem as interested in cruising as anything else. The solicitous killer of *In the Line of Fire* catches the cop whose attention he desires in a helpless position and teases him by wrapping his mouth around the barrel of the cop's gun. The heartless corporate climber of *Robocop* supervises the creation of the cyborg cop with an eroticized glee. He holds Robocop's arm to his chest in a close embrace. "Come here often? How're you doing?" Robocop shakes and begins to crush his hand. "Aagh! He's got a hell of a grip."

"It's four hundred foot-pounds," says the lovely female doctor, slowly. "He could crush every bone in your hand."

The criminal becomes thoroughly excited. "I like that," he says, looking Robocop up and down. "You're going to be a bad motherfucker!" Later: "I fucking love that guy!"

Criminals can be openly salacious with other men. One seems almost to be cruising in *Hard Target*, "I've been looking all over for you."

The hero: "You've been looking in all the wrong places."

"Good. I know you wouldn't want to hurt my feelings." The two men fire away at each other, the criminal finally expiring in a hail of bullets fired from below into his crotch and abdomen with a series of groans and gasps worthy of a porn soundtrack.

A mountain-man criminal in *Death Hunt* cruises a cute young sidekick: "Yeah, everyone here is vicious . . . except pinkcheeks here. Yeah, you're real civilized. We don't get many pretty young white boys like you up here. There's only one thing you're good for," he says, looking the cop up and down. He kisses his prey aggressively and gets beaten for his trouble.

A criminal in *Stone Cold* sizes up the undercover cop trying to penetrate his biker gang, "My, my, my, what do we got here? . . . You sure are pretty. . . . Oh no, no, you're a real pretty boy. Ain't he a pretty boy?" The cop slowly waves a long pool cue in front of him. "You got a real pretty face, huh?" The criminal grabs the end of the cue. "How'd you like me to fuck it up for you?" The cop poses as an ex con and the criminal mocks him, "A pretty boy like you must have done some painful time." The cop looks particularly offended; and the criminal clarifies his challenge: "Are you going to use that stick, —you want to dance with me?" Later, the cop watches another biker throw a knife into a photograph of a naked ass, stabbing it between the cheeks to general approval. He presents the criminal boss with a bullet-proof vest, which the criminal notes is "government issue." The cop notes the same of "that piece in your pants." The horseplay goes on and on, metaphors for cruising, sodomy, and safe sex piling high before the leering men blow each other away. On both sides, criminal and cop, men love and hate one another and spend much of their time in a physical intimacy readable as erotically charged. However similar the behavior of cop and criminal, though, only the latter tend to embody "fag" stereotypes of dress and demeanor characteristic of the effete rich. Those are the men who perish by film's end. Thus could the genre displace and deny any queer identity among its heroes.

Other analysts do not focus on the scapegoating of particular "fag" characters but look instead to family, race, location, comedy, and violence as means by which movies displace the erotic heat between cops. For instance, Cynthia Fuchs argues that "contemporary cop-buddy movies emphatically hetero-sexualize their homosocial protagonists (through off-screen ex-wives or girl friends who die on-screen) while settling other differences."[21] She argues that, in *Off Limits,* "their mutual erotic desire . . . is, again typically, displaced by comedy."[22] She argues further that, in *Lethal Weapon,* "homoerotic tension is displaced most obviously on to race and class."[23] Robyn Wiegman also argues that movies can ward off the threat of homosexuality with fag jokes, recalling the scene from *Shoot to Kill* in which one man rubs his bare body against the other's to prevent frostbite and jokes, "Ain't you heard about us country boys?" In such cases, Wiegman argues, "they laugh, and the threat of homosexuality is simultaneously foregrounded and averted."[24]

Of similar value, in this analysis, is the camera's discretion with the bodies of cops. Of *Lethal Weapon*'s hero, Wiegman argues that,

> in denying the sight of the penis [we see the hero's ass but not his dick] the film both represses the construction of the spectator's gaze within a homosexual economy of desire and reinscribes the penis as the phallus. . . . The white male body achieves power and privilege in its reconstruction as stand-in for the absent penis.[25]

One can certainly regard men as ambulatory scrota, not least when they call each other "dick head." Nevertheless, the argument has it that movies defuse troubling erotic charges both by shifts to comedy and by visual discretion. Thus does the genre maintain a heterosexual status quo and retain for cop heroes some privilege in a homophobic world.

In this displacement logic, then, the pleasures of cop action work at cross purposes. The homoerotic bonding, parade of manly ass, and bloody penetration threaten to turn good men into sodomites. The genre then does everything it can to straighten them out, "erasing" or "repressing" sexual play. In cinema generally, Steve Neale links "the repression of any explicit avowal of eroticism in the act of looking at the male . . . to a narrative content marked by sado-masochistic phantasies and scenes."[26] About cop action more specifically, Christine

Holmlund argues that in *Tango and Cash* "a homosexuality lurks beside heterosexuality" in the scenes among men, but that the movie "displace[s] the anxiety" created by that display of male flesh with cutaways to chase scenes and fire fights.[27] Through their macho mayhem these movies distract viewers from the erotic spectacle they make of men's bodies and turn attention instead to bloodshed.

Indeed, analysts demonstrate little interest in the genre's violence other than to argue that it distracts from weightier matters.[28] In Michael Paul Rogin's influential discussion of cinema, the " 'sensory overload' of 'superficial' spectacle allows phenomena such as 'race' to structure a movie without making audiences aware of the racism of their enjoyment, by 'burying history.' "[29] This part of the larger displacement hypothesis imputes a politically damaging ignorance—lack of story, lack of history, lack of critical insight or political engagement. In this argument the genre offers its society only the most dim-witted and self-ignorant responses to the resentments that animate it and keeps its heroes straight while ignoring their hot and hard homosociality.

Yvonne Tasker sums this up with her observation that in many cop action movies "a dichotomy can be seen to develop in which the anxieties provoked by the physical display of the white male hero are displaced either through the use of comedy . . . or through the deployment of images of torture and suffering."[30] Movies direct tensions between men that might have opened up space for queer affirmation or inspired critical thought, toward a morally purifying and mind-numbing violence. Cop action, like "fag-bashing" by straight men in the throes of queer panic, gives both an alibi and a steam vent for lusts between men in a world that wants fags dead. Cops kill effete, well-dressed and nicely coifed criminals for the sins of fagginess. Perhaps penetrative combat with these bad guys consoles cops for the more tender moments that hero and side-kick might share were they not so straight. Buddies instead pursue lethal liaisons with enemies, for which they find reward in each other's arms (the juicy bear-hugs in *Die Hard* and *Lethal Weapon,* or the mock flirting in *Tango and Cash,* the stroll into the sunset in *The Last Boy Scout,* the sentimental good-bye scenes in *Red Heat, Midnight Run,* and *Black Rain*). Movies deny the male bonding and mutual attraction that might have affirmed some sort of gay existence, turn them into violent play, and cleanse them of subversive force. Self-contradictory cops loom large in this analysis: What the genre giveth it taketh away through a spectacle that wipes away sodomite stain but bears no other message.

This analysis attends to a tried and true method of managing manhood in a homophobic world.[31] Married, divorced, sleeping around, bickering with girlfriends, even widowered, heroes can claim some sort of heterosexual status even as they ditch those women for the wilder side of manly play. Fags are the problem, the genre seems to say, and if we can wipe out the fags then some of our problems might go away. For so long as many blame lost ground on lesbian and gay movements, destructive energy aimed at the effete, homophillic criminal class can answer to a desire to straighten up the world. Certainly this fits the "Prop 9" logic reviewed in Chapter 1, which supposes an outgroup invading the halls of power to corrupt ruling institutions from within. Fags, conceived as upper-class dandies with little regard for rational governance and social justice, make nice scapegoats, and heroes blow them away. The genre might speak to the fantasy that the rich make good targets not just because they are rich but because they are perverts, the perversion being worse than the greed. Cops might use such rich men to displace the faggotry of their own bonds because the halls of power just happen to house more fags. The status of the criminal class as a well-networked group of upper-class white men might simply flow from an older association between riches and sodomy. The genre would thus be more homophobic than anti-elite, and the heroism in question more heterosexual than working class.

These all make for worthy hypotheses. They each define a relation between cop action and its social context. They hold that violent play works against the illumination of coherent narrative and moral logic. Notice, however, the curious immunity here to the pleasures of violence, alongside the contradiction logic that I prefer to avoid. Christian Chensvold, for instance, worries over the sensory thrills of *Speed* in a manner reminiscent of warnings about gay men and AIDS: "*Speed* represents a great corruption of film. It has guessed that it is a means to excite weary nerves—and with that it has made film sick. . . . perhaps someday the thriller will thrill itself to death."[32] D. A. Miller, in his study of the Victorian sensation novel, calls Chensvold's sort of repulsion a kind of "Cartesian scholarship, in which pulp-as-flesh gets equated with pulp-as-trash."[33] He suggests that the sensations produced by these novels have a way of "feminizing" the reader, and hence we should expect that male critics put off by such sexual responses would remain silent on the subject of the meaning of the violence.

Richard Dyer and Carol Clover argue much the same as Miller, and I find their observations helpful. Clover suggests of horror movies that sensations produced by terrible sights and sounds on the bodies of their viewers have a way of "feminizing" them, at least from the perspective of the "one sex" logic that equates bodily vulnerability with womanhood and strict control with manhood.[34] Clover notes the film theorists' disinterest in the relation between cinema and the male spectator. She blames this on the popular equation of male sexuality with sadism toward women. Many analysts take this link for granted as though it were natural and ignore male perversion as too trivial or deviant too explain. The displacement argument may very well affirm straight manhood as the only game in town by refusing to acknowledge anything else. It waves away the many men who like to tussle with other men.

Dyer, however, celebrates the subversion of the "enforced passivity" of the theater seat, in which viewers find themselves "ecstatically manipulated" by the rush of manly action. "Come to think of it," he argues, "for the male viewer action movies have a lot in common with being fellated." In his brief analysis of *Speed* and the violent rush as white male turf, he notes that

> men cherish the illusion that their masculinity is not compromised by being fellated. Yet it's the other person doing the work, really being active. So it is with action movies. In imagination, men can be Arnie or Keanu [cop action actors]; in the seat, it's Arnie or Keanu pleasuring them. Now that's what I call speed."[35]

(I quibble merely with the notion that masculinity proves more illusory than anything else. If the "men" in question find the position of being blown manly, then so it is, whoever might be working hard and craning his neck.) Many in the audience, fans or analysts, might prefer not to think too hard on the more perverted end of the genre's thrills. They might prefer to turn away from what the violent play could teach us.

Whatever the disparate motives of their authors, displacement arguments partake of a "contradiction" logic that I reject. Though both they and I attend to strain, displacement arguments impute strain to the producers and stories, finding them duplicitous, confused, senseless. I would rather impute these hard times to the cops and their lives, as an ethnographer must. Committed as I am to allowing the genre to make a rough sense as a subculture, I will read it in another way before moving on. What might the genre look like if we presumed no duplicity on its part? What might the tricky, hammering sexuality of these men say to a larger world in turmoil? If the displacement arguments provide the best ways to read the genre, then guilt falls on the heads of queers and not the greedy. If displacement arguments are right, then cop action keeps to self-ignorant scapegoating and can teach us nothing of value. If the displacement hypotheses give way to another reading, however, then a different heroism emerges. Do cops regard themselves as responsible men deserving of the authority they think they have lost? I argue that heroes seek not authority but attention and pleasure. They are less upstanding than childlike, and they have a hard time dealing with adults. They'd rather run off and play rough with rich, white men.

Hard-ons for Criminals

Cops love to kill lusty men in power. Even when the main criminals are not white, as in one movie in six, they are mostly rich and guilty as such. Cops identify their victims by their corruption and then blow them all away. This sacrifice points a demagogic finger at those who abuse their positions of authority and privilege. While cops hate unreasoning lust in the halls of power, they love sodomite bonding too much to pose themselves as straight-arrow solutions to governmental problems. They will not replace the corrupt men they kill as worthy leaders or responsible stewards. Cops do not scapegoat eroticized bonding (as the displacement argument suggests). Instead, they run with the sodomites among them as the brutal, useless deviants they prefer to be. Cops slaughter criminals for their filthy rich sins, to be sure, but not to become paragons of righteous exchange. They could scarcely be taken for the white knights of an orderly capitalism. Cops kill criminals in this way because they can. They have the skills; they must banish xenophobic, military-industrial predation; and they enjoy it. I turn next to the nature of this fun and the light it casts on straight white men as responsible citizens.

Though displacement arguments register in their own way the hard time that cops have making sense to anyone looking, they look suspiciously like the "repression" hypotheses famously countered by Michel Foucault's observation that sex is all over the place and so cannot really be said to be repressed.[36] "Repression" arguments suppose homoerotic impulses concealed by heterosexual romance stories, transformed into death by spectacular violence, never freed to run their queer courses from forces of containment. But, let's just admit that perverted violence lines these movies and makes them fun. Rather than view movies as panicked engines of repressed desire, blowing fags away to ward off scary perversity, I would like to appropriate Foucault's language to consider that these violent men might be in actual fact, and directly, perverse.[37] They do not wrestle and tear at each other because they must to seem normal. They do it because it's a rush.

Cops make no artificial or "homophobic" connection between violence and sex. On the contrary, cops show that violence and sex belong together on the job. For why should gunplay and eroticism oppose each other? Violence need not seem either a punitive substitute for, or a prohibitive lid on, sex (unless straight men really do just want anal/genital contact and don't know it). Men take sex the way they take their work—with violence. Physical injury does not discipline or sublimate anything. It just feels oh so right. Rather than stand in for taboo embraces, body slams and beatings provide the embraces cops want. The more conventional "sexuality" that cops do in their off-hours might actually sublimate this more savage male intimacy.

In this logic, cops remove deviant male bonding from the homes of families and halls of power, where it hurts women and cycles resources between privileged men. Cops make their sodomite violence a distinctly working-class male job, where it can screw no one but the (mostly white) men who so richly deserve it. Cops return deviant male bonding to the ground of manly violence where they can savor it to their hearts' content and their bodies' limits, without having to feel so much like the oppressors that others tell them they are. Rather than distract from race, gender, and class relations, then, violence helps cops deal with them in their own way.

Return for a moment to Smith's analysis of *Tightrope,* mentioned in Chapter 4. Smith argues that the movie's clever critique of compulsory heterosexuality fizzles into a standard ending: The cop murders the male serial killer and strolls away from the scene with his (feminist!) lover.[38] Smith argues that this turn, from a critique of violence against women to yet another wrestling match between men and then to a heterosexual happy ending, sidesteps or displaces the movie's main point. Rather than explore the hero's guilt, in other words, the movie lets him off the hook and sends him away with one of the victims of that male violence and thus absolves him of male predation.

Rather than suppose, however, that the cop's brutal, homosocial law enforcement sublimated the abuse of women, one could imagine the reverse, that the serial killing of women sublimates (covers up the underlying) aggression between men, and that the cop merely reverses the process. Why not homoerotic violence as the ground from which other desires flow? Perhaps the cop desublimates misogynist violence (a misogyny that he shares) and so turns it back toward men. Perhaps the female self-defense instructor who takes this bloodied cop in hand believes that he has returned his sadistic energies from women and back to where they belong, among men. In other words, perhaps cops jump on male criminals, not because they stand for and displace someone else, but simply because they are male. Maybe that's the point.

The displacement hypothesis tells of homoerotic currents diverted into a violence supposedly less sexy; and I must note here that I do not share my colleagues' experiences. I often find fire storms, fist fights, and car chases exciting in visceral ways not separable from erotic rush. Hence, only in the light of some "healthy" standard for the operation of sexual metaphor in film need one condemn the murderous sodomite activity as dishonest or homophobic. Suppose, for instance, one chose to celebrate the fights not merely as the punishment of evil but also as pleasure one could enjoy. Suppose one left life-affirming sympathies behind, in which safety and survival mark virtue, and followed combatants into the dark heart of their conflict to enjoy the sensations they share. As Leo Bersani puts it in his speculative sermon on anal erotics and homophobia, suppose this sodomite violence were rooted in a male fantasy of "insatiable desire" or "unstoppable sex,"[39] a dream of pounding, thrusting, explosive fucking that need never end. Cop action can look suspiciously like Bersani's recreational, masochistic, "anal sex (with the potential of multiple orgasms having spread from the insertee to the inserter, who, in any case, may always switch roles and be the insertee for ten or fifteen of those thirty nightly encounters)."[40] After watching dozens of movies in which men shoot and are shot, beat and are beaten, stab and are stabbed many times, shifting roles and positions for many encounters per movie, I can take Bersani's account for a loose description of a cop action plot. Certainly he could have the payoff scenes in mind: all sweaty groping, spurting fluids, and sodomite slang. Cops flaunt this delicious disorder. Their sodomy marks both male business gone horribly wrong and the wild play of cop combat, not to sublimate something else but as its own undisciplined, irresponsible reward for men losing the ground under their feet.

Analysts have thus perhaps misconceived the sex *versus* violence debate. To suggest that this genre features either an eroticized violence or a sexuality tainted with brutality presumes this distinction. Perhaps cop action contributes a synthesis of the two, at least for men. The coincidence of the meanings of the verb "to fuck" may tell cop action's deepest truth, and all nonsexual or nonviolent meanings offer only a part of the story. In cop action to kill is to fuck is to penetrate is to commune is to give pleasure and pain in an exchange in which currents of respect, insult, fear, courage, affection, desire, and disgust never stop long enough for any man to be simply good or utterly bad, cop or criminal. The pleasure comes in the hostile mix as men hunker down and blow each other away.

Problems with this view would inhere in any dependence on yet another notion of underlying or root desire; and I do not propose to have uncovered any hidden, deeper sexual fantasies at work here. Cop action gives no final answer to the problem of a lack of a sexual relation, social relations, or anything else for that matter. I merely suggest that we pause to read the genre in this way before rushing off to psychoanalyze its displacements and defense mechanisms. If Martin of *Lethal Weapon 2* says that he will fuck a man's ass, later takes it in the thigh with a large knife, rams the blade back into his opponent's chest, and then drops a trailer on him with a happy smile, then maybe that's the sort of fucking Martin likes to do. Next, a criminal shoots Martin many times, and sidekick Roger blows that criminal away. Roger cradles the wounded Martin in his arms; the two seem happy as the sidekick gently strokes his bleeding hero and they joke about the danger of smoking cigarettes. They giggle as Martin tells Roger what a beautiful man he is and asks him for a kiss.

One finds conventional "sex" in these movies, to be sure, though not often, and viewers so inclined might find pleasure in either the domestic caresses between male cop and female lover or the gentler moments between sidekick and cop. But why take this as license to interpret the genre as antihomosexual at heart? If we take them at their words, then most of the "fucking" takes place between male couples. This is their sexuality. This is what they want. This is how they live and die hard. The payoff scenes for which people know this genre leave straight gentleness behind and give over to the wilder side of physical play: the wrenching, sodomite trauma to manly bodies that bring these movies to their collective climax.

Notice the light this throws on cop citizenship in a world

turned rotten. If cops wade into hot action less to displace sex drives than to enjoy the deviant pleasure, then what must we think of them as responsible people? Or, in terms borrowed from Jack Katz's study of the seductions of crime, if cops engage in sodomite slaughter, not because they must in order to seem like good guys, but rather because it provides the most antisocial moral satisfaction, then how can they merit moral authority?[41] The theory of sodomy as a sign of chaos suggests that, in a patriarchy, women do not count for as much in collective worries over the passage of resources. Men hold and trade most of those resources—wealth, authority, esteem, and opportunities to gain more. Hence, men loom large in our anxieties about privilege and its abuse. Certainly this makes sense of the general absence of women from the most spectacular violence. Who cares whom women shoot, hold, or love or with what ethics they do it? So long as they do not withdraw when men need them for supportive affection, tending of wounds, making of meals, to trade to other men, and so on, we need not care about their tastes for physical bonding. Further, though women come into play as victims (serial killers want their attention and torture them for it), they cease to matter as subjects of violence. So long as women have little to lose or exchange, no one need care what they do with their aggression.[42] Their absence from the terrain of hostile combat makes them attractive to heroes as domestic refuge.

Cops crave nurturance from women from time to time but long to spend their days in hot, hard action in the company of men. Male bonding drives the cop action world, and it matters how disordered and destructive that bonding is. Male intimacies both circulate resources in a patriarchal society and lead to disease and destruction. They provide the basis of a modern order and always, potentially, that order's scourge. This makes men important and their choices interesting. It merits them the attention that the genre and its citizens give them. If cop male bonding destroys life and property, if it earns the contempt of men in authority, then that bonding may not be such a good way to run a state. What then shall white men do about the positions of authority they feel they are losing?

With the rest of this chapter, I argue that working-class, straight, white, male cops, anxious to grapple with other men around them, pose themselves as both unworthy of and too interesting for the formal authority against which they define their rebellious action. They desire instead a large spotlight trained on their bloody work. Cops want a turf of their own, in full view of many, on which they can revel in their inability and refusal to do anything but rise to sodomite slaughter. Heroes look to outrageous violence, not to purify themselves of sodomite taint nor to camouflage their true intent, but to bathe in it and so present a hard sexuality, one that enjoys the sodomite violence that it uses to slaughter the criminal class, and one that strains against the proscription of their desire for men.

Point Break

Point Break tells the story of a bunch of white guys who wrestle with their desires for one another and their hatred of authority. Our hero, Johnny, begins as a rookie FBI agent in a wet T-shirt. He rolls through the mud, cocks his weapon in a manly fashion, and shoots targets with skill. As he does this, another young dude surfs to soaring synthesizer music. They both look great. Johnny has the usual troubles with his boss: Though fine on the firing range, Johnny doesn't follow rules. "You're a real blue flame special, aren't you son? Young and dumb and full of cum. I know," says his disgusted boss, who grows more abusive of Johnny as the story moves along.

The criminals turn out to be bank robbers, one of whom bares his ass for a video camera during a heist. Johnny can hardly look away, freezing the tape on it. "Good moves," he murmurs, as he studies the stranger's flesh. These criminals aren't such bad guys in cop action terms, as it happens.

Johnny's sidekick, Angelo, tells him, "They never go for the vault. They never get greedy." In fact, Angelo suspects surfers of the crime. Why? As this salty older cop scoffs at modern Los Angeles, where "the air got dirty and the sex got clean," he peers again at that bare ass on the screen: "It's in our face," he says. "Look at the tan line on this guy." Also, someone found Sex Wax on the scene, which surfers rub on their boards.

Johnny ponders this: "Sex wax. You're not into kinky shit are you, Angelo?"

"Not yet." Their job will provide much kinky fun as they chase men who move money around in improper ways. Tying these surfers to a deviant male subculture, Angelo advises Johnny that they form a "tribe" with "their own language. You can't just walk up to those guys. You got to get out there and learn the moves, get into their head."

And of course this will be dangerous, as deadly as the hero's infiltration of the New York City gay club scene in *Cruising*. "I'm going to learn to surf or break my neck," boasts Johnny to a surfing informant, a woman named Tyler who as her name suggests can do double-duty as a man (not to mention a go-between among them) in this subculture in which gender can shift in funky ways. Johnny uses Tyler as his entré and through her meets a great surfer, Bodhi, "a modern savage . . . a real searcher" for "the ultimate ride," as Tyler describes him. "He's even crazier than you, Johnny." Though Johnny doesn't know yet that Bodhi robs banks for kicks, he bonds with him immediately and for the rest of the movie will tail him, wrestle with him, and let loose with him.

So, the cops comb the beaches for criminals while Johnny moves in on Bodhi and shares a wresting match against other buff young guys on the beach. Angelo collects evidence while spewing fag jokes. Soon, Johnny attends a party in which Bodhi offers him Tyler as a lover: "What's mine is yours." Later, Johnny becomes even more intrigued while Bodhi's buddies talk sex and death, as they spray each other with the white foam of their beer cans. "Big wave riding's for macho assholes with a death wish," snorts Tyler, who as a woman does not feel the pull.

"No it's not," says one of Bodhi's surfer/bank robber dudes. "It's the ultimate rush. There's nothing that comes close to it, not even sex."

"Maybe that's 'cause you're not doing it right, Roach." Tyler gives the young dude a knowing look. She understands the deadly male intimacy but doesn't approve.

Johnny, however, cannot resist. Joining the phallic crowd, he jumps into the conversation: "So what's the biggest?"

"If you want the ultimate," says Bodhi with reverence, "you've got to be willing to pay the ultimate price. It's not tragic to die doing what you love."

"That's how I want to go," cheers a dude.

"Hell, I ain't going to live to see thirty," brags another.

Tyler, and one of the other women, whom the boys generally ignore, look troubled. "There's too much testosterone here," she says. Johnny follows her as she stalks off but cannot stop thinking about Bodhi. She can tell. "—bunch of goddamn adrenaline junkies," she sneers. "—hope you're not buying into this *banzai* bullshit like the rest of Bodhi's moonies. . . . You've got that *kamakaze* look, Johnny. I've seen it. Bodhi can smell it a mile away. He'll take you to the edge— past."

"Johnny has his own demons, don't you Johnny?" says Bodhi, who understands Johnny's tastes as well as Tyler does. Johnny is the only one who seems not to know where his relationship with Bodhi is going. That night they surf in the darkness, a truly dangerous sport.

"I've got to be fucking crazy," says Johnny. "I can't see shit out here. I'm going to die." As Bodhi shows him how to move, a wave takes Johnny. "Shit, —die now. I'm going to fucking die now!" He catches the wave. "Fuck me! . . . . Whoa! I'm fucking surfing. Yeah! Check it out!" Pounded and tossed, nearly to death in Bodhi's company, Johnny talks like he's found the meaning of his life.

"Isn't that the best feeling on earth?" gasps Bodhi.

"Yeah!" Totally turned on, Johnny notices that Tyler, in a wet suit with hair slicked back, now looks just like him. They make out as Bodhi leaves them alone together. The next morning, perhaps still turned on, Johnny runs off to bust nazi surfers, most of whom cops shoot point blank in a vicious gun fight as one screams, "Oh shit! Shit! We're fucked!" Johnny tussles with one. He gropes, smashes, nearly gets his face pulped by a lawn mower while the nazi straddles him from behind in a sodomite wrestling match. Cops kill and otherwise maim the nazis. Johnny pants in triumph.

That night, in bed, Tyler looks like a man, well muscled, cropped, a perfect companion for Johnny. Still, she's no great-looking male surfer, and Johnny stays awake, his thoughts far away. Bodhi shows up unannounced and invites Johnny for another surf with his guys. One moons Johnny, who makes the connection: bare ass, surfer, bank robber, his guys. He wants them.

He and Angelo stake out a bank Bodhi frequents and catch the masked boys in the act. Johnny tumbles with Bodhi, who keeps his dudes from shooting Johnny and even pauses during a chase to let Johnny catch up and wrestle with him. The chase ends when Johnny hurts his ankle. Suddenly impotent, he limps to the ground, points his gun at Bodhi, who gives him a soft, blue-eyed look back, and then discharges his weapon into the air with a frustrated yell. He can't shoot Bodhi but he sure wants to let it rip with his piece. As his wad of bullets fly into the Southern California sky and Bodhi, still masked, lopes away, Johnny knows an intimate frustration.

Angelo can see what's happening to his partner, and he doesn't like it: "I want you to know something. When you shoot, you don't miss."

"I missed," says Johnny, lying.

"No. I believe you're either scared, or you're getting too goddamn close to this surfing guru buddy of yours." And after a meaningful pause, nose to nose with his errant hero, Angelo says like a jealous man, "I don't believe you're scared." Nevertheless, he supports his hero. "Hey, I want you to go home, and get some rest. You look like hammered shit. [Sodomy puns abound.] And if I get anything that resembles your boy, I'll beep you." So Johnny goes home to think about his boy some more. By this time Tyler, neglected long enough to figure out who Johnny really is, leaves him in disgust at his duplicity. He has lied to her, telling her that he's just a lawyer who likes to surf. Understanding that he used her to get to his guy, she tells him off.

The movie kicks into romantic high gear when Bodhi and his boys, now unmasked, stop by the next morning to take Johnny skydiving. Johnny accepts. They know he's a cop. He knows they're criminals. They leave their identities open secrets, however, for the purpose of a little bonding, like straight guys angling for forbidden fruits, so to speak. In fact, I defy anyone to make sense of such scenes without recourse to a romantic entanglement between the men, which drives them to all kinds of sacrifices for and pretenses around each other. Far from gay, these guys hardly look straight either, if one defines straight as only interested in intimate physical contact with the opposite sex. On the four-minute free-fall (cop action jumps last longer than ours) Johnny seems to forget himself utterly. He holds hands with his criminal quarry and screams at the top of his lungs, "Amazing! Fucking amazing!" He and Bodhi tease about not pulling the parachute cord on the way down, flirting with death and the ultimate sacrifices that they might make for each other. As he lands in the water Johnny wonders at how far he's come from his upstanding FBI agent days: "Jesus Christ. —got to be fucking losing it."

"The closest you'll ever get to God," says Bodhi.

The fun over, however, Bodhi plays a trump card and turns up the heat between them. He has kidnapped Tyler, who, mannish no more, fumes in her underwear as a captive of

Bodhi's boys. Bodhi, content no longer to lure Johnny with promises, now drags him deeper into deviance with threats. Johnny must rob a bank with him or lose Tyler for good. So Johnny does, and during the fatal heist two men die: one of Bodhi's dudes, and an off-duty cop in the wrong place at the wrong time. Now for the first time Bodhi's economic antics cost lives, and Johnny determines to take him down for crossing the line barring dizzy deviance from cop action evil. He and Angelo chase him across town to an airfield where more men will die: Angelo, when he tries to shoot Bodhi against Johnny's wishes; and another of the dudes.

Johnny and Bodhi fly to Mexico ("We are going to ride this all the way, Johnny, you and me, so let's go. Get the fuck up!") where a goon holds Tyler, and as they near Johnny begs Bodhi to let her go. Cop action morality almost always excuses women from these affairs, and Johnny says, "She's served her purpose. Do it man, you owe me that much!"

Apparently to provoke Johnny, Bodhi refuses. He won't release Tyler until he's on the ground. He pushes a wounded dude out the airplane, readies his own parachute, leaving Johnny with none, and taunts him. "I know it's hard for you Johnny," he says with an amused look. "I know you want me so bad it's like acid in your mouth. But not this time. Adios amigo!"

Obsessed beyond reason, Johnny cannot bear to let Bodhi go. "Fuck it!" he vows and jumps from the airplane with no parachute. He speeds through his free fall toward Bodhi's backside, takes him from behind in a forcible bear hug, and the two plummet face-to-face in an intimate, life-threatening embrace in which Bodhi refuses to pull his own parachute cord. They fall to earth amidst the linen folds of Bodhi's parachute, grunting and panting. "Jesus Christ, Bodhi," says Johnny, his man in his clutches again.

"Goddamn, you are one radical son of a bitch," admires the criminal. But, he turns to flee. "I'm out of here, Johnny."

Johnny struggles and falls lame again. "That knee again, huh. That's too bad. —Looks like this time you won't be getting your man. This game we both lose." He leaves his man behind as Johnny, furious to see Bodhi go, comforts Tyler.

Any straight movie might have ended there, killed Bodhi and left him dead on the ground, just as *Point Break* kills Bodhi's wounded surfer dude, who seems to have expired while Bodhi and Johnny fell to earth. The bloody corpse lies amidst stolen dollars, a testament to what's wrong with Bodhi's sense of fun. To risk life to protect others is one thing, but to endanger people for money earns almost everyone violent death. A straight movie might also have ended with Tyler restored to Johnny's care, terrorized into submission by the protection racket. But, *Point Break* will take Johnny to the ends of the earth for his boy and leaves us no doubt about his priorities. He leaves Tyler far behind and many months later has tracked Bodhi to Australia, for the "fifty year storm," which can kill anyone who plunges into its mighty waves. Now the two men look just alike, with matching hair, beards, and expressions of grim determination to risk their lives for sport. Standing next to each other, profiles matched, they may not be twins but they do look like soul mates in vice.

Still, Bodhi has abused a position of responsibility, stained himself with the blood of others shed for money; and so Johnny lays down the law: "You crossed the line and people trusted you and they died."

"Yeah it went bad, it went real bad," admits Bodhi. "Life sure has a sick sense of humor doesn't it?" To illustrate his point, he asks, "Still surfing?"

"Every day." Johnny has come all this way, not to wipe out the vice he has come to love, but rather to keep it where it belongs—between working-class men and away from either the women it hurts or the exchange that it corrupts. "Come on, Bodhi, it's time to go. You know you've got to go back with me."

"Sorry my friend." They fight in the surf, beat and grope each other one last time. Johnny wins and Bodhi begs him: "No! You know there's no way I can handle a cage, man."

"I don't care," Johnny shouts. "You got to go down. It's got to be that way."

Bodhi arranges to avoid jail (where men go down in a less dignified way, as cops like to joke) but die in the surf where he can find God instead. Like any hero, Johnny understands the impulse to self-importance and allows Bodhi to paddle to a grander death. He stalks off and throws his FBI badge into that very surf, having given up everything for his boy and his "fuck me!" joy rides: his sidekick, his job, his girlfriend, his adherence to conventional law. Now he trades only in deadly male fun. He'll take down any man who does it for money, but he will not give it up himself.

Just to set this engaging movie back in its context let me note that another one, *Tequila Sunrise,* covers similar ground with its strapping guys in trouble on the beach. It also offers two white men and sets them, a cop and the criminal whom he likes very much, against each other (in this movie they are longtime friends and the criminal deals drugs rather than bank notes). It also associates their male bonding with lethal violence and the Southern California beach (and with Ping-Pong, a game that commences after one criminal catches another in a bathrobe with a juicy bear-hug from behind). This movie also has its cop and criminal exchange a woman between them as a pawn ("—you want to fuck your friend?" she objects to the cop. "Then fuck him, not me"). Finally, this movie also gives the hero a sidekick who acts like a jealous lover and gets shot in the back when he tries to kill the cop's favorite criminal (though in *Tequila Sunrise,* the cop does the killing himself to protect the man he really loves by murdering a fellow officer of the law).

Tequila Sunrise differs mainly by letting the friendly criminal live to see the final sunrise, killing off his Latino partner in crime instead (who met his drug-dealing buddy, provocatively enough, in a Mexican jail, saving his ass, and who wonders why anyone would ever stigmatize a man for his deviant love: "No man should be judged for whatever direction his dick goes," he argues. "That's like, uh, uh, blaming a compass for pointing north, for Christ's sake!"). The surviving criminal (who lives perhaps because he appears never to have killed anyone for money or for sport) splashes around in the surf with the woman rather than die a Viking's death in the waves.

Both stories feature heroes who use women to get to men, whose lives revolve around rituals of male bonding always described in terms of deviance, Southern California beaches where men get wet together, and physical danger (all of *Tequila Sunrise*'s victims die on the water, where the bonding climaxes with a fiery explosion). These heroes break the law for their criminals; both take on, use, and then ignore girlfriends for their criminals; both prefer danger and male bonding to lawful domesticity. Errant employees and lousy lovers, they make great cop heroes. They have wet, hard times copping to their sins. They have such hard times living with nurturers and running their society that they pretty much give up both. Most of all, though, they have good hard times tussling with and killing white men. *Point Break* and *Tequila Sunrise* suggest that what (mostly white) men do for fun lures cops, kills men, and screws the world around them. Why do cops like it so much? How does such play address the problems of lost ground? We need to look longer at the violence, blood, and guts to see.

Fuck Whitey

In *Downtown*, a white male patrolman busts a snooty, well-connected man in a speeding Porsche. His bosses punish him with an ouster from his toney suburb to the nonwhite precinct of the movie's title. There in that alien land, residents beat, strip, and debase him in public. At home that night, back in a white town, he tells his wife that he has had the time of his life: "Lori, Lori, Lori, will you just listen to me?" he says. "You should have seen this place. They're cops, real ones. I mean, they're smart."

"If they're so goddamned smart," Lori wonders, "how come they're not working out here?"

"Because nothing happens out here. Look, I'm fine, really. I can learn a lot from these guys. I think I can be that good."

Lori notices his shirt, borrowed from the precinct house. "It's quite lovely," she says in scorn. "I especially like how someone wrote 'FUCK WHITEY' on the sleeve."

The cop thrives in his new work, and never more so than when pressed to his limits by abuse from nonwhites and his perverse criminal quarry. After hoods nearly pulp him in a tree shredder and one slurps through the machine with an impressive "splat," he lies in a hospital in bed next to his wounded black male partner, right where he wants to be. Along the way, he destroys a white man's enterprise, ruining the pillar of his community who smuggles drugs and had the hero sent downtown to begin with (this movie's version of lost ground). Poor Lori never does know what he likes about his work, or why a day of combat and sexual shame before a crowd of nonwhites should thrill him so. Though she pointedly cannot see why, whitey fucked is a happy man.

Note the difference between cop action and the less bloody sensitive-men genre. In Fred Pfeil's convincing analysis, the latter movies begin with upper-class straight white men, put them through traumatic changes, give them the free therapy familiar to cops, and then leave them to pursue their privileged lives. The men reform into childlike versions of their exploitive selves but give up little other than a few callow white male friends or corrupt jobs for others of equal value. In other words, these guys gain the love of those they have exploited in the past without having to give up much in turn. The hero of

Hook (1991), for instance, "holds out the promise or ideal of a masculinity whose arrested development and deliberate regression are the guarantee of its power and its right to rule."[43] Thus does the sensitive men genre take a meditation on white manhood and turn it into a reform story, leaving the white guys pretty much where it finds them, socioeconomically, or at least on track back up that ladder.

Contrast this to cops' stories, in which the working-class heroes defy themselves out of their jobs—quit or are fired—in forty movies. They face serious trouble, including potential prosecution at the ends of another thirteen stories. All told, heroes find love from sidekicks, welcome from families, respect at work, and defeat of the criminals, all together, in less than a third of their stories. Criminals still run free in one movie in five, and another one in six leaves the cops with no family or romantic life at all. Reintegrated happiness, while widely pursued and often found, is not assured in cop action. Certainly, the action leads up no economic ladder. Few heroes wind up with any more authority than they had at the stories' beginnings, and often they face more trouble. What, then, do the less socially successful cops gain from this combat? Simply, the violent testing ground provides its own reward, even though this indulgence can alienate cops further from management and family. Cops want less the respect due patriarchs than a high-profile version of the status of skilled blue-collar workers—protectors of the very families and communities that they should not try to head.

Pfeil analyzes the first two *Die Hard* and *Lethal Weapon* movies and notes the terrain of erotic male combat at their hearts, "a hot spot . . . a place where some of the bad guys as well as the good, and black guys as well as white, both care and kill—kill, indeed, *because* they care . . . —and where race doesn't matter anymore."[44] Pfeil moves on when the topic of this eros among men arises, but I would like to stay a while and consider more fully why men pummel each one another in their sodomite fashion.

What do white men want? The meanings of manhood, whiteness, class identity, and proper male intimacy and exchange seem to have been thrown into doubt by current events. Some of the authority with which such men speak has been sapped, even if the distributions of other resources go largely unchanged. These movies respond to crises of confidence and negotiate, through metaphors of anal engagement, a new, erect yet receptive, hard and hot male heroism. For any cop tough enough, the violence affirms some privilege (after all, only those in secure positions can enjoy submission; only to the privileged is it a game) and gives those privileged few their well-deserved comeuppance. Guys eat their beef and have it too, variously beaten, shocked, stabbed, shot, burned, blown apart, dropped, crushed, mangled, mulched, and otherwise mutilated. Why test cops with this terrible violence, especially if it taints them with the deviance of their criminal prey? The answer lies in the tribute that this self-mortification provides.

Other genres work the terrain of the visceral. Classical Hollywood women's films, horror, and pornography offer "low" embraces of onlookers' bodies.[45] While porn aims for the crotch, melodramas route their melodramatic appeal through the characters' emotional trauma, and horror through bodily injury. Of Victorian sensation novels, D. A. Miller notes that the stimuli tended to "feminize" readers, and that most novels appealed to and reaffirmed their masculinity by flattening out this affect toward the end of the story, assuaging anxieties of liberal subjects (defined there as those who feel controlled or affected from without and nervous about it).[46] Cop action, however, seems to dampen hysteria (in which men feel feminine) by heading in just the opposite direction, away from comfort and toward macho trauma. Beyond the "feminized" state of "melodramatic" torment, cop action offers a thrill-seeking abandon that promises to make a hero of whomever can stomach it. For the most part, expressions of angst accompany two scenarios: furious grief over the murder of loved ones and angry defense of insulted pride. To be sure, these scenarios pack their own visceral power as good guys in crisis cry, scream, and promise pain to those they hunt. Still, these moments always (and perhaps this always defines this genre's appeal) lead to violence, just as surely as foreplay leads to coitus in porn. Once finished with the strictly emotional frisson with intimates, cops turn to explosive sensation by punishing the bodies of men. I refer here not only to the sights of men in pain but also the sounds of crunching bones, torn flesh, and screams. I call these gut shots.

Linda Williams writes of the importance of the "money shot" (of a penis spewing semen) to pornography.[47] She describes the lengths to which characters go to produce such spectacle, the sexual truth the shots imply, and the proof of pleasure they offer. All of this she terms "the frenzy of the visible," and "frenzy" seems an apt term for the "numbers" in action movies. Numbers pay off genre movies, bringing them to their climaxes: songs in musicals, sex scenes in porn, emotional confrontations in melodrama. Cop action pays off by screwing with a male body (the visibility of whose injury may provide the most common measure of the generic quality of the movie among fans).[48] Spectacles of pain can work as teaching tools, ways to know and believe something about one's world. Gut shots tell us something about cops' hard times and brand the thoughts into onlookers' bodies.

These are the gut shots. In *Blade Runner,* one man breaks another's fingers, one by one. Men slowly hack and chew each other's extremities in *Black Rain, Sharky's Machine, Showdown in Little Tokyo,* and *Stone Cold.* In *The Last Boy Scout,* one man puts a gun to a another's hand and blows a hole in it. The hero of *Marked for Death* breaks his wailing opponents' arms in hand-to-hand fights. The title character of *Predator 2* has an arm hacked off and later screams as he cauterizes the bloody stump in acid. In *Robocop,* criminals blow the cop's arm off for sport. He gasps, spouts blood, screams, and thrashes while they blow his body to pieces. Another man explodes in fountains of blood as bullets riddle his body, and yet another melts into viscous goo as toxic waste eats him alive. In the sequel, a doctor tortures a cop to death on an operating table with a scalpel. In *Total Recall,* the hero drives a spike through a man's skull and rips another's arms off, holding the bloody stumps as they rain blood. Later a man dies in slow agony as he decompresses and his eyes pop from his skull. In *Die Hard,* the hero pulls shards of glass from his bloody foot and in the sequel jams an icicle into an opponent's eye, pausing for a moment to look before moving on. In the next sequel, a flying cable bisects a man and the hero paints himself in the blood of his opponents in a close-quarters gunfight. Later still he tugs a long metal sliver from the gory flesh of his arm. *Shoot to Kill* features a gunman who aims for the eyes, and onlookers survey the carnage with care. In *Blade Runner,* one man pops another man's eyes out of his skull while he screams. The same occurs in *Marked for Death* and *Under Siege.* Killers knife naked men in *Basic Instinct* and *Cruising;* blood spouts from the many wounds as victims writhe and wail. *Lethal Weapon, Showdown in Little Tokyo,* and *Tango and Cash* feature long scenes of the electroshock torture of barely clad cops. Movies such as *Innocent Blood, Se7en,* and *Wolfen* feature long scenes in morgues with mutilated corpses.

Gut shots must affect onlookers in many ways, but certainly they testify to the hard times cops have. At first repellent to me, the sight, for instance, of a criminal twisting a large knife in a cop's thigh and the sound of his screams, or another falling into the rotors of a helicopter (or tree mulcher, or crop thresher, or jet engine, or propeller—this "splat" approach to law enforcement amounts to a cop action cliché) begin after a while to seem like the only sensible conclusions to protracted physical struggles. Gut shots often play like the final resolution to a major key after a movement in a minor one (a musical move that sometimes accompanies the final gut shot). In these punishing moments, the genre offers a hardness, a sex-inflected resilience to violent contest. The pain is generally less affective and more visceral: pounding meat, exploding limbs, rattled joints, and squashed bodies. It is a sign of cops' double claim to survival skill and victimhood. The materiality of the sinewy bodies of the heroes, not least the insides of those bodies freed to spout across the room, amount to invitations to belief in the cops' stories. They gesture toward a world where the heroic act *matters* in every sense of the word. The blood that flies from the entry point of a bullet or the cold-cocked character's mouth, the thud of a fist in a stomach or a club on a head, a cop's cry as a knife twists in his flesh, these quick-cut moments of injury and pain—each proves the hardness of the hero's times and the moral ambiguity of those who explode in showers of blood before us.[49]

Cops have lost ground in their blue-collar sector and must deal with the fact that skilled workers get nailed by the greedy unless someone takes some action. "Regular people suck," and cops want credit for doing what only men can do. They feel they are not getting it in a labor market more interested in service and information than in hard physical work. Worse, these service and white-collar jobs too often serve the very organizations that have corrupted their society for money. In a world with little frontier left, and without the miserable nineteenth century conditions of proletarian labor against which they might prove their resilience, working-class, straight white men have a hard time feeling irregular. They look to combat with oppressors as routes to a new place in their world.

Jude Davies notes that the frustrated white men of *Falling Down,* cop and criminal alike, hearken back to a time "when experience could be relied upon, when hard work was rewarded, and before technology made people like himself obsolete; . . . the jungle boots [worn by the criminal with whom the cop empathizes] represent masculine practice versus effete theory."[50] Working-class men can prove themselves with violence in a world of professionals and bureaucrats whose work fails to use and thus glorify their bodies, work that fails to protect against the ravages of bad white men. Without such protection from vice, what can cops offer their world? Not much, as they know too well. Cops dream of jobs that test their bodies and offer evidence for beleaguered workers' claims. The action proves with pain both that the corrupted world really has fucked whitey over and that it needs the only thing he was ever good at. The world needs him to slaughter the very forces that put him where he is today, in his position of contested, screwed-up privilege. This drama may require bandages or a stay in the hospital later, and may occasionally take a hero's life; but things could be worse. "Regular people suck," as the hero puts it in *Running Scared*. Brutally contested privilege looks a hell of a lot better than life as one of the women they abandon or community members they defend. It beats cleaning toilets, raising kids, selling shoes, or flipping burgers. Cops dream of a skilled, taxing, vital labor they can call their own, and gut shots show us that work with a vengeance.

Thus, bloody moments close stories of frustrated workers—working-class white men mostly—who draw the undivided attention of everyone around and stage the punishment of elites, all as a way to address, though not exactly reverse, their loss of authority over their worlds. Heroes and criminals taunt one another with their shared frustrations and deviance and then get into it in the most visceral manner. The battles allow cops to embrace corrupted, bad white manhood and then burn it up for all to see. The Aryan criminal of *Cobra* goads the cop with his vision of a fascist new world order: "Let's play, Pig. . . . We are the hunters. We kill the weak, so the strong survive. . . . Your filthy society will never be rid of people like us. It's breeding them. We are the future."

"No!" retorts the cop. "You're history." The cop locks the criminal in his gun sight, but the latter foolishly tries to cloak himself in the social order that the cop would shrug off. "You won't do it, Pig," he gloats. "You won't shoot. Murder is against the law. . . . The court is civilized, isn't it, Pig?"

"But I'm not," the cop corrects him. "This is where the law stops and I start, Sucker." Visions of order compared, they choose chaos. The strapping white men grope, wrestle, and beat each other unmercifully as hot liquids steam and drip around them. The criminal threatens the cop with a huge knife and they grapple over it, face-to-face and staring into each other's eyes—two white men, both contentious, crazy, built for rough trade, and each doing what he does best. The cop grabs the criminal in a bear hug, impales him through the rear on a large foundry hook, and roasts him alive. The scene reverberates with the criminal's screams and the genre soaks in torn flesh as men fight over the highest stakes. More than disputes over rational governance, labor market status, or familial authority, these become battles for life and death. They may begin as debates over legal authority and systems of justice, but they end with wailing men on hooks buttfucked for good. The hero of *Cobra* tortures his mirror to death, sullies himself with the exchange, and so trades one moral ambiguity (respectable employee of the state) for another (useful nut).

Though the law demands that cops serve criminals for trial, they mostly (93 percent of the time) do not. *Wanted Dead or Alive* ends with the famous "Fuck the bonus" line, with which the cop chooses the fun of one last (orally penetrative) murder over the money promised him for the Semitic criminal's live delivery. Another movie ends with an Aryan criminal's plea to the hero who has bested him. Impaled from the rear on an erect pipe from which white fluid spurts and drips, the blond alien roars in pain for quite a long time before the white male cop picks up a large gun and prepares to finish the job. The criminal gives the line for which the movie is named: "I come in peace."

"And you go in pieces, asshole," retorts the cop as he delivers his coup de grâce, blowing the criminal away in an explosion of flesh. The jokey malevolence of the line suggests a lack of moral purpose, and one could counter my argument by suggesting that the hero merely needs an excuse to practice his deadly art against a man of no moral significance. Perhaps heroes shoot such criminals just because they can. Or perhaps they deny and project their responsibility for a world losing ground onto any scapegoat around, fighting for some unmarked white male supremacy. These make worthy hypotheses; but my favorite story tells of a hero who shoots for these reasons: (1) The cop knows very well that he is good for little but summary execution and had best show that skill off before he gets his ass downsized by a world falling to service work and corporate corruption; (2) he knows that moneyed white men pose danger and deserve to die; (3) because he shares some of their guilt, he can have as much fun tearing into Aryan men as being beaten by them; and (4) the studied outrageousness of his violence demonstrates a self-conscious disaffection from the rational and responsible world.

By this last reason, I mean that cops drive a hard bargain with the world they defend. They will fight for moral order as long as they can do it in the most disordered way and banish all pretense to instrumental considerations, even the most murderous, by the proud assertion of undisciplined work. I am not suggesting a lack of method to the manly madness. Rules govern greed, xenophobia, and the role of women in combat. Cops enforce these rules with their guns. Rather than random, I mean, the methods seem simply, pointedly, beyond the law. The righteous moral dizziness of deviance is the privilege for which cops fight.

By "dizziness," I refer to an influential piece of criminological theorizing that supposes that (noncinematic) men engage in unruly, often violent crime not because they must but because it feels good.[51] Whatever their class status, nearly any man can relate to the sense of having been disrespected by his society. Katz discusses the apparent foolishness with which murderous men pursue trivial conflict and press themselves where they are not wanted. Dizzy with moral deviance, they would rather play the rebel until beaten or shunned than seem to cave in to a corrupt society—the very society that has shamed them with its lack of deference. Rather than roll over in the face of disrespect, heroic men don mantles of wrathful gods. In moments conducive to violence, they deem themselves morality's last hopes, they take last desperate stands, and hurl themselves into chaos. So it goes in cop action. These are the moments in which fists and bullets fly. Disrespected by losing ground, cops wade into combat with little thought for personal safety, bosses' opinions, or lovers' wishes. Dizzy with deviance, even as they take blows and spit blood, they stand tall again: They won't just knuckle under. They seem fools to those around, but they will not submit. This dizziness, the joy with which heroes loose disorder on the world around them, both founds and flows from their heroic hard times. They did not choose lost ground, but they merrily escalate the conflict, reshaping their own, more heroic, hard times.

What sort of white male politics is this? On one hand, we see a conventional re-empowerment. Action movies famously stage fantastic revenge, in which the hero's abuse merits him brutal resumption of his former standing. Domestic grand slams—families reunited, lovers come to heel, and homes restored—occur by way of protection rackets in a sixth of the movies. Heroes accept awards for valor in another dozen, and many heroes accept free therapy from the sidekicks whom they often leave in service positions. One might certainly read in these the reintegration of cops into a world that had abandoned them, a retaking of ground lost to corruption.

Further, heroes endure beating after beating (I have yet to see Clint Eastwood reach the end of an action movie without a stern thrashing), but only to climb to their feet once more and chew their opponents to pieces. They first mortify themselves in the most intimate ways, testify to the world their ruined status, cede responsibility for the worst excesses of white male supremacy to their more xenophobic and greedy brethren, and then right the world as best they can.[52] Wiegman argues for this as a reaffirmation of white male authority. She says of *Lethal Weapon* (and its refusal to show the hero's dick):

> The white male body achieves power and privilege in its reconstruction as stand-in for the absent penis. In the specularization of [hero] Riggs's body, the white masculine, in effect, multiplies itself, the missing penis finding its way back into the scene as the much-sought-after phallus. The film's various moments of looking at Riggs—reclining, running, falling, fighting, shooting—are affirmations that the threat of castration has not simply been averted but that the body has now become the phallus, literalizing itself in various displays of phallic authority as the "lethal weapon."[53]

Thus may the genre's violence work to reaffirm an authority lost. Cops take their punches, to be sure, but usually, like Rambo, come out on top.

Whatever such "power and privilege" may add up to, however, I also see a serious abdication occurring here, in which cops disgusted with the world wash their hands of its corrupt and unmanly politics and walk away as though they were both too bad (as in too white and male) and too good (as in too proudly deviant) for it. Consider Pfeil's reading of the *Die Hard* and *Lethal Weapon* movies:

> The rhythms of excitation and satisfaction in these films . . . asserting male violence and/or death-trip spectacle again and again, even as their own speeded-up processes of gratification undermine any claim to male authority . . . evoke, with various admixtures of pride, embarrassment, and wistfulness, the resonance of skills discounted or dismissed in the new late-capitalist Processed World of L.A., within films that go on to reassert the ongoing value, even necessity, of such skills and savvy in the struggle against international criminal-commercial enterprise.[54]

Pfeil's reading certainly works for me, and I would apply it to the larger genre.[55] It evokes the complicated stance of proud entitlement and embarrassed admission of white manhood that cops offer. Many of these guys reintegrate, to be sure, binding lovers and families through protection rackets only to lose them later and find new ones if they are lucky. They befriend sidekicks and take comfort in the free therapy. They even draw accolades from managers in a few movies. But they count dizzy deviance as their bread and butter, the prize of work well done. The "speeded up processes of gratification" lead to the orgasmic gut shots and parade their uncivilized bents. The sodomite violence offers cops not only a turf of their own but also an escape from the burdens of stewardship. Heroes never do get down to the serious business of rebuilding the world that they feel has lost so much ground and rejected them. Instead, they admit their inadequacies, reject the job of ruling in turn, and stalk off to the margins to play. The violent expulsion of the effete, wealthy, feminine, nazi within comes to a head as they blow the criminals away and take so much abuse themselves. Governance is pointedly not on their minds, since such concerns would taint these sodomites with corruption again. Faced with the choice between the restoration of their patriarchal authority and the brutal pleasures of nailing the criminal class, cops choose dizziness every time.

This is male-bonding utopia, the corollary to the "pornotopia" of Williams's analysis of the porn genre. This is the space in which cops are (mostly) men and the criminals had better be scared. It certainly brings the heroic cop and his loyal sidekick as close as they ever get. Near the endings of such movies as *Black Rain, Die Hard, Lethal Weapon, Stone Cold,* and *Under Siege,* sidekicks acquit themselves expertly and save their heroes' lives. In *Lethal Weapon,* for instance, Roger catches bare-chested Martin in his arms ("I've got you partner, I've got you") and guns down the criminal with Martin's help. In *The Last Boy Scout,* the hero and sidekick both do their parts saving family members and public officials, and each suffers his own awful wound in the process. At the close of these movies, cop and sidekick trade affection and respect, often walk off into the sunset, ultimately to find more bad guys, more beatings at their hands, more satisfaction at their deaths, and so on. The action need never end, the heroes need never be regular and need never suck. They stride off into a world that's learned what they're made of, where the only things they were ever good at will serve as their tickets to a marginal turf where manhood is dizzy but not so tainted by greed.

For all of the anxiety over autonomy in the bureaucratic jungle of their work lives, these heroes still lose themselves in the manly crowds that undermine their status as upstanding straight men.[56] Cops take themselves to the limits, explore the extremes, less because it will restore their authority, disavow their guilt, or otherwise confuse their audiences than because it feels so right and puts them in the spotlight as the skilled workers they long to be. Barbara Ehrenreich observes that noncinematic men seem to have given up on the nuclear family in which they stand as head.[57] Along with this, of course, they are only too happy to give up the responsibility for making sure that the society runs in a responsible manner. Likewise, deposed from positions of comfortable authority, cops want to take their toys and leave home, heading into the fire fights in which a different sort of dizzy hardness awaits them. Some of them return, to be sure. Cop action offers twin utopias of reintegration through their protection rackets and free therapy on one hand, and painful removal from governance through criminal intimacies on the other.

Tired of the cultural wars that have left many white men feeling buffeted and abused, heroes long for the thrill of surrender to white-boy brutality. They fall into a mass of beefy, murderous bodies with a sort of hateful implosion. Their own brutality rebounds against the racist, greedy, misogynist bodies that maintain and profit from it, and beats them up. Fuck

whitey, indeed. The joyous masochism, in which cops re-
nounce some of their historic privileges, allows them a more
infantile claim in a society that may now give less deference to
patriarchal authority. A cop is being beaten and will shortly
crawl home to lick his wounds, try to find a woman to comfort
him as he weeps for fallen friends, and see if he can't get himself some good home-loving. For now, though—the now that
the genre stretches out as long as possible—he can throw his
head back and howl while knives skewer thighs, fists pounds
faces, and bullets rip flesh. Cops call this manly turf their own.
They earn it by killing criminals and living to play another day.
Only those who can identify and get along with white men belong. Nobody else has so much privilege and guilt to wrestle.
No one else proves as interesting to the moral logic that gov-
erns cop action.

Conclusion: Good Guys?

Cops feel forsaken by the supports they recall with nostalgia. Their children doubt them; their bosses, coworkers, and wives demand skills they do not have. Cops fess up to their paranoia to sidekicks, find criminals on whom to practice their one trade, and so regain as much ground as they can. They bond across their differences with sidekicks and then identify with and don the rage of the oppressed against the criminal class. Finally, cops target white men in positions of authority as the source of their biggest problems. The bigoted and reckless bonding of criminals causes the problems that have cost straight, white, working-class men so much public legitimacy in the first place. Exposure of their corruption has led sidekicks, bosses, families, and community members to blame white men as bullies and to distance from them as such. These men know that they cannot return to the status of "normal" or "human"; white manhood must bear the stain of their sins. Nevertheless, they can round up the baddest of white men, blow them away for public show, and claim the attention they want with their self-hating immolation. They save for themselves this terrain of sodomite violence on which they do their politically charged work. Rituals of self-expulsion light cityscapes with fire, testify to the pain of ground lost, and affirm their unique ability to suffer another day as they fight the good fights.

I can see why cops strike so many analysts as bundles of contradiction. The men admit to incompetence as lovers and own up to their sexism, yet still push women from their job turf. They enjoy sodomite bonding and thus queer fun, yet destroy such bonding among the rich men around. White cops face their racism and serve nonwhite communities, yet grab center stage when the action heats up. But, if we allow for a fiery mix of shame and pride, all of these contradictions can blend into a coherent moral logic.

Cops wade into battle against the most resentful and over-privileged of their own kind. There they earn the attention on which they thrive by expressing the shame they cannot avoid. Hard times come of a slew of ills: the predations of the rich, deviant male bonding and lapsed female support, nonwhite encroachment into job and domestic turf, and emasculation by women in their professions. These problems mark the unmarked, "normal" men as political players and leave cops with wounds they can lick in the public spotlight. Cops must acknowledge their sins and limitations, strain against them, and move forward with their penance and revenge. What other analysts regard as the genre's confusions, displacements, and evasions, I see as the cops' ornery but mindful self-hatred. Cops know what they do; they just do not like it or themselves very much.

I have argued that cops become heroes not merely through displacement and erasure of the practices that benefit their class but also through acknowledgment of political struggle. Certainly they must hold onto some status and comforts along with everyone's attention. Doubtless they wish for more. Still, cops look their troubled world in the face, in obvious comparison with the scurrilous criminal class, dare anyone to see the common ground between them, and then blow those counterparts away. Whether they live alone at the end matters less than how they meet their demons and spit in their faces. Diagnoses of "erasure" will not do here. Universal, "normal" status has slipped away and cops must talk about their resentment over ground lost to them. Racism, misogyny, capitalist exploitation, police authoritarianism, and homophobia loom too large in this genre, called what they are, for straight white manhood to seem very natural or for its moral authority to escape unstained.

Certainly, by blowing the greedy white men around them to bits, cops may seem to disavow their membership in that race- and gender-bound group. They may seem to strain toward the liberal, unmarked status of the privileged. One could also read the rejection of organizational constraint and bonds with women and nonwhite men, who call them to account and make them feel like oppressors, as gestures toward a world with no race, gender, or class. As such analyses suggest, it may be that the genre shrugs off critical conversation and forgets the racist abuse that cops hurl at others. Perhaps, as they chase a privilege lost, cops forget who they are and fool onlookers into doing the same. Many view cop movies this way.

An analysis of *Dirty Harry* provides a case in point. Unimpressed with cop self-consciousness, Paul Smith reads the moral logic of some as liberal individualism of the most reactionary sort. He first notes that the *Dirty Harry* tradition takes a "populist line" to "underscore an ideology of individual power and rectitude and to promote a distrust of institutions."[1] He argues that such movies are "fascist" when they address the problems of a community with the "fantasized ideal of the white male father who ruthlessly ensures security and carries out the right kind of vengeance . . . on 'our' behalf." Then, because he reads the criminal class as liberal-to-left rather than a capitalist/nazi ruling class, Smith regards the genre as morally illogical. That is, the killing of dirty cops—bad white men with badges (as in *Dirty Harry's* sequel *Magnum Force*)—seems to Smith to sit "uneasily with" the cop's status as just another "individual killer white male . . . offered as our protector."[2] Thus does the genre contradict itself in Smith's view. The use of an individual white man to protect a community works against a critique of organized white male violence against that community.

Though I dislike Smith's logic, I can sympathize (see the Appendix for a fuller discussion of "contradiction" arguments). Heroes' exploits solve few problems, and as political planners they amount to little. If our judgment of them bears on the extent to which they return the costs of oppression to the privileged, then cops have an uneven record. Capitalists die, and cops suffer in their own ways, to be sure, but the machinery of domination runs on. The unreciprocated attention from sidekicks and lovers to cops certainly offends. Cops seem to think that such people have nothing to do but provide free therapy.

They blow away a fair number of owners and robber barons, but cops take little interest in the redistribution of wealth or any collective action that could press for it. Heroes usually ignore the underclass who suffer for capitalism's sins, unless there is killing to be done. Having established that they cannot rule in good faith, cops run off to pound flesh and leave the rest of the world to pick up the pieces. Heroes shrug off management while swearing loyalty to their trade and replace the order that management represents with their gut instincts that rich white men should die. This abdication of managerial responsibility may appear noble to those wishing white men to give up authority; but it also refuses to rebuild that authority in a better way. White men suck up the attention like vacuum cleaners and then take their toys to go play by themselves before they have even addressed the major problems of inequality.

I am disappointed also by the general exclusion of women as fighters from the combat. The guys include many black and Latino cops, but women need still not apply, as though cops would not know how to stand tall if women were not shorter than them on the battlefield. One wonders what cops fear that violent women would do. Would a world full of female heroes define the male criminal class more broadly than cops would like? Or would such women refuse in greater numbers to stand by male heroes as lovers, the unsung and unpaid cornerstones of nurturing families?

The point is that guys do little lasting good in this genre. Cops intend more to slaughter criminals than to torch the inequities that both cause and result from crime—those that placed straight white men on our dominant culture's center stage in the first place. They are nobody's revolutionaries. Instead, they make for figures in a fantasy of lost ground regained, sort of. By this I mean that the status of professional class men with happy homes and esteem in a community of equals is not their goal. In fact, rejection of any such egalitarian utopia remains central to the ornery, dizzy, xenophobic cop character. Cops' work yields neither personal success nor social justice for all or even most. Instead, they rehearse fantasies of heroic strain, hard times for petulant stars. Their work makes them "heroes" in the sense that people may look at them, see their guilt and the hard time they have living with the stigma, and appreciate that work. They do not find unmarked identities in any traditional sense. Cops need oppression in their world because their guilt makes them dramatically interesting and sets up the violence that they enjoy and for which they get paid.

Dramas and Dreams

To what extent do cops or those around them consider their heroism or hard times authentic as opposed to theatrical? Sometimes others mock them for their investments in popular drama. "Who are you?" taunts *Die Hard*'s German criminal. "Just another American who saw too many movies as a child? Another orphan of a bankrupt culture who think he's John Wayne, Rambo, Marshall Dillon?"

The cop John McClane responds, "I was always kind of partial to Roy Rogers, actually. I really like those sequined shirts." Heroes seem to know very well what an act theirs is. Against a classical Hollywood standard of naturalism, cop action remains self-reflexive. *Lethal Weapon*'s hero listens to a television ad for "hero" cologne in between *Three Stooges* episodes. *The Hard Way* features a pampered and childish action-movie actor who learns to be a mythical cop. *Last Action Hero* sends its hero out of his movie world to meet Arnold Schwarzenegger, the actor who plays him. (The character scorns the acquaintance: "Look, I don't really like you, all right?" he tells the privileged actor. "You've brought me nothing but pain.") The fantastic nature of this pain, the spot lit suffering from which cop action ressentiment and all of its violence flows, becomes a hero most. Heroes acknowledge the fantastic nature of their happy endings and keep on working anyway.

As always, disagreement arises. Susan Jeffords hesitates to credit cops with awareness of their fantastical nature. Of the criminal quoted above she writes:

> To Gruber's credit, he recognized what many did not, that the foundation for this resurgence of power lay in the images of a mediated past, images produced by earlier eras equally in need of heroes to rely on. Following in the footsteps of those projected heroes, Rambo, Martin Riggs, and John McClane declare themselves to be the new heroes of the Reagan era. Their greatest act of heroism, as it turns out, is in believing that not only their historic predecessors but they themselves are real.[3]

I sympathize with the skepticism but prefer to take the hero at his word. He probably just likes those sequined shirts. The deviant and phony heroism, the silly subordination of others, and the whining about his lovers and bosses liven his hard times. If he must play to a politically hip audience and own up to guilt, then he might as well have some fun.

Cops care about heroism; after all, the alternatives degrade them ("regular people suck"). Still, "real" in cop action seems to include fraudulent, performative, or self-consciously posed. They have pointedly "lost" their traditional, secure identity, if indeed they ever had it. Guys, at least these guys, often seem to keep this in the backs of their minds as they pose and wink their ways through this political theater. They care little how genuine or natural their heroism may seem. In the absence of legitimate models of unmarked white masculinity, the hard times they have acting normal or natural are the whole point. In his appreciation of *Total Recall*, Robert Miklitsch argues that "the loss of loss that suffuses the film is driven not by some 'authentic' historical desire (say, for a real 50s, whatever that might mean) but for the 50s as mediated by, precisely, the mass media."[4] Cops play as cartoon subjects of the losing ground society, their losses "losses" and their sufferings "sufferings." The self awareness of the genre knows no bounds, as cops seem to understand their ambitions as fantasies.

At the story's end, *Total Recall*'s hero stands atop a red mountain in which abused workers lie entombed, one now turned green and fertile by the force of his mighty hand. All of his dreams fulfilled, he suddenly thinks "a terrible thought," that this green world may be just a dream. He fears that he is just a character in a drama written by a frustrated, working-class, white guy whose heroics do naught but entertain a man stuck in a nowhere job with little to hope for but bland consumption and prefab daydreams on the daily train ride to work. (I refer here to Doug Quaid, the movie's unhappy, dreamy construction worker.) This may amount to the genre's final shot at its manhood: That which seems most genuinely heroic also strays far from it and leaves us instead in the cold arms of a bigoted capitalism. All of this suggests an undercurrent of sly knowingness to the moral panic over losing ground. Cops offer defensive scorn about appearing stupidly xenophobic. They do not mind copping to paranoia, arrogance, misogyny, and racism; and they can sometimes reckon the stakes of the game—the costs to others of the attention and other privileges cops enjoy.

I have not discovered some unique hard time here, so much as a sense of crisis by men, the cops, who seem to savor the drama of their collective tantrum. These self-aware "men in crisis" have lost ground and will make spectacles of themselves for their own entertainment. If the world will not accord them the authority they thought they deserved, then they can just walk away. Sure, cops care and feel pain. They demand support and suck up attention. They chafe under constraint and long to be seen as more talented than the next guy. They rage at women who love them too little and bristle at incursions into their turf. They acknowledge racist paranoia and then line up with oppressed groups whose righteousness they envy. Finally, they identify the sources of their problems and gleefully mow them down, spraying guts and blood in the process. They know they haven't the skills to rebuild their world, so they grunt and walk away from the task. They know that they have faked a crude, nasty heroism, and they do not care. We regular people, who suck, can clean up the mess.

What It All Means

This book steers clear of "why" questions for the most part, hesitating to ponder the push and pull between the United States and the cop action world. These two cultures coexist and affect each other in many ways, and scientists have not amassed the kinds of evidence we would need to suggest much about how. I conducted this research, not because it stood a chance of answering those questions, but because I grew tired of people trying to answer them without paying close attention to the movies in the first place. This sort of genre study can only provide a single, important link in the larger chain that we humanists must build to know what popular culture and real people do to each other. The complexities of those relationships puzzle us still, and though others feel free to speculate, I shall mostly leave that to them. I shall blow by the important questions of causes and effects by adding a thought about the lure of the genre's bloodshed, one that remains strong for me.

Probably any reader who lasted through this conclusion, with its comments on cop refusal to put a corrupted world back together better, figures that movies present irresponsible fantasies with visceral appeal simply because that is what people want from their entertainment—stimulating fun. At least, I would agree that is part of the story. Even if some critical mass of U.S. citizens really did want to foment revolution and design a society that did not do what the dirty cops and criminals do, they would not necessarily pay money to see movies about it. Social engineering bores most of us to tears, and even those who do not approve of screen violence experience its visceral force and have to admit that it is more stimulating than the achievement of consensus or parliamentary procedure. So, we consume a genre that stages fantasies more immediately appealing, fantasies that answer questions like "Who's to blame here?" and "What do they deserve?" with the moral force of public violence. Cop action focuses rage with its firepower, gives satisfaction in both the punishment of evil and the occasional rewards given virtue. I like these movies because the best of them provide some of the most complex and satisfying bits of moral instruction available in our popular culture. I do not agree with all of their lessons, to be sure, but I never tire of the fun-house mirror that cop action holds up to a collective moralism. The bloodshed tells us why so many of us work bad jobs, why our families grow estranged, innocents die, and money disappears into corporate black holes. The carnage tells us who really sucks and who has earned the right to take it in the ass.

Along those lines, I have been thinking about a bloody cop movie that I would like to see. In my own movie, a college-student right-wing group drifts from Republican partying to bombing abortion clinics and deprogramming queer students by any means necessary. Related murders at campuses around the country catch the attention of the FBI, which dispatches as a "student" a young woman reminiscent of the hero of *Betrayed*. Cops happily dig up organized dirt behind bizarre murders; and our undercover hero investigates Republican funding channels to expose the interrelations of conservative Christian, pro-capitalist, white-supremacist, and anti-homosexual organizing nationwide. She finds, with the help of a disaffected college Republican who turns sidekick, links between grass-roots organizing across the country, top-down funding from national groups and their corporate sponsors, protection from rightists in the state, and rampaging by the most deranged. Conspiracy theories form the bread and butter of cop action, and our hero figures out who's screwed the world around her by linking lost ground to corruption at the top. In a related subplot, two groups of queer bashers, one from the right-wing college group and one from the local community, operate independently. Charismatic young men lead each one, working as bait to draw marks to their doom, their violence an unintended consequence of the shrill homophobic preaching in the community.

Eventually stakes increase as both the FBI and right wingers decide that the battles on campus symbolize their respective potencies. The body count rises; the hero speaks on morality between fire fights; someone slaughters the sociology department. Ultimately, students choose sides en masse and pickets turn to riots. The twin gangs of queer bashers inadvertently bait each other, and the two hot young homophobes slice each other to ribbons in an ecstasy of self-abuse. The hero destroys most of the campus in order to save it and then turns on the community pillars who back the right-wing activism. Wealthy homes shatter as entrepreneurs die, mountains of profits doing them no good. The administration building goes out in its own high style, a fireball spreading body parts over the lawn. Someone breaches the animal-testing labs and violates the experimenters in unspeakable ways. Cop action dearly loves its vengeance.

The hero finds a place among those she defends for a while. She moves on to other assignments, though, until one day a boss orders her to put down an insurrection among working people with whom she can sympathize. She turns on the FBI, defends the community against it, murders her bosses, and quits in disgust. She surveys the dozens of deadend job opportunities before her and goes to work for a nonprofit lefty foundation or something else low paying but satisfying. One day she meets a hard man and gives him enough attention to explain that there's more to politics than mass murder, even if bad people, the rich white men of our world, bear its brunt. Her own hard time, and maybe his after he's thought about it, involves harder work. They'll have to better the lives blighted by corrupting greed and not just suck up attention as they savage their demons.

Appendix: Using Movies

Genre

The hero of *Dirty Harry* sizes up his new sidekick: "Just what I need, a college boy. Get your degree?"

"Sociology."

"Sociology! Well you'll go far—that's if you live. Just don't let your degree get you killed."

The stakes are never small in cop action movies. "This ain't no game, 'Flash'—real guns, real bullets. It's dangerous," says "the last Boy Scout." I suppose then that I should be careful what I say about the cop action world. I treat the genre as a culture that can make as much sense as any other if we look at it closely, one with characters who share a moral logic that tells them right from wrong. In a world in which people blame others for most of their troubles, we should understand this. I look not to the conditions of the genre's Hollywood production for meaning but to the events within the genre itself and try to understand the rules and ideals that cops share. Before I get too far into the details of interpretation, however, I should explain what I mean by "cop action."

I collect movies by viewing any that center on cops and feature serious violence. References come from the literature on the genre, recommendations of colleagues, and the video store shelves that I browse. Because I have had no difficulty following such references, I believe that I have at my disposal close to the whole of the genre, taking into account the blurred nature of its boundaries. For the sake of limiting this study's scope, however, I exclude "direct-to-video" movies and include as data only the 193 films made by U.S.-based producers and

213

given international theatrical release between 1980 and 1997 as noted in the British journals *Monthly Film Bulletin* and *Sight and Sound*.[1]

I limit the study to movies given international release for three reasons. First, the direct-to-video market contains hundreds of movies available only in larger video stores. These movies are more difficult to obtain, and inclusion of them would have inflated the scale of this project even further beyond reason. Second, because these videos are marketed selectively, they are not as widely seen. Certainly they do not reach the large and diverse cinema audiences. Third, in narrative terms these movies are often considered a genre unto themselves. Perhaps their inclusion would alter my analysis. I find direct-to-video cop action slower and less violent than their cinematic cousins and thus less fun to watch.

Hollywood movies about the business of policing date to the Keystone Cops and gangster movies; but films marked by a coherent set of cop action themes first appeared in the late 1960s.[2] As Robert Reiner describes the early crop, "in almost all the cop movies of the 1960s and 1970s the hero is a lone-wolf, lower rank policeman (occasionally with one partner) working *against* the organisational hierarchy."[3] In those movies, most of these cops could be considered "liberals" fighting for civil rights against a bigoted police establishment. Then, the Nixon years saw these lone wolves assume a more ambivalent stance on punks and scum. *Bullitt* (1968) marks the transition as well as any. A white male homicide detective searches for a murderous mobster. In a precursor to the buddy relations for which cop action became famous, Detective Bullitt and a black surgeon tending his wounds silently acknowledge the shared harassment by managers. Later, Bullitt's girlfriend complains that his life is too "dirty." As the cop action genre bloomed in the 1980s, these supportive-sidekick and disapproving-girlfriend characters became commonplace.

Movies such as *The Chase* (1966), *In the Heat of the Night*

(1967), *Coogan's Bluff* (1968) and *Madigan* (1968) featured cops who fought against racial, sexual, and economic corruption. Most broke laws to get their jobs done,[4] and *Coogan's Bluff* pointed toward the pared-down hero-versus-criminal storyline of *Dirty Harry* (the same actor/director team made both). *Dirty Harry* (1971) most famously grounds the genre we know today. The sullen hero shoots criminals and seems to live for little else. The famous scene in which he taunts a black man has shot with a Russian roulette dare ("You got to ask yourself one question: 'Do I feel lucky?' Well do ya, punk?") became a tough cop cliché. Inspector Harry Callahan is a big city homicide cop, a widower who has lost interest in family contact, and a moralist who just wants to put the bad guys away. He argues with his superiors over proper procedure and survives his partners as they fall in the line of duty. A serial-killing sniper is loose and Harry must defy his conciliatory bosses to catch and kill him. Harry spends most of his time, assisted by a fearful Latino cop, stalking the criminal. The sequels—*Magnum Force* (1973), *The Enforcer* (1976), *Sudden Impact* (1983), and *The Dead Pool* (1988)—stick to the plot and feature Harry tracking serial killers, teamed with partners either nonwhite or female, enjoying brief sexual liaisons with women, and having a hard time with his bosses. In these ways, Harry set parameters for heroes to come.

In the throes of economic crisis but buoyed by the success of the late 1960s movies mentioned above, U.S. filmmakers produced and released a small crop of cop thrillers in 1971 along with *Dirty Harry*. That year saw the release of *Klute* (another harbinger of the serial killer subgenre to blossom in the 1980s), the famous blaxploitation movie *Shaft,* and *The French Connection*. The unprecedented success of these movies (including major awards for *The French Connection* and *Klute*) resulted in the production and release of a dozen more in 1973, including the first of the *Dirty Harry* sequels, *Magnum Force;* the first paranoid-detective-in-a-dirty-department movie,

Serpico; and the beginning of another cop action franchise, *Walking Tall.* But, as brightly as the genre burned in these early years, cop action could not draw enough attention to survive and soon went the way of its blaxploitation cousin. By 1976, only three cop movies saw release in any given year, and by 1979 all was quiet.

The gunplay resumed in 1980 with the most hated cop movie ever. Its double entendre title suggested that *Cruising* would explore the link between law enforcement and erotic male bonding; and the genre has done just that for the past eighteen years, amounting to a vast and popular meditation on the problems of whiteness, masculinity, class privilege, and male sexual exchange run amok. I study the 193 movies of the period 1980–1997, the second wave of cop action. They include, among others, the last two "dirty" Harry movies, a sizeable serial killer subgenre, and countless paranoid detectives working in corrupt departments. The resurgent genre started the 1980s slowly, with an average of four movies each year. By 1988, though, the average had risen to fourteen. And by the end of 1998, this popular genre showed little sign of flagging.

I study a genre because the meaning of any single case lies in the context of a larger group. Though cop-centered violence informs these movies, the genre mixes and matches its plots. A run-of-the-mill cop action movie includes elements of martial arts (reluctant but awesomely skilled hero fights criminals to defend or avenge loved ones), western (skilled hero defends a community in which he has no comfortable place), traditional detective (investigator discovers "whodunit" and brings guilty party to justice), neo-noir (lowlife man confronts attractive embodiments of his paranoid fantasies who then corrupt him) prison (innocent person abused until release or escape), horror (scenes of suspense lead to grisly death), war rescue (hero saves hostages from an enemy nation), blaxploitation (black hero kills crackers and other enemies with style), and disaster (hero saves people from freak accidents amid the destruction of property).[5] (See the list of movies on pages 235–47.)

Because the plot structure fits some of these movies better than others, a list was difficult to compile. How do we know a real cop action movie from one with just a few cop action themes driving it? What sort of generic hybrids count? This variation and the difficulty of drawing lines indicates the unstable nature of genre. For my purposes, however, anything recognizable as a set of repeated images or narratives counts. Fredric Jameson argues that genre includes no "original" to study, but only the fact of repetition.[6] Carol Clover also defines genre in terms of

> the free exchange of themes and motifs, the archetypal characters and situations, the accumulation of sequels, remakes, imitations. This is a field in which there is in some sense no original, no real or right text, but only variants; a world in which, therefore, the meaning of the individual example lies outside itself.[7]

Meaning lies in the cultural context in which actions repeat over and over again in different situations. Repeated themes, images, and character types constitute the genre and include such themes as the fractured home life, disrespectful bosses, and cross-race/gender/class pairings of law enforcement personnel; such character traits as the emotionally scarred, wise-cracking hero and the suave, remorseless criminal; such images as the orange fireballs set against blue-gray urban steel, or the shattering windows and flying bodies; and such aural devices as female screams, thudding fists, sodomite profanity, and rattling gunfire.

Cop action elements wander into movies commonly classified into other genres. For instance, *Basic Instinct* is cop noir. Its hero belongs to cop action, quick with the trigger and wisecrack, hassled by his boss, and in conflict with his loving sidekick; but he stumbles through a film noir universe and obsesses over a femme fatale. Critics and video store operators often consider *Basic Instinct* an "erotic thriller." It looks like a remake, with a different ending, of *Sea of Love,* which itself looks like a heterosexual remake of *Cruising.* These movies feature police officers drawn into whirlpools of paranoid violence by figures of deviant sexuality.

   Blade Runner and *Total Recall* began as science fiction stories rewritten (from Phillip K. Dick stories) as cop action plots. *Judge Dredd* loosely remakes the former. *Runaway,* the *Robocop* movies, and *Univeral Soldier* also involve science fiction, mostly in the construction of high-tech cops. "Rape revenge" themes characterize *Cop, Copycat,* and *Sudden Impact.* Good-but-paranoid-cop-against-the-system plots, descended from *Serpico,* characterize *Code of Silence, Fort Apache: The Bronx, Internal Affairs, Q & A, The Untouchables,* and *Year of the Dragon. Action Jackson, Low Down Dirty Shame, New Jack City,* and *Vampire in Brooklyn* revive blaxploitation, hearkening back to the musical interludes, comic walk-ons and bravura, as well as the cautionary antidrug preaching, of that short-lived genre. *Death Warrant* and *Tango and Cash* edge into prison-movie territory (though not the women-in-chains genre). Their cop heroes do hard time and trade sodomite threats with lusty criminals. Finally, comedies such as *Dead Heat,* the *Ghostbuster* movies, *The Hard Way,* and *Last Action Hero* parody cop action but form less a genre unto themselves than extreme examples of a self-reflexive bent.

   While I trace the outlines of the genre, I should distinguish cop action from close relatives: First, male "buddy" movies do not all qualify. For instance, the buddy movies of the 1960s and 1970s concerned lawless men. These include *Butch Cassidy and the Sundance Kid* (1969), *Easy Rider* (1969), *Midnight Cowboy* (1969), *Mean Streets* (1973), *Thunderbolt and Lightfoot* (1974), and the recent entry *Harley Davidson and the Marlboro Man* (1991).[8] They also feature juicy male bonding and plenty of violence but do not necessarily offer the same ways to negotiate lost ground. I restrict my analysis to those films whose heroes do law enforcement and safety work.

Furthermore, not all cop movies suffice. Though their interest in sexuality and class link them to the genre, movies such as *Partners* (1982) and *Someone to Watch Over Me* (1987) lack the stimulating violence, with nary an explosion to liven their scenes. Many contemporary comedies and dramas feature cops. I restrict this study to those that stage the loud and gruesome physical battles for which people remember such fare as *Lethal Weapon* and *Die Hard*.

Military adventure movies such as *Rambo: First Blood Part II* (1985) and *Rambo III* (1988) spill much blood and incorporate many cop action elements (awesomely skilled but reluctant hero saves hostages from militaristic bad guys and blows them all away). Spy movies such as *True Lies* (1994) and *Mission Impossible* (1996) feature agents of enforcement but take a more worldly, Bond-like approach. Both of these genres distinguish themselves with their more historical and international concerns. Though the cop action movies *Off Limits, Outbreak,* and the *Under Siege* series feature military officers, I avoid the saving-hostages-from-foreign-countries genre here. *Uncommon Valor* and *Missing in Action* are typical.

Finally, "sensitive men" movies also relate, featuring as they do the redemption of white men through intimate contact with nonwhite men. Like their cop action brethren, sensitive men suffer for their crimes and deride the white patriarchs around them. Unlike cops, however, sensitive men hail from the upper class, may enjoy familial warmth, and abjure the violence on which cops thrive (though *Hook* [1991] provides a cartoonish exception to that last rule). *The Doctor* (1991), *Jerry Maguire* (1996), and *Regarding Henry* (1991) provide examples.

The cop action genre takes shape amid thousands of movies that bear subsets of relevant themes. I base this study on those movies that feature the plot structure outlined above and the shocking violence. Movies such as *Cobra* and *Die Hard* exemplify the genre, and many others cleave closely to their structure. In a genre study, movies find meaning within the larger pool.

Interpretation

If movies are going to provide evidence for an argument, then we will have to make them talk, and researchers have made progress interrogating genres. Stanford Lyman reads movies as a contemporary dialogue with classic myth—one that registers the demoralizing effect of World War II on heterosexual relations.[9] In a similar vein, John Cawelti and Will Wright discern the relation between generic narratives and economic change.[10] Wright finds in westerns evidence of a shift from individualist heroics to more corporate organization of action. Theorists of fantasy argue that stories draw engaged response when they appeal to questions posed and conflicts felt by their audience.[11] When impossible questions need asking, people tell stories. Elizabeth Cowie, in her summary of this fantasy theory, quotes Roland Barthes: "Isn't storytelling always a way of searching for one's origins, speaking one's conflicts with the law, entering into a dialectic of tenderness and hatred?"[12]

Gina Marchetti suggests that "particular genres tend to be popular at certain points in time because they somehow embody and work through those social contradictions the culture needs to come to grips with and may not be able to deal with except in the realm of fantasy."[13] This train of argument fits an extensive literature on movies in which theorists suppose that social conflict drives movie storytelling. Cinema fantasies can take shapes that may never arise in conversation or even in conscious thought. Movies can articulate the hopes and anger we share. This utopian bid allows analysts to read in them parts of a political culture. The desires that movies address may differ from those than find expression in plainer language; perhaps we could find whole realms of fantasy circulating through popular movies because they can run these particular courses nowhere else. Presumably the development of film study from audience research outward to industry and then to narrative study has created theoretical room to use a genre as data. All we need, then, is a way to interpret.

To put it in the abstract for a moment: I judge the worth of interpretations by whether they make the character's behaviors comprehensible, in terms of contemporary social problems as I have interpreted those. I approach with a concern for lost ground and contested privilege, and so the genre looks the way it does to me. Take, for example, the scene from *The Last Boy Scout* with which I open chapter 1, the encounter between Joe and the lighter-wielding thug. Why would Joe submit himself to the abuse? He threatens those who mete it out with death; why does he ask for more? I must find a logical framework, one related to contested privileges, in which this makes sense (a sense that might differ from one offered by a producer or fan unconcerned with such issues, but one that illuminates the way in which generic patterns seem "right" to so many people).

So, I impose on what I watch a frame of narrative logic, to which I compare the movies' events. Any time something happens that does not make sense, I try a new frame, thus basing my own interpretation on my own choice of frames. This tautology, in which I guide my own experience of a movie, lies at the heart of all interpretation, as the meaning of an object arises only in the relationship between it and a logical frame that a viewer imposes. Switching frames allows me to view Joe's behavior with the thugs in different ways until it makes significant sense. In relation to a logical frame that equates heroism with invincibility and avoidance of injury, Joe's behavior seems silly. In relation to a frame that equates brutal crime with straight masculinity, neither do the tinkling of the piano and the whispery purring of the thugs fit very well. Within a moral logic that equates heroism with a desire to endure pain, and criminality with sexual deviance, however, the movie seems to follow a logic and thus belong to a culture worth exploring. (I discuss such scenes and their import more fully in Chapter 7.)

The remainder of this Appendix presents the details of my interpretive process and the contingent nature of the "sense" that data make to researchers thinking in terms drawn from the very culture that they analyze. As I note in Chapter 1, I prefer to treat cop action as a subculture that makes sense if you let it. Certainly there is more than one way to look at it right, but there are also many ways to look at it wrong. If we are going to learn anything from cops, about their troubles or about ours, then we should take them seriously when they talk about themselves and NOT assume that they are always deceitful or stupid. Let's look at a couple of ways in which analysts tend to look at these movies wrongly, why they do it, and why they should not.

First Temptation: To Find Them Simple and Evil

Though we can draw simple conclusions about what movies mean, claims for their transparency and ideological closure ring false. Wright's axiom, for instance: "In life meaning is problematic, in narrative it is not" does little justice to the difficulties of the task at hand.[14] It pays little attention to the tautological nature of interpretation (its origin in the relationship between an object of study and the frame imposed by an interpreter) or the open nature of meaning (the possibility of imposing an infinite number of frames). For instance, Michael Ryan and Douglas Kellner impute simplicity to *Death Wish* (1974), a cousin of cop action in which a man slaughters criminals after some attack his wife and daughter. "The narrative is fairly univocal," they write, "the cinematography is unsullied. The decisiveness of the isolated subject's will, the purity of his motives, is thus reinforced."[15] One might respond that if

Death Wish seems to offer a reactionary assurance of one right way of viewing anything, then it does so only because the analysts construct this tunnel vision and then impute it to the film as its meaning.

I sense here a wish that meaning can be simple; for instance, aspects of political evil line up in single file behind various movies or characters and thus achieve a moral simplicity. A character who seems to be pro-male, then, should also be white-supremacist, U.S.-supremacist, homophobic, pro-capitalist, and so on. For instance, Susan Jeffords finds pro-Reagan political messages throughout the cop action movies she studies. No matter whom cops fight, those heroes stand in for Reagan.[16] No matter how much like the white-collar robber barons of the S&L scandal criminals appear to be, Jeffords finds that criminals always stand in for the outgroups whom Reagan stigmatized: blacks, women, queers, the poor. She theorizes other tendencies as misdirections or trivia (to the extent that Jeffords imputes deceit, she employs the second tempting strategy, which I review below).

One solution to the problem of imputed closure raises yet another version of this temptation to find movies evil. That is, analysts can portray movies as evil in order to present themselves as relatively innocent. This works by way of a Marxist cultural theory that proposes that alongside a cultural object's "dominant" and "preferred" (guilty) interpretations we find opportunities for "oppositional" or "resistant" (innocent) readings, opportunities in which specific audiences may find revolutionary models.[17] For instance, after supposing that a "dominant" (read: white) audience takes *Beverly Hills Cop* to depict a color-blind world in which a black cop bears no racial stigma (allowing them to ignore and perpetuate racism), we could further suppose that the movie offers a different, "resistant" reading to its black audiences, in which racism seems more evident and more wrong (see Chapter 4 on this example). Or, one could suppose that the "dominant" reading of cop action male-buddy-relationships sees straight men bonding in sexless camaraderie and then further suppose that a "resistant" reading of this same bonding defines it as queer (see Chapter 7). Both of these analyses suppose dominant audiences affirming the common sense of dominant groups (e.g., white entitlement, heterosexuality), and alongside them resistant readings which counter the former in the interests of disenfranchised and rebellious groups (e.g., antiracism, queer visibility).

The theory supposes "dominant" or "preferred" readings to work within the "codes" (the common sense, including the moral logic) of the producers, such that they reaffirm political interests of, say, a capitalist class by their consumption. Though resistant readings abound among all groups, dominant readings circulate with more authority, in part because they are legitimate ("explicit" as opposed to "implicit," or, more important, "really there" as opposed to having been "read into it") within the dominant common sense, which this theory supposes roughly to match the common sense of the producers. This match and the practices that maintain it amount to what they call "hegemony." Oppositional readings, in contrast, violate the rules of this common sense and work "against the grain" by rearranging plot structures, elevating minor characters to heroic status, ignoring the endings of movies, and so on.[18] This is resistance.

One could recommend this theory for the manner in which it ties meaning to competition among groups for authority. Meaning is neither simple nor closed but instead changes with the social locations and purposes of the viewers. Some interpretations may circulate with more authority than others, at least in particular contexts.[19] Whatever "dominance" might mean, however, both the meanings and their authority too often congeal into qualities inhering in objects rather than in analysts' interpretations of them. This reification marks analyses unsupported by data on audiences and their activities, the authors of which must thus base attributions of "dominance" and "resistance" on other criteria. As Janet Staiger and Stuart Hall have complained, no one has advanced useful standards for applying these terms (even for those armed with audience-data), and Hall's advice that we abjure reception study and "read as much as [we] can, as neutrally as [we] can get," doesn't help.[20] So, what criteria do analysts use?

It strikes me as more than coincidental that Marxist analysts nearly always attribute racism, homophobia, colonialism, and misogyny to the "dominant" or "preferred" meanings of the objects they study. In the light of this, I can only speculate that such analysts yield to a temptation to turn their politically engaged research into an elaborate identification with the innocence of the oppressed. (See Chapter 5 for the cop action version of this, in which heroes align with the oppressed not for the moral purity but for the license to kill. My theoretical objections aside, perhaps academics should stick to the former.) That is, analysts may be ranking their own interpretive responses in terms of their distance from the authority of privileged groups. Apparently, when an analyst working within this framework responds to a movie in a way that would seem to celebrate the interests of a putative dominant group (generally racist, sexist, homophobic, bourgeois, nationalist, etc.), they simply code this response as "dominant" or "preferred." Analysts may then regard any contrary responses, which might undermine the authority of a dominant group, as "resistant" or "oppositional." Analysts seem to assume with little basis that the interpretive codes of the producers and their mass audiences are always racist, misogynist, and so on. Thus "dominant" may simply reduce to a label for responses that do not confirm the analysts' desired sense of working outside these ruling-class codes. This would allow analysts to criticize movies as hegemonic and view themselves in sympathetic solidarity with political underdogs.

I can relate to the sympathy, but such a stance comes at some cost to our analyses. Regarding the posturings of researchers, Tania Modleski counsels attention to what researchers might share with the societies in which our interpretive habits form rather than ways in which we differ. She argues that we should "acknowledge how much we ourselves are implicated within those very structures we set out to analyze."[21] Why should movies be objects of academic abuse? I prefer that we regard these movies as our own, in some ways at least, treating them as ideas to be considered for what they reveal about us, rather than as alien (dominant) objects of derision and foils for our hyper-moral (resistant) standing. The circular path of interpretation runs along the relationships between analysts and masses and producers with no clear lines drawn between them and us. Appreciating this, one can perhaps become less concerned with treating research as an opportunity to contrast one's political consciousness to those of one's neighbors and the popular culture all share.

We can see such moral posing outside of pop-cultural analysis. In an interesting corollary, Charles Kurzman found that ethnographic interpreters imputed powerful "social determination" (distinguished from "resistant agency") to the behavior of their subjects when they disapproved of them.[22] Researchers were more willing to impute agency when they approved of and wished to affiliate with their subjects' behavior, especially when they regarded the behavior as "progressive" in some respect. Kurzman argues that the analyst's wish to identify with a political subculture drives the assignment of labels analogous to "dominant" and "resistant."

If this is true in cultural studies, then the use of this dominant/resistant theory arranges data and interpretation in ways that manage the analyst's political identity. Interpretations and identities line up the following way:

Implicit	Explicit
Resistant	Dominant
Oppositional	Preferred

Emergent	Hegemonic
Reactions of which analysts feel proud	Reactions of which analysts feel embarassed
Analysts and marginal groups with whom they identify	Producers and masses

This represents a very interesting combination of activism and research, one directed toward invidious distinctions between the habits of the masses and ruling class on one hand and the interpretive practices of the resistant researcher and oppressed groups on the other.[23]

Response: Shaking Things Up a Bit

Movies are complicated, often more so than criticism of them. The best analyses will avoid simplicity and refuse to present movies as objects mastered and exhausted of their import. Humility, or at least respect, before the complexity of even those movies that enrage us seems called for if we want also to learn from our data and not simply elaborate our initial assumptions no matter what movies actually do. We should allow data to teach us about ourselves rather than use them as objects of politicized scorn. (Clearly, I assume a different stance toward the analytic work of others than to objects of research.)

Imputations of simplicity seem to slide too easily into (and perhaps root in) accusations of evil. I am bothered less by the coherent picture of their data that such analyses present, than I am by the way in which analysts seem to assume that the various demons of the progressive ideals that we share (the political right, racism, sexism, etc.) line up neatly at all times no matter what. The genre seems to do a great deal of work making the political landscape more messy; and it seems a shame to see such work ignored in the drive to read monolithic oppression into it.

My desire to be accountable for, as well as respectful in, my interpretive choices leads me to make political aspirations and implications plain in a different way, without configuring my methodology and arranging my data on behalf of the accomplishment of an underdog persona. Hostile imputations of hegemonic force and intended racism, and so on, to complex interactions do not seem to add much to our understandings. Certainly this wrangling over dominance and resistance in the study of the macho, low-brow action genre provides more scorn than help.

What I like about action movies—for instance, the contempt and destruction aimed at the white, male, bearers of wealth—I like, not because it amounts to some effective "resistance" distinguishable from "conformity," but because it makes it fun for me to think about privilege and a world in contest over it. I sometimes cheer heroes to their victories, find comfort in their heterosexual unions, and enjoy the destruction of sexually sadistic criminals. But I need hardly call these responses products of hegemonic forces held over me by heterosexual/white-supremacist movies. Nor need my responses to the contrary seem uniquely and always resistant (queer, profeminist, anti-racist). Imputations of dominance and resistance are red herrings in the search for moral logic; and labels such as left versus right wing, patriarchal versus feminist, homophobic versus queer, or white supremacist versus antiracist could never fit. Certainly, it would not do to use the dominant versus oppositional logic of cultural studies to make them fit, as with the recalcitrant puzzle piece and the convenient hammer. Such labels make better moral pokers than analytic lenses. The genre earns all of them in ways that break down the distinctions upon which they rest.

This said, let me note that efforts to police interpretation will quickly run aground. Though I might hold analysts responsible for their impositions of logical frames, I do not intend that meaning lies only within this or that individual interpreter, or that analysts should follow therapeutic fashion and write in "I" statements. Such arguments would also require the separation of object, interpreter, and context. I suggest instead that we understand that these always come together. As Barthes writes, "I am not hidden within the text, I am simply irrecoverable from it."[24] This insight implies the effect that interpretation can have on the meaning of the interpreter as well as the object of it. We can do better than claim our own innocence by projecting guilt onto our culture.

Second Temptation: To Find Them Senseless and Deceitful

Unfortunately, avoiding the temptation to impute monolithic evil can lead to another temptation, one that also makes use of the dominant/resistant dualism. Claiming that slips and contradictions can subvert a movie's own narrative logic, researchers impute "dominant" meanings (such as the triumph of white power) and then regard countervailing action (such as its ridicule) as either obfuscating "recuperation" to penetrate or resistant "excess" to champion.[25] Either way, this anlaysis takes any lack of correspondence to the analyst's choice of logical frame to indicate tension inhering in the cultural object rather than in the analyst's choices.

For instance, as I describe in Chapter 7, Christine Holmlund argues that in *Tango and Cash* a "homosexuality lurks beside heterosexuality" in the scenes among men. The movie both "displace[s] the anxiety" raised by peeks at male flesh through cutaways to chase scenes and firefights, and "contain[s] the homoeroticism" by "positioning [the male cops] as 'family' " rather than as lovers.[26] This logic first supposes, after those enticing shower scenes that lead many of us to choose a homoerotic logical frame, that the characters might have some gay potential but then finds them looking pretty straight after all and so accuses the movie of backing away from its subversive promise.

This seems fair enough. The guys flirt but never come out as gay. However, only by first positing conflict among sexualities within a movie can one then accuse it of narrative "homophobia"[27] when it fails to resemble the gay cinema to which one might have hoped its male bonding would lead. But thus do analysts accuse cop action of narrative contradiction, cowardly or deceitful, whenever it does not blossom into either the dominant or the oppositional cinema it might have first seemed to be.

Though Clifford Geertz rightly urges that we not make a fetish of abstract order, I assume that any widely shared culture makes a rough sense to those willing to make sense of it.[28] While its members might define a subculture as "ironic," "paradoxical," or "internally conflicted"; apart from such imputations from within, a culture will contradict itself only to an interpreter looking for contradiction from without (the position of a researcher, in this case). I view such a search as hostile because, if I may speculate, analysts often seem to hurl imputations of contradiction across ideological lines. Especially when researchers do not defend their choice of the logical frames in which "contradictions" arise, these arguments seem to have as their first function selling analysts as more ideologically consistent than the ostensibly confused objects of their research. Where the first tempting misuse of movies helps us look more innocent, this one helps us look smarter. Political distaste precedes accusation of senselessness, such that one first finds a movie noxious and then puts it down by finding it contradictory. We are more likely to find sense in our own ideologies and senselessness in the enemy's.

Let me back up and note that I would not dismiss the concept of contradiction out of hand. For well-defined purposes one might want to see what a movie looks like held against a standard different from the ones that guide its production by artists, its reception by fans, or its rendering as a sensible culture by analysts. The analyses mentioned above can certainly give a sense of the moral difficulties and the hard time that cops have making sense to anyone. My objection to this sort of analysis now is that it mostly just measures the difference between analysts' logical frames and the movies they view, too often to judge the movies lacking in ideological honesty and value. Slogans could read: Analyst smart, movie dumb; derision fun, understanding not. Dismissal of the data and the cultural formations they represent seems to be both motive for and outcome of such research.

Analysts have found other ways to find movies senseless. Some accuse movies not of saying too much but of saying nothing at all. An interesting cultural analysis looks for "explicit" depictions of political struggle and then argues that movies that lack them "erase" important social forces or "forget" history. Thus such movies constrain interpretation by foreclosing the possibility of historical or political thought among their audiences. Michael Paul Rogin has developed Roland Barthes' theory of the historically forgetful effect of myth into an analysis of "political amnesia" in film. In this argument, ahistorical entertainment "permits repetition of pleasures that, if consciously sustained in memory over time, would have to be called into question."[29] Rogin cites Guy Debord's argument that the "society of spectacle" provides illusory entertainment by "distracting attention from producers and from classes in conflict."[30] Protected by this burial from a history that might rebuke them, viewers can enjoy their guilty pleasures (homophobic, misogynist, or white supremacist ones, for instance, in the analyses cited above) with none of the guilt. This is a corollary of the popcritic's assertion that a movie has "no plot," that it's "all style and no substance" and thus morally bankrupt.

As false consciousness arguments go, I can certainly sympathize with "amnesia" theory. No one wants to see the history of inequality buried by forgetful films. But I am struck by the irony that the histories supposed to be missing or erased must have arisen in some way during the films and their interpretation in order for researchers even to think to look for "explicit" depictions or neglect of them. We might ask, then: What is it that inspires analysts watching movies to think about racism or any other historical practice—the supposedly forgetful films or the omnipotent analysts? Either these movies do refer to the histories they are accused of forgetting and thus stimulate analysts to think of them (who then accuse the movies of forgetting them), or the analysts wish primarily to distance themselves from the movies and the more forgetful or easily fooled masses. In any case, analysts (who perhaps disagree with me about the tautological nature of interpretation) condemn movies as "ideological" or "ahistorical." In my view, imputations of closure misdirect responsibility for responses away from the analytic scene and toward the movie or its producers, a redirection that presumes the separation of analysts from their observations.[31]

Response: Fandom

My own method finds coherence by selecting frameworks for narrative logic against which the movies appear to make sense (in terms of the social problems that I study) rather than assume the genre's duplicity when it fails to confirm my initial expectations. I approach movies in the same way that I would approach human communities or interview subjects—as objects that make sense within some discoverable set of terms, terms that I am obliged to learn. Referring to members of a culture under study by an outsider to it, Geertz defined the data for which we provide "thick description" as "our own constructions of other people's constructions of what they and their compatriots are up to."[32] The rendering of such constructions will certainly benefit from the assumption that we can find coherent accounts, even if in actual practice life grows messy and complicated. I must find a moral logic (which will not be the only one, and which may have little to do with the intent of any movie's producer or the conversations among its fans) that bears on contested privilege and within which this genre roughly coheres, rather than trumpet my own greater consistency or perceptiveness by imputing contradiction or deceit. We should avoid, as Geertz charges we do, the "construction of impeccable depictions of formal order,"[33] but we should not see lies and confusion behind every action that does not flatter our initial assumptions or political sympathies.

I believe that my fandom gives me an edge in the rendering of valid and useful analyses. I learned as a fan to devour with pleasure the little moments that can make movies significant. My appetite makes it all the more easy to pore over them as a researcher should.[34] Still, one might ask here, if interpretation remains unstable and tautological, of what use are mine to others, however scrupulously framed they might be? As "dirty" Harry angrily warns, "Opinions are like assholes; everybody's got one." Whatever the depth of my investment in this genre, I do not mean my fandom to stand in for the responses of others. My readings might strike many as perverse. Instead, I note the significance to my work that I share some mundane, "whoa, good crash!" responses with other fans and lean on those. My research moves under the steam of that which I try to illuminate—not some generic fan-response but instead the unstated assumptions, informed by negotiation over privilege, that make sense of cop action. As a member of this torn society and a lover of violent movies I become part of what I study. I take generic heroes seriously.

Generic Heroes

I have objected to trends in cultural studies toward contempt for popular genres and what they might teach us. Sociologists have always sought to view particulars in the light of the groups in which they take shape, and I hope that this research shows the effects that situating individual cops and their stories in the context of the larger group can have. Analysis of cultural forms can offer more than a forum for analytic disdain steeped in ignorance of a cultural logic. Awful as they are, cops make attractive targets for derision; but one would think that their status as data in scholarly work would shield them from the operational assumption of their political stupidity. Cops say much about the construction of their world and their role in it. A decent genre study takes note. We need not like what cops have to say in order to admit that they speak.

Perhaps this genre's political complexity makes it seem incoherent to many. Racism does not always line up in formation with the other evils of the world as judged from the political left in which so many of us busy ourselves. Capitalism, colonialism, sexism, homophobia, anti-Semitism do not always accompany each other as reliably as so many pop cultural analyses seem to expect. When white guys join antiracist causes and line up against misognyist serial killers, they may confuse our simplest notions of good and evil. The dominance/resistance framework has forced many of us into this corner where one believes that a person does one or the other and that one must figure out which and when. Cops would force us from that corner at gunpoint. They claim not so much righteousness or omnipotence as guilt, pain, and infantile self-regard.

The political axes that analysts grind do not ruin their arguments. I grind the same ones. This study differs from others mostly in its scope and its commitment to the fictional moral community with much to teach its neighbors. By taking cop action as a large society of characters worthy of the respect that I would grant to any set of interview subjects, for instance, I allow these crowds to shout down my misconceptions, gang up on me, and force their moral logic into view. A genre of 193 movies can cow one who thinks he already understands it before he wades in. In this way, a genre that seemed fairly simple after I had savored those initial viewings of *Die Hard* and appreciated Fred Pfeil's analysis grew before my eyes into a complex culture, filled with exceptions to every rule, subpopulations not accounted for in the most popular movies, a scattering of greedy heroes, and a moral logic more fine-grained than I had anticipated. None of this discounts the importance of summary and generalization; but it does demand that we tune those sweeping statements to the sounds of all of these characters rather than a haphazardly chosen few.

Genre study offers just this apprehension of a massive culture. Its long-established tradition and debates could swallow this study whole; yet one rarely comes across ethnographies of fictional cultures. Many of us have celebrated Carol Clover's work with horror genres for its sensitivity to the patterns that emerge when one looks at masses of data.[35] Surely, this approach to cultural analysis has more rewarding surprises in store. Analysts need only drop their professional class scorn for their data, roll up their sleeves, and wade in. The best work keeps pressure on the popular culture that entertains us. Whether my account of this genre proves the most sensitive is hardly the point. Others could improve upon it in short order, I am sure. Instead, I would like us to value the work and avoid the dismissiveness that I find in the cultural studies literature. To read everything around us as senseless domination and everything within us as omniscient resistance seems silly. Queer theory made such a big splash in part, I think, because it suggested that popular culture has more to offer than endless portraiture of Big Brother's iron cage. I wish for a cultural studies as complex as the cultures it studies, and I believe that a painstaking appreciation of generic contexts holds a key.

The Movies

Cop Action, 1980–1997

Above the Law. Written by Steve Pressfield, Ronald Shusset, and Andrew Davis. Directed by Andrew Davis. Produced by Steven Seagal and Andrew Davis. Warner Bros., 1988.

Action Jackson. Written by Robert Reneau. Directed by Craig R. Baxley. Produced by Joel Silver. 20th Century Fox/Lorimar: 1988.

Alien Nation. Written by Rockne S. O'Bannon. Directed by Graham Baker. Produced by Gale Anne Hurd and Richard Kobritz. 20th Century Fox, 1988.

Another 48 Hours. Written by John Fasano, Jeb Stuart, and Larry Gross. Directed by Walter Hill. Produced by Lawrence Gordon and Robert Warks. Paramount, 1990.

Another Stakeout. Written by Jim Kouf. Directed by John Badham. Produced by Jim Kouf, Cathleen Summers, and Lynn Bigelow. Buena Vista, 1993.

Assassination. Written by Richard Sale. Directed by Peter Hunt. Produced by Pancho Kohner. Cannon, 1986.

Backdraft. Written by Gregory Widen. Directed by Ron Howard. Produced by Richard B. Lewis, Pen Densham, and John Watson. Universal, 1991.

Bad Boys. Written by Michael Barrie and Jim Mulholland and Doug Richardson. Directed by Michael Bay. Produced by Don Simpson and Jerry Bruckheimer. Paramount, 1995.

Basic Instinct. Written by Joe Eszterhas. Directed by Paul Verhoeven. Produced by Alan Marshall. TriStar, 1992.

Bestseller. Written by Larry Cohen. Directed by John Flynn. Produced by Carter DeHaven. Orion, 1987.

Betrayed. Written by Joe Eszterhas. Directed by Constantin Costa-Gavras. Produced by Irwin Winkler. MGM/UA, 1988.

Beverly Hills Cop. Written by Danilo Bach and Daniel Petrie Jr. Directed by Martin Brest. Produced by Don Simpson and Jerry Bruckheimer. Paramount, 1984.

Beverly Hills Cop 2. Written by Larry Ferguson and Warren Skaaren. Directed by Tony Scott. Produced by Don Simpson and Jerry Bruckheimer. Paramount, 1987.

Beverly Hills Cop 3. Written by Steven de Souza. Directed by John Landis. Produced by Mace Neufield and Robert Rehne. Paramount, 1994.

The Big Easy. Written by Daniel Petrie Jr. and Jack Baran. Directed by Jim McBride. Produced by Stephen Friedman. King's Road Entertainment/HBO, 1986.

Black Rain. Written by Craig Bolotin and Warren Lewis. Directed by Ridley Scott. Produced by Stanley Jaffe and Sherry Lansing. Paramount, 1989.

Blade Runner. Written by Hampton Fancher and David Peoples. Directed by Ridley Scott. Produced by Michael Deeley. Warner Bros., 1982.

Blink. Written by Dana Stevens. Directed by Michael Apted. Produced by David Blocker. New Line, 1994.

Blown Away. Written by Joe Batter and John Rice. Directed by Stephen Hopkins. Produced by John Watson, Pen Densham, and Richard Lewis. MGM/UA, 1994.

Blue Steel. Written by Kathryn Bigelow and Eric Red. Directed by Kathryn Bigelow. Produced by Edward R. Pressman and Oliver Stone. MGM/UA, 1990.

Blue Thunder. Written by Dan O'Bannon and Don Jakoby. Directed by John Badham. Produced by Gordon Carroll. Columbia, 1982.

The Border. Written by Deric Washburn, Walon Green, and David Freeman. Directed by Tony Richardson. Produced by Edgar Bronfman Jr. Universal, 1981.

Borderline. Written by Steve Kline and Jerrold Freeman. Directed by Jerrold Freeman. Produced by James Nelson. ITC, 1980.

Broken Arrow. Written by Graham Yost. Directed by John Woo. Produced by Mark Gordon, Bill Badalato, and Terence Chang. 20th Century Fox, 1996.

Bulletproof. Written by Joe Gayton and Lewis Colick. Directed by Ernest Dickerson. Produced by Robert Simonds. Universal, 1996.

City Heat. Written by Sam O. Brown. Directed by Richard Benjamin. Produced by Fritz Manes. Warner Bros., 1984.

Cliffhanger. Written by Michael France and Sylvester Stallone. Directed by Renny Harlin. Produced by Alan Marshall and Renny Harlin. Columbia/TriStar, 1993.

Cobra. Written by Sylvester Stallone. Directed by George P. Cosmatos. Produced by Menahem Golan and Yoram Globus. Warner Bros., 1986.

Code of Silence. Written by Michael Butler and Dennis Shryack. Directed by Andrew Davis. Produced by Raymond Wagner. Orion, 1985.

Collison Course. Written by Frank Darius Namei and Robert Resnikoff. Directed by Lewis Teague. Produced by Ted Field and Robert W. Cort. De Laurentis Entertainment Group/HBO, 1989.

Colors. Written by Michael Schiffer. Directed by Dennis Hopper. Produced by Robert H. Solo. Orion, 1988.

Con Air. Written by Scott Rosenberg. Directed by Simon West. Produced by Jerry Bruckheimer. Buena Vista, 1997.

Cop. Written and directed by James Harris. Produced by James Harris and James Woods. Paramount, 1987.

Cop Land. Written and directed by James Mangold. Produced by Cary Woods, Cathy Konrad, and Ezra Swerdlow. Buena Vista, 1997.

Copycat. Written by Ann Biderman and David Madsen. Directed by Jon Amiel. Produced by Arnon Milchan and Mark Tarlov. Warner Bros., 1995.

Cruising. Written and directed by William Friedkin. Produced by Jerry Weintraub. United Artists, 1980.

Dead Bang. Written by Robert Foster. Directed by John Frankenheimer. Produced by Steve Roth. Warner Bros., 1989.

Dead Heat. Written by Terry Black. Directed by Mark Goldblatt. Produced by Michael Meltzer and David Helpern. New World, 1988.

The Dead Pool. Written by Steve Sharon. Directed by Buddy Van Horn. Produced by David Valdes. Warner Bros., 1988.

Death Hunt. Written by Michael Grais and Mark Victor. Directed by Peter Hunt. Produced by Murray Shostak. 20th Century Fox, 1981.

Death Warrant. Written by David S. Goyer. Directed by Deran Sarafian. Produced by Mark DiSalle. MGM/UA, 1990.

Deep Cover. Written by Michael Tolkin and Henry Bean. Directed by Bill Duke. Produced by Pierre David and Henry Bean. New Line, 1992.

Demolition Man. Written by Daniel Waters and Robert Reneau and Peter M. Lenkov. Directed by Marco Brambilla. Produced by Joel Silver, Michael Levy, and Howard Kazanjian. Warner Bros., 1993.

The Devil's Own. Written by David Aaron Cohen, Kevin Jarre, and Vincent Patrick. Directed by Alan J. Pakula. Produced by Robert F. Colesberry and Lawrence Gordon. Columbia, 1997.

Die Hard. Written by Jeb Stuart and Steven de Souza. Directed by John McTiernan. Produced by Lawrence Gordon and Joel Silver. 20th Century Fox, 1988.

Die Hard 2. Written by Steven de Souza and Doug Richardson. Directed by Renny Harlin. Produced by Lawrence Gordon, Joel Silver, and Charles Gordon. 20th Century Fox, 1990.

Die Hard with a Vengeance. Written by Jonathan Hensleigh. Directed by John McTiernan. Produced by John McTiernan and Michael Tadross. 20th Century Fox, 1995.

Donnie Brasco. Written by Paul Attanasio. Directed by Mike Newell. Produced by Mark Johnson, Barry Levinson, Louis DiGiaimo, and Gail Mutrux. Columbia/Tristar, 1997.

Double Team. Written by Don Jakoby and Paul Mones. Directed by Tsui Hark. Produced by Moshe Diamant. Columbia/Tristar, 1997.

Downtown. Written by Nat Mauldin. Directed by Richard Benjamin. Produced by Charles H. Maguire. 20th Century Fox, 1990.

Drop Zone. Written by Peter Barsocchini and John Bishop. Directed by John Badham. Produced by D. J. Caruso, Wallis Nicita, and Lauren Lloyd. Paramount, 1994.

8 Million Ways to Die. Written by Oliver Stone and David Lee Henry.

Directed by Hal Ashby. Produced by Steve Roth. Producers Sales Organization/20th Century Fox, 1986.

Eraser. Written by Tony Puryear and Walon Green. Directed by Charles Russell. Produced by Arnold Kopelson and Anne Kopelson. Warner Bros., 1996.

Excessive Force. Written by Thomas Ian Griffith. Directed by John Hess. Produced by Thomas Ian Griffith. Columbia/New Line, 1992.

Executive Decision. Written by Jim Thomas and John Thomas. Directed by Stuart Baird. Produced by Joel Silver, Jim Thomas, and John Thomas. Warner Bros., 1996.

Extreme Justice. Written by Frank Sacks and Robert Bons. Directed by Mark L. Lester. Produced by Frank Sacks. HBO/Vidmark, 1993.

Extreme Prejudice. Written by Deric Washburn and Harry Kleiner. Directed by Walter Hill. Produced by Buzz Feitshans. TriStar, 1987.

An Eye for an Eye. Written by William Gray and James Bruner. Directed by Steve Carver. Produced by Frank Capra Jr. Embassy/New Line, 1981.

Face/Off. Written by Mike Werb and Michael Colleary. Directed by John Woo. Produced by David Permut, Barrie M. Osborne, Terence Chang, and Christopher Godsick. Buena Vista, 1997.

Fair Game. Written by Charlie Fletcher. Directed by Andrew Sipes. Produced by Joel Silver. Warner Bros., 1995.

Falling Down. Written by Ebbe Roe Smith. Directed by Joel Schumacher. Produced by Arnold Kopelson, Herschel Weingrod, and Timothy Harris. Warner Bros., 1992.

Fargo. Written by Joel and Ethan Coen. Directed by Joel Coen. Produced by Ethan Coen. Polygram, 1996.

Fatal Beauty. Written by Hilary Henkin and Paul Reisner. Directed by Tom Holland. Produced by Leonard Knoll. MGM/UA, 1987.

The Fire Down Below. Written by Jeb Stuart. Directed by Felix Enriquez Alcala. Produced by Julius R. Nasso and Steven Seagal. Warner Bros., 1997.

The First Deadly Sin. Written by Mann Rubin. Directed by Brian G. Hutton. Produced by George Pappas and Mark Shanker. Warner Bros., 1980.

The First Power. Written and directed by Robert Resnikoff. Produced by David Madden. Orion, 1990.

Flashback. Written by David Loughery. Directed by Franco Amurri. Produced by Marvin Worth. Paramount, 1989.

Fled. Written by Preston A. Whitmore II. Directed by Kevin Hooks. Produced by Frank Manusco Jr. MGM, 1996.

Fort Apache: The Bronx. Written by Heywood Gould. Directed by Daniel Petrie. Produced by Martin Richards and Tom Fiorello. 20th Century Fox/HBO, 1981.

48 Hours. Written by Roger Spottiswoode, Walter Hill, Larry Gross, and Steven de Souza. Directed by Walter Hill. Produced by Lawrence Gordon and Joel Silver. Paramount, 1982.

The Frighteners. Written by Fran Walsh and Peter Jackson. Directed by Peter Jackson. Produced by Jamie Selkirk and Peter Jackson. Universal, 1996.

The Fugitive. Written by Jeb Stuart and David Twohy. Directed by Andrew Davis. Produced by Arnold Kopelson. Warner Bros., 1993.

Gang Related. Written and directed by Jim Kouf. Produced by John Bertolli, Brad Krevoy, and Steven Stabler. Orion, 1997.

Ghostbusters. Written by Dan Aykroyd and Harold Ramis. Directed and produced by Ivan Reitman. Columbia, 1984.

Ghostbusters 2. Written by Dan Ackroyd and Harold Ramis. Directed and produced by Ivan Reitman. Columbia, 1989.

The Glimmer Man. Written by Kevin Brodbin. Directed by John Gray. Produced by Steven Seagal and Julius R. Nasso. Warner Bros., 1996.

Hard Target. Written by Chuck Pfarrer. Directed by John Woo. Produced by Sean Daniel, James Jacks, Daryl Kass, and Sam Raimi. Universal, 1993.

Hard to Kill. Written by Steven McKay. Directed by Bruce Malmuth. Produced by Gary Adelson, Joel Simon, and Bill Todman. Warner Bros., 1990.

The Hard Way. Written by Daniel Pyne and Lem Dobbs. Directed by John Badham. Produced by Rob Cohen and William Sackheim. Universal, 1991.

Heart Condition. Written and directed by James D. Parriott. Produced by Steve Tisch. New Line: 1990.

Heat. Written and directed by Michael Mann. Produced by Michael Mann and Art Linson. Warner Bros., 1995.

Heaven's Prisoners. Written by Harley Peyton and Scott Frank. Directed by Phil Joanou. Produced by Albert S. Ruddy, André E. Morgan, and Leslie Greif. New Line, 1996.

The Hidden. Written by Bob Hunt. Directed by Jack Sholder. Produced by Robert Shaye, Gerald T. Olson, and Michael Meltzer. New Line, 1987.

Homicide. Written and directed by David Mamet. Produced by Michael Hausman and Edward R. Pressman. Columbia, 1991.

The Hunter. Written by Ted Leighton and Peter Hyams. Directed by Buzz Kulik. Produced by Mort Engelberg. Paramount, 1980.

I Come in Peace. Written by Jonathan Tydor and Leonard Mass Jr. Directed by Craig R. Baxley. Produced by Jeff Young. Vision/Media Home Entertainment, 1989.

Impulse. Written by John De Marco and Leigh Chapman. Directed by Sondra Locke. Produced by Albert S. Ruddy and Andre Marco. Warner Bros., 1989.

Innocent Blood. Written by Michael Wolk. Directed by John Landis. Produced by Lee Rich and Leslie Belzberg. Warner Bros., 1992.

Internal Affairs. Written by Henry Bean. Directed by Mike Figgis. Produced by Frank Manusco Jr. Paramount, 1990.

In the Line of Fire. Written by Jeff McGuire. Directed by Wolfgang Petersen. Produced by Jeff Apple. Columbia, 1993.

The Jackal. Written by Chuck Pfarrer. Directed by Michael Caton-Jones. Produced by James Jacks, Sean Daniel, Michael Caton-Jones, and Kevin Jarre. Universal, 1997.

Jennifer 8. Written and directed by Bruce Robinson. Produced by Gary Lucchesi and David Wimbury. Paramount, 1992.

Judge Dredd. Written by William Wisher and Steven de Souza. Directed by Danny Cannon. Produced by Charles Lippincott and Beau E. L. Marks. Buena Vista, 1995.

Just Cause. Written Jeb Stuart and Peter Stone. Directed by Arne Glimcher. Produced by Lee Rich, Arne Glimcher, and Steve Perry. Warner Bros., 1995.

K-9. Written by Steven Siegel and Scott Myers. Directed by Rod Daniel. Produced by Lawrence Gordon and Charles Gordon. Universal, 1989.

Kindergarten Cop. Written by Murray Salem, Herschel Weingrod, and Timothy Harris. Directed by Ivan Reitman. Produced by Ivan Reitman and Brian Grazer. Universal, 1990.

Kiss the Girls. Written by David Klass. Directed by Gary Fleder. Produced by David Brown and Joe Wizan. Paramount, 1997.

L. A. Confidential. Written by Brian Helgeland and Curtis Hanson. Directed by Curtis Hanson. Produced by Arnon Milchan, Curtis Hanson, and Michael Nathanson. Warner Bros., 1997.

Last Action Hero. Written by Shane Black and David Arnott. Directed by John McTiernan. Produced by Steve Roth and John McTiernan. Columbia, 1993.

The Last Boy Scout. Written by Shane Black. Directed by Tony Scott. Produced by Joel Silver and Michael Levy. Warner Bros., 1991.

The Last of the Finest. Written by Jere Cunningham, Thomas Lee Wright, and George Armitage. Directed by John MacKenzie. Produced by John A. Davis. Orion, 1990.

Lethal Weapon. Written by Shane Black. Directed by Richard Donner. Produced by Richard Donner and Joel Silver. Warner Bros., 1987.

Lethal Weapon 2. Written by Jeffrey Boam. Directed by Richard Donner. Produced by Richard Donner and Joel Silver. Warner Bros., 1989.

Lethal Weapon 3. Written by Jeffrey Boam and Robert Mark Kamen. Directed by Richard Donner. Produced by Joel Silver and Richard Donner. Warner Bros., 1992.

Lone Wolf McQuade. Written by B. J. Nelson. Directed by Steve Carver. Produced by Yoram Ben-Ami and Steve Carver. Orion, 1983.

The Long Kiss Goodnight. Written by Shane Black. Directed by Renny Harlin. Produced by Renny Harlin, Stephanie Austin, and Shane Black. New Line, 1996.

Low Down Dirty Shame. Written and directed by Keenan Ivory Wayans. Produced by Joe Roth and Roger Birnbaum. Buena Vista, 1994.

Mad Dog and Glory. Written by Richard Price. Directed by John McNaughton. Produced by Barbara De Fina and Martin Scorcese. Universal, 1992.

Manhunter. Written and directed by Michael Mann. Produced by Richard Roth. Warner Bros., 1986.

Maniac Cop. Written and produced by Larry Cohen. Directed by William Lustig. Shapiro Glickenhaus/Elite, 1988.

Maniac Cop 2. Written and produced by Larry Cohen. Directed by William Lustig. Live, 1990.

Marked for Death. Written by Michael Grais and Mark Victor. Directed by Dwight Little. Produced by Michael Grais, Mark Victor, and Steven Seagal. 20th Century Fox, 1990.

Married to the Mob. Written by Barry Strugatz and Mark R. Burns. Directed by Jonathan Demme. Produced by Kenneth Utt and Edward Saxon. Orion, 1988.

Maximum Risk. Written by Larry Ferguson. Directed by Ringo Lam. Produced by Moshe Diamont. Columbia, 1996.

Men in Black. Written by Ed Solomon. Directed by Barry Sonnenfeld. Produced by Walter F. Parkes and Laurie MacDonald. Columbia/Tristar, 1997.

Metro. Written by Randy Feldman. Directed by Thomas Carter. Produced by Roger Birnbaum. Buena Vista, 1997.

Midnight Run. Written by George Gallo. Directed and produced by Martin Brest. Universal, 1988.

The Mighty Quinn. Written by Hampton Fancher. Directed by Carl Schenkel. Produced by Sandy Lieberson, Marion Hunt, and Ed Elbert. MGM/UA/CBS, 1989.

Mississippi Burning. Written by Chris Gerolmo. Directed by Alan Parker. Produced by Frederick Zollo and Robert F. Colesberry. Orion, 1988.

Money Train. Written by Doug Richardson and David Loughery. Directed by Joseph Ruben. Produced by Jon Peters and Neil Canton. Columbia, 1995.

Mulholland Falls. Written by Peter Dexter. Directed by Lee Tamahori. Produced by Richard D. Zanuck and Lili Fini Zanuck. MGM, 1996.

Murder at 1600. Written by Wayne Beach and David Hodgin. Directed by Dwight Little. Produced by Arnold Kopelson and Arnon Milchan. Warner Bros., 1997.

Murphy's Law. Written by Gail Morgan Hickman. Directed by J. Lee Thompson. Produced by Pancho Kohner. Cannon/Media Home Entertainment, 1986.

Narrow Margin. Written by Earl Fenton Jr. Directed by Peter Hyams. Produced by Jonathan A. Zimbert. TriStar, 1990.

National Lampoon's Loaded Weapon 1. Written by Don Holly and Gene Quintano. Directed by Gene Quintano. Produced by Suzanne Todd and David Willis. New Line, 1993.

New Jack City. Written by Thomas Lee Wright and Barry Michael Cooper. Directed by Mario Van Peebles. Produced by Doug McHenry and George Jackson. Warner Bros., 1991.

Nighthawks. Written by David Sheber. Directed by Bruce Malamuth. Produced by Martin Poll. Universal, 1981.

No Man's Land. Written by Dick Wolf. Directed by Peter Werner. Produced by Joseph Stern and Dick Wolf. Orion, 1987.

No Mercy. Written by Jim Carabatsos. Directed by Richard Pearce. Produced by Michael Hausman. TriStar, 1986.

Off Limits. Written by Christopher Crowe and Jack Thibeau. Directed by Christopher Crowe. Produced by Alan Barnette. 20th Century Fox, 1988.

On Deadly Ground. Written by Ed Horowitz and Robin U. Russin. Directed by Steven Seagal. Produced by Steven Seagal, Julius R. Nasso, and A. Kitman Ho. Warner Bros., 1994.

Outbreak. Written by Laurence Dworet and Robert Roy Pool. Directed by Wolfgang Petersen. Produced by Arnold Kopelson, Wolfgang Petersen, and Gail Katz. Warner Bros., 1995.

Passenger 57. Written by David Loughery and Dan Gordon. Directed by Kevin Hooks. Produced by Lee Rich, Dan Paulson and Dylan Sellers. Warner Bros., 1992.

Physical Evidence. Written by Bill Phillips. Directed by Michael Crichton. Produced by Martin Ransohoff. Paramount, 1988.

Point Break. Written by W. Peter Iliff. Directed by Kathryn Bigelow. Produced by Peter Abrams and Robert Levy. 20th Century Fox, 1991.

Predator 2. Written by Jim Thomas and John Thomas. Directed by Stephen Hopkins. Produced by Lawrence Gordon, Joel Silver, and John Davis. 20th Century Fox, 1990.

The Presidio. Written by Larry Ferguson. Directed by Peter Hyams. Produced by D. Constantine Conte. Paramount, 1988.

The Protector. Written and directed by James Glickenhaus. Produced by David Chan. Warner Bros., 1985.

Q & A. Written and directed by Sidney Lumet. Produced by Arnon Milchan and Burtt Harris. TriStar, 1990.

Rapid Fire. Written by Alan McElroy. Directed by Dwight Little. Produced by Robert Lawrence. 20th Century Fox, 1992.

Raw Deal. Written by Gary DeVore and Norman Wexler. Directed by John Irvin. Produced by Martha Schumaker. De Laurentis Entertainment Group/HBO, 1986.

Red Heat. Written by Harry Kleiner, Walter Hill, and Troy Martin. Directed by Walter Hill. Produced by Walter Hill and Gordon Carroll. TriStar, 1988.

Renegades. Written by David Rich. Directed by Jack Sholder. Produced by David Madden. Universal, 1989.

Ricochet. Written by Steven de Souza. Directed by Russell Mulcahy. Produced by Joel Silver and Michael Levy. Warner Bros., 1991.

Rising Sun. Written by Philip Kaufman and Michael Crichton and Michael Backes. Directed by Philip Kaufman. Produced by Peter Kaufman. 20th Century Fox, 1993.

Robocop. Written by Edward Noumeier and Michael Miner. Directed by Paul Verhoeven. Produced by Arne Schmidt. Orion, 1987.

Robocop 2. Written by Frank Miller and Walon Grein. Directed by Irvin Kirshner. Produced by Jon Davidson. Orion, 1990.

Robocop 3. Written by Frank Miller and Fred Dekker. Directed by Fred Dekker. Produced by Patrick Crowley. Orion, 1993.

The Rock. Written by David Weisberg, Douglas Cook, and Mark Rosner. Directed by Michael Bay. Produced by Don Simpson and Jerry Bruckheimer. Buena Vista, 1996.

The Rookie. Written by Boaz Yakin and Scott Spiegel. Directed by Clint Eastwood. Produced by Howard Kazanjian, Steven Siebert, and David Valdez. Warner Bros., 1990.

Runaway. Written and directed by Michael Crichton. Produced by Michael Rachmil. TriStar, 1984.

The Running Man. Written by Steven de Souza. Directed by Paul Michael Glaser. Produced by Tim Zinnemann and George Linder. TriStar, 1987.

Running Scared. Written by Gary DeVore and Jimmy Huston. Directed by Peter Hyams. Produced by David Foster and Lawrence Turman. Universal, 1986.

Rush. Written by Pete Dexter. Directed by Lili Fini Zanuck. Produced by Richard D. Zanuck. MGM/UA, 1991.

Sea of Love. Written by Richard Price. Directed by Harold Becker. Produced by Martin Bregman. Universal, 1989.

Se7en. Written by Andrew Kevin Walker. Directed by David Fincher. Produced by Arnold Kopelson and Phyllis Carlyle. New Line, 1995.

Shakedown. Written and directed by James Glickenhaus. Produced by J. Boyce Harman Jr. Universal, 1988.

Sharky's Machine. Written by Gerald Di Pego. Directed by Burt Reynolds. Produced by Hank Moonjean. Warner Bros., 1981.

Shoot to Kill. Written by Harv Zimmel, Michael Burton, and Daniel Petrie. Directed by Roger Spottiswoode. Produced by Ron Silverman and Daniel Petrie. Buena Vista, 1988.

Showdown in Little Tokyo. Written by Stephen Glantz and Caliope Brattlestreet. Directed by Mark Lester. Produced by Mark Lester and Martin Caan. Warner Bros., 1991.

The Silence of the Lambs. Written by Ted Tally. Directed by Jonathan Demme. Produced by Kenneth Utt, Edward Saxon, and Ron Bozman. Orion, 1991.

Silent Rage. Written by Joseph Fraley. Directed by Michael Miller. Produced by Anthony B. Unger. Columbia, 1982.

Speed. Written by Graham Yost. Directed by Jan DeBont. Produced by Mark Gordon. 20th Century Fox, 1994.

Speed 2: Cruise Control. Written by Randall McCormick and Jeff Nathanson. Directed by Jan De Bont. Produced by Jan De Bont, Steve Perry, and Michael Peyser. 20th Century Fox, 1997.

Stakeout. Written by Jim Kouf. Directed by John Badham. Produced by Jim Kouf and Cathleen Summers. Buena Vista, 1987.

Stone Cold. Written by Walter Doniger. Directed by Craig R. Baxley. Produced by Yoram Ben Ami. Columbia, 1991.

Strange Days. Written by James Cameron and Jay Cocks. Directed by Kathryn Bigelow. Produced by James Cameron and Steven-Charles Joffe. 20th Century Fox, 1995.

A Stranger Among Us. Written by Robert Avrech. Directed by Sidney Lumet. Produced by Steve Golin, Sigurjon Sighvatsson, and Howard Rosenman. Buena Vista, 1992.

Striking Distance. Written by Rowdy Herrington and Martin Kaplan. Directed by Rowdy Herrington. Produced by Arnon Milchan, Tony Thomopoulos, and Hunt Lowry. Columbia, 1993.

Sudden Death. Written by Gene Quintano. Directed by Peter Hyams. Produced by Moshe Diamant and Howard Baldwin. Universal, 1995.

Sudden Impact. Written by Earl E. Smith and Charles B. Pierce. Directed and produced by Clint Eastwood. Warner Bros., 1984.

Switchback. Written and directed by Jeb Stuart. Produced by Gale Anne Hurd. Paramount, 1997.

Tango and Cash. Written by Randy Feldman. Directed by Andrei Konchalovsky. Produced by Jon Peters and Peter Guber. Warner Bros., 1989.

10 to Midnight. Written by William Roberts. Directed by J. Lee Thompson. Produced by Pancho Kohner and Lance Hool. Cannon, 1983.

Tequila Sunrise. Written and directed by Robert Towne. Produced by Thom Mount. Warner Bros., 1987.

Terminal Velocity. Written by David Twohy. Directed by Deran Sarafian. Produced by Scott Kroopf and Tom Engelman. Buena Vista, 1994.

Thunderheart. Written by John Fusco. Directed by Michael Apted. Produced by Robert De Niro, Jane Rosenthal, and John Fusco. TriStar, 1992.

Tightrope. Written and directed by Richard Tuggle. Produced by Clint Eastwood and Fritz Manes. Warner Bros., 1985.

Timecop. Written by Mark Verheiden. Directed by Peter Hyams. Produced by Moshe Diamant, Sam Raimi, and Robert Tapert. Universal, 1994.

To Live and Die in L.A. Written by William Friedkin and Gerald Petievich. Directed by William Friedkin. Produced by Irving H. Levin. MGM/UA, 1985.

Total Recall. Written by Ronald Shusset and Dan O'Bannon, and Gary Goldman. Directed by Paul Verhoeven. Produced by Buzz Feitshans and Ronald Shuset. TriStar, 1990.

Turner & Hooch. Written by Dennis Schryack and Michael Blodgett; Daniel Petrie Jr.; and Jim Cash and Jack Epps Jr. Directed by Roger Spotiswoode. Produced by Raymond Wagner. Touchstone, 1989.

Under Siege. Written by J. F. Lawton. Directed by Andrew Davis. Produced by Arnon Milchan, Steven Seagal, and Steven Reuther. Warner Bros., 1992.

Under Siege 2: Dark Territory. Written by Richard Hatem and Matt Reeves. Directed by Geoff Murphy. Produced by Steven Seagal, Steve Perry, and Arnon Milchan. Warner Bros., 1995.

Universal Soldier. Written by Richard Rothstein, Christopher Lietch, and Dean Devlin. Directed by Roland Emmerich. Produced by Allen Shapiro, Craig Baumgarten, and Joel B. Michaels. TriStar, 1992.

The Untouchables. Written by David Mamet. Directed by Brian De Palma. Produced by Art Linson. Paramount, 1987.

Vampire in Brooklyn. Written by Charles Murphy and Michael Lucker and Chris Parker. Directed by Wes Craven. Produced by Eddie Murphy and Mark Lipsky. Paramount, 1995.

Virtuosity. Written by Eric Bernt. Directed by Brett Leonard. Produced by Gary Lucchesi. Paramount, 1995.

Wanted Dead or Alive. Written by Michael Patrick Goodman, Brian Taggert, and Gary Sherman. Directed by Gary Sherman. Produced by Robert C. Peters. Starmaker, 1987.

Who Framed Roger Rabbit? Written by Lowell Ganz, Babaloo Mandel, Jeffrey Price, and Peter S. Seaman. Directed by Robert Zemeckis. Produced by Frank Marshall and Robert Watts. Buena Vista, 1988.

Witness. Written by Earl W. Wallace and William Kelly. Directed by Peter Weir. Produced by Edward S. Feldman. Paramount, 1985.

Wolfen. Written by David Eyre and Michael Wadleigh. Directed by Michael Wadleigh. Produced by Rupert Hitzig. Warner Bros., 1981.

Year of the Dragon. Written by Oliver Stone and Michael Cimino. Directed by Michael Cimino. Produced by Dino De Laurentis. MGM/UA, 1985.

Other Movies Cited: Early, Nonviolent, and Non-Cop

Bullitt. Written by Alan Trustman and Harvey Kleiner. Directed by Peter Yates. Produced by Philip D'Antoni. Warner Bros., 1968.

Butch Cassidy and the Sundance Kid. Written by William Goldman. Directed by George Roy Hill. Produced by John Foreman. 20th Century Fox, 1969.

The Chase. Written by Lillian Hellman. Directed by Arthur Penn. Produced by Sam Speigel. Columbia, 1966.

Coogan's Bluff. Written by Herman Miller, Dean Riesner, and Howard Rodman. Directed and produced by Don Siegel. Universal, 1968.

Dave. Written by Gary Ross. Directed by Ivan Reitman. Produced by Ivan Reitman and Lauren Shuler-Donner. Warner Bros., 1993.

Death Wish. Written by Wendell Mayes. Directed by Michael Winner. Produced by Hal Landers, Bobby Roberts, and Michael Winner. Paramount, 1974.

Dirty Harry. Written by Harry Julian Fink, P. M. Fink, and Dean Riesner. Directed and produced by Don Siegel. Warner Bros., 1971.

The Doctor. Written by Robert Caswell. Directed by Randa Haines. Produced by Laura Ziskin. Buena Vista, 1991.

Easy Rider. Written by Peter Fonda, Dennis Hopper, and Terry Southern. Directed by Dennis Hopper. Produced by Peter Fonda. Columbia, 1969.

The Enforcer. Written by Stirling Siliphant and Dean Riesner. Directed by James Fargo. Produced by Robert Daley. Warner Bros., 1976.

The Fisher King. Written by Richard LaGravenese. Directed by Terry Gilliam. Produced by Debra Hill and Lynda Obst. Tri-Star, 1991.

The French Connection. Written by Ernest Tidyman. Directed by William Friedkin. Produced by Philip D'Antoni. 20th Century Fox, 1971.

Ghost. Written by Peter Barsocchini. Directed by Jerry Zucker. Produced by Howard W. Koch, Jr. and Lisa Weinstein. Paramount, 1990.

Groundhog Day. Written by Danny Rubin. Directed by Harold Ramis. Produced by Trevor Albert. Columbia, 1993.

Harley Davidson and the Marlboro Man. Written by Don Michael Paul. Directed by Simon Wincer. Produced by Jere Henshaw. MGM/UA, 1991.

Hook. Written by Jim V. Hart, Nick Castle, and Malia Scotch Marmo. Directed by Steven Spielberg. Produced by Kathleen Kennedy, Frank Marshall, and Gerald R. Molen. Columbia, 1991.

In the Heat of the Night. Written by Stirling Silliphant. Directed by Norman Jewison. Produced by Walter Mirisch. United Artists, 1967.

Jerry Maguire. Written and directed by Cameron Crowe. Produced by James L. Brooks, Richard Sakai, Laurence Mark, and Cameron Crowe. Columbia, 1996.

Klute. Written by Andy K. Lewis and Dave Lewis. Directed and produced by Alan J. Pakula. Columbia/Warner Bros., 1971.

Madigan. Written by Henri Simoun and Abraham Polonsky. Directed by Don Siegel. Produced by Frank P. Rosenberg. Universal, 1968.

Magnum Force. Written by John Milius and Michael Cimino. Directed by Ted Post. Produced by Robert Daley. Warner Bros., 1973.

Mean Streets. Written by Martin Scorcese and Mardik Martin. Directed by Martin Scorcese. Produced by Jonathan T. Taplin. Warner Bros., 1973.

Midnight Cowboy. Written by Waldo Salt. Directed by John Schlesinger. Produced by Jerome Hellman. United Artists/MGM, 1969.

Michael. Written by Nora Ephron, Peter Dexter, and Jim Quinlan. Directed by Nora Ephron. Produced by Nora Ephron, Sean Daniel, and James Jacks. New Line, 1996.

Missing in Action. Written by Steve Bing, James Bruner, and Alan Sharp. Directed by Joseph Zito. Produced by Yoram Globus and Menahem Golan. MGM, 1984.

Mission Impossible. Written by William Huyck, Gloria Katz, David Koepp, Robert Towne, and Steven Zallian. Directed by Brian DePalma. Produced by Tom Cruise and Paula Wagner. Paramount, 1996.

Partners. Written by Francis Veber. Directed by James Burrows. Produced by Aaron Russo. Paramount, 1982.

The Prince Of Tides. Written by Jay Presson Allen, Pat Conroy, and Becky Johnston. Directed by Barbra Streisand. Produced by Cis Corman, Andrew S. Karsch, James T. Roe III, and Barbra Steisand. Columbia, 1991.

Rambo: First Blood Part II. Written by Sylvester Stallone and James Cameron. Directed by George P. Cosmatos. Produced by Buzz Feitshans. EMI/Carolco, 1985.

Rambo III. Written by Sylvester Stallone and Sheldon Lettich. Directed by Peter MacDonald. Produced by Buzz Feitshans. EMI/Carolco, 1988.

Regarding Henry. Written by Jeffrey Abrams. Directed by Mike Nichols. Produced by Scott Rudin and Mike Nichols. Paramount, 1991.

Serpico. Written by Waldo Salt and Norman Waxler. Directed by Sidney Lumet. Produced by Martin Bregman. Paramount, 1973.

Shaft. Written by Ernest Tidyman and John D. F. Black. Directed by Gordon Parks. Produced by Joel Freeman. MGM, 1971.

Someone to Watch Over Me. Written by Hector Babenco, Danilo Bach, Howard Franklin, and David Seltzer. Directed by Ridley Scott. Produced by Thierry de Ganay and Harold Schneider. Columbia, 1987.

Thunderbolt and Lightfoot. Written and directed by Michael Cimino. Produced by Robert Daley. United Artists, 1974.

True Lies. Written and directed by James Cameron. Produced by Stephanie Austin and James Cameron. 20th Century Fox, 1994.

Uncommon Valor. Written and directed by Ted Kotcheff. Produced by Buzz Feitshans and John Milius. Paramount, 1983.

Walking Tall. Written and produced by Mort Briskin. Directed by Phil Karlson. Cinerama/Lightning, 1973.

Notes

Preface

1. About male privilege and anal sex, see Christopher Castiglia, "Rebel Without a Closet," in *Engendering Men: The Question of Male Feminist Criticism*, ed. Joseph Boone and Michael Cadden (New York: Routledge, 1990); D. A. Miller, "Anal Rope," in *Inside/Out: Lesbian Theories, Gay Theories*, ed. Diana Fuss (New York: Routledge, 1991); and Eve Kosofsky Sedgwick, *Epistemology of the Closet* (Berkeley and Los Angeles: University of California Press, 1990).

2. My favorites from among the several dozen cop action studies include: Christopher Ames, "Restoring the Black Man's Lethal Weapon: Race and Sexuality in Contemporary Cop Films," *Journal of Popular Film and Television* 20 (1992): 52–60; Kwame Anthony Appiah, " 'No Bad Nigger': Blacks as the Ethical Principle in the Movies," in *Media Spectacles*, ed. Marjorie Garber, Jann Matlock, and Rebecca L. Walkowitz (New York: Routledge, 1993); Richard Dyer, *White* (New York: Routledge, 1997); Cindy Patton, "What Is a Nice Lesbian Like You Doing in a Film Like This?" in *Immortal, Invisible: Lesbians and the Moving Image*, ed. Tamsin Wilton (New York: Routledge, 1995); and Fred Pfeil, *White Guys: Studies in Postmodern Domination and Difference* (New York: Verso, 1995).

3. See Ames, "Restoring the Black Man's Lethal Weapon"; Pfeil, *White Guys;* and Robyn Wiegman, *American Anatomies: Theorizing Race and Gender* (Durham, N.C.: Duke University Press, 1995).

4. A subgenre of the literature takes on the sci-fi elements of such movies as *Blade Runner, Robocop,* and *Total Recall,* articulating the relations between cinema technology, psychoanalytic theory, political fantasy, and individual subjectification. That I do not engage this aspect of the literature very much probably says more about the disciplinary divide between humanists and social scientists than anything else. At least it gives a sense of where I call home.

Chapter One

1. When I use the phrases "lost ground" and "losing ground," I am referring to a time when the corruption of privileged groups wrecks people's

251

lives and makes them fear for their nation's health. Publicity given to "identity" politics and nationalisms, maintenance of affirmative action, movements of minorities and women into professional turf and the popular media, overpaid and factory-closing CEOs, and worries over the nuclear family, as well as a perceived slide in standards of living, add to this sense of "losing ground." Charles Murray locates our problems in "the culture of poverty" in his book *Losing Ground* (New York: Basic Books, 1984). But people find lots to blame: the military industrial complex, the drift from Victorian family values, the feminist and lesbian/gay rights movements, the exportation of blue-collar jobs, a secret organization of Jews, and so on. Many people, whomever they blame, can relate to "losing." From all corners of a society, people hurl accusations of mismanagement and corruption at those whom they regard as overly privileged, particularly as they feel their own entitlements slipping away.

2. By "corruption," I mean the abuse by those in positions of authority who keep resources from circulating in legal, rational, and meritocratic manners and keep them instead to themselves. The privileges in question result from the discriminating distribution of resources, which include esteem, freedom, authority, and wealth—all that we used to get somewhere in life. Anyone can define anyone else as privileged by perceiving some inequality—believing that someone else has more resources.

3. See, for instance, Jerry Adler, "Taking Offense," *Newsweek*, December 24, 1990, pp. 48–54; David Gates, "White Male Paranoia," *Newsweek*, March 29, 1993, pp. 48–53; John Taylor, "Are You Politically Correct?" *New York*, January 21, 1991.

4. Williams writes of structures of feeling: "This is a way of defining forms and convention in art and literature as inalienable elements of a social material process . . . which may in turn be seen as the articulation (often the only fully available articulation) of structures of feeling which as living processes are much more widely experienced." See Raymond Williams, *Marxism and Literature* (Oxford: Oxford University Press, 1977), p. 132.

5. See Robert Hughes, *The Culture of Complaint: The Fraying of America* (New York: Oxford University Press, 1993).

6. See David Ashley, "Postmodernism and the 'End of the Individual': From Repressive Self-Mastery to Ecstatic Communication," *Current Perspectives in Social Theory* 10 (1990): 195–221; Barbara Ehrenreich, *Fear of Falling: The Inner Life of the Middle Class* (New York: Harper, 1989); James Davison Hunter, *Culture Wars: The Struggle to Define America* (New York: Basic Books, 1991).

7. See Marc Cooper, "Queer Baiting and the Culture War," *The Village Voice*, October 13, 1992, p. 30. Measure 9, denying state protection to

people denied housing or jobs because they are homosexual, nearly won an Oregon election. The Oregon Citizens Alliance sponsored the measure.

8. Ibid., p. 32.

9. Ibid., p. 34.

10. The group "No on 9" fought against passage of the state bill and defended local lesbian and gay equal rights laws.

11. Ibid., p. 35.

12. Ibid., p. 29.

13. Ibid., P. 29.

14. Wendy Brown, "Injury, Identity, Politics," in *Mapping Multiculturalism,* ed. Avery F. Gordon and Christopher Newfield (Minneapolis: University of Minnesota Press, 1996), p. 158.

15. See Fred Pfeil, *White Guys: Studies in Postmodern Domination and Difference* (New York: Verso, 1995), on the "sensitive man" movie genre of the 1990s.

Chapter Two

1. These movies with no lead white guy cops include three of the neo-blaxploitation movies (*Action Jackson, Low Down Dirty Shame,* and *Vampire in Brooklyn*), as well as seven other movies in which the white male criminal gets a lot of screen time being bad (see Chapter 4) and thus preserve the focus on white male guilt and rage.

2. Indeed, no one breaks the rule until the fugitive black male cop in 1998's *U.S. Marshalls* takes a white girlfriend. Miscegenation rules do not, of course, work the other way, against white men and their options. As Tomás Almaguer describes the Califonia history that begat cop action, women of color were always the "exotic prize that many Anglo men arrogantly believed were part of the spoils of conquest." See Tomás Almaguer, *Racial Fault Lines: The Historical Origins of White Supremacy in California* (Berkeley and Los Angeles: University of California, 1994), p. 59.

3. Carol J. Clover, "*Falling Down* and the Rise of the Average White Male," in *Women and Film: A Sight and Sound Reader,* ed. Pam Cook and Philip Dodd (Philadelphia: Temple University Press, 1993), p. 139.

4. Ibid., p. 145.

5. Ibid., p. 143.

6. The fortunes of heroes mirror those of the noncinematic industrial economy over the last few decades. As Avery Gordon observes, "the corporation['s] decline and fragmentation . . . decline in union-driven managerial relations, the increasingly symbolic and cultural nature of economic products, and the attendent split between a high wage/skill and low wage/skill

work force create the conditions for a serious crisis of authority within the firm." See Avery Gordon, "The Work of Corporate Culture," *Social Text* 13, 3 (1995): 5. As I argue in this and subsequent chapters, the approaches taken by cop heroes both resemble and differ from those taken by the noncinematic corporate multiculturalists Gordon describes. Cops focus on the problems of white manhood to the neglect of the underclass sacrificed by the systems against which they fight. On the other hand, cops oppose management in a way that not only champions individualism but also derides the authority of white men in general, however liberal that authority might be.

7. *Die Hard*'s hero mentions a "man upstairs," the hero of *Above the Law* attends a Roman Catholic church, and the hero of *Hard to Kill* leads his son in a bedtime prayer (and later looks a lot like a Catholic Christ as he rises from his extended coma to kick holy butt). The title character of *The Glimmer Man* practices Buddhism. A boss in *Cop* presents himself as a "born again" Christian. Also, heroes in *A Stranger Among Us, Thunderheart,* and *Witness* take shelter with orthodox adherents of various faiths and are each touched, though none converts.

8. The cop strips to the jockstrap, grabs a weapon hidden beneath, and shoots a criminal in the leg. I discuss erotic law enforcement in Chapter 7.

9. See Houston A. Baker, *Blues, Ideology, and Afro-American Literature: A Vernacular Theory* (Chicago: University of Chicago Press, 1984), p. 65.

Chapter Three

1. The supervising officer in this case is also the movies' hero, a juxtaposition of character types made possible in part by the casting of a black man. No white hero ever takes on this aggressive managerial role. Though the heroes of *Heat* and *Tequila Sunrise* run the Special Crimes unit and Narcotics Bureau on Los Angeles, respectively, neither abuses his subordinates (though the latter shoots a superior in the back for reasons I describe in Chapter 7).

2. In three movies, sidekicks catch up in violence to heroes who are not white males. These exceptions include *Beverly Hills Cop*, in which the working-class black hero sets the example for the professional-class, milk-toast white sidekick to follow; *Low Down Dirty Shame*, in which a black female sidekick finally helps the black male hero; and *A Stranger Among Us*, in which a Hasidic man sworn to pacifism finally aids the white female hero by shooting a criminal. In each of these exceptional cases, then, cops and sidekicks cross some divide: class, gender, or culture.

3. As I note above, though, cops cannot depend upon such reconciliation. For every movie in which a cop receives acclaim for a job well done, another

sees a hero quit, fired, transferred, or retired. I deal with these more serious rifts between cops and employers, which have less to do with management and more to do with disagreement about who the criminals are, in Chapter 5.

4. See Stuart Kaminsky, *American Film Genres* (Chicago: Nelson-Hall, 1985), p. 114.

5. Curiously, I have found no analysis of the cross-gender bondings that comprise nearly a third of all the cop pairings. Analysts of cop action racism include Ann Ardis and Dale M. Bauer, " 'Just the Fax, Ma'am': Male Sentimentality in the *Die Hard* Films," *Arizona Quarterly* 47, 2 (1991): 117–29; Donald Bogle, *Toms, Coons, Mulattoes, Mammies, and Bucks: An Interpretive History of Blacks in American Films* (New York: Continuum, 1991); Paul S. Cowen, "A Social-Cognitive Approach to Ethnicity in Films," in *Unspeakable Images: Ethnicity and the American Cinema,* ed. Lester D. Friedman (Chicago: University of Illinois Press, 1991); Susan Jeffords, *Hard Bodies: Hollywood Masculinity in the Reagan Era* (New Brunswick, N.J.: Rutgers University Press, 1994); Tania Modleski, *Feminism Without Women: Culture and Criticism in a "Postfeminist" Age* (New York: Routledge, 1991); Andrew Ross, "Cowboys, Cadillacs, and Cosmonauts: Families, Film Genres, and Technocultures," in *Engendering Men: The Question of Male Feminist Criticism,* ed. Joseph Boone and Michael Cadden (New York: Routledge, 1990); Robyn Wiegman, "Black Bodies/American Commodities: Gender, Race and the Bourgeois Ideal in Contemporary Film," in *Unspeakable Images,* ed. Friedman, and *American Anatomies: Theorizing Race and Gender* (Durham, N.C.: Duke University Press, 1995), Mark Winokur, "Black Is White/White Is Black: 'Passing' as a Strategy of Racial Compatibility in Contemporary Hollywood Comedy," in *Unspeakable Images,* ed. Friedman.

6. See Wiegman, "Black Bodies/American Commodities," and *American Anatomies.*

7. Houston A. Baker, *Blues, Ideology, and Afro-American Literature: A Vernacular Theory* (Chicago: University of Chicago Press, 1984), p. 65.

8. Ardis and Bauer, " 'Just the Fax, Ma'am,' " p. 124.

Chapter Four

1. A civilian contemplates the genre's elasticity in *Robocop 3:* "Sarge, you've got a Robocop. Do you got an alien cop? Huh? Do you got a ghost cop?"

The sergeant frowns upon mockery of his culture. "Leon, I told you. I don't have time for this."

"Do you got a vampire cop?"

The genre features all of these life-forms as cops or criminals or both at some point, and throws in some zombie cops to boot.

2. See, for instance, Christopher Ames, "Restoring the Black Man's Lethal Weapon: Race and Sexuality in Contemporary Cop Films," *Journal of Popular Film and Television* 20 (1992): 52–60; Carol J. Clover, *Men, Women and Chainsaws: Gender and the Modern Horror Film* (Princeton, N.J.: Princeton University Press, 1992); Susan Jeffords, *Hard Bodies: Hollywood Masculinity in the Reagan Era* (New Brunswick, N.J.: Rutgers University Press, 1994); Kaja Silverman, "Back to the Future," *Camera Obscura* 27 (1992): 109–34; and Yvonne Tasker, *Spectacular Bodies: Gender, Genre, and the Action Cinema* (New York: Routledge, 1993).

3. I draw anecdotal support from the frequency with which viewers describe the genre's villains as nonwhite. They do this for a dozen reasons, I am sure, perhaps confusing cop, war, and spy movies. For instance, the spy movie *True Lies* (one of the international-intrigue movies that I bar from the genre) poses as criminals a group of terrorist Semitic Muslims and seems to deal more with fears of international impotency than with domestic oppression and shame.

4. Tasker, *Spectacular Bodies*, p. 45.

5. Christopher Ames "Restoring the Black Man's Lethal Weapon," p. 57.

6. Clover *Men, Women, and Chainsaws*, p. 135, n21.

7. Ibid., p. 161.

8. Silverman, "Back to the Future."

9. Jeffords, *Hard Bodies*, p. 53.

10. Ibid., pp. 56, 139.

11. Ibid., p. 139.

12. In only three movies does a slasher direct aggression toward men: In *Cruising*, one targets men whom he picks up for sex; in *Sea of Love*, a jealous husband sexually assaults and shoots his ex-wife's male lovers; and in *Basic Instinct*, one of the four female lead criminals in the genre ice-picks men to death as part of a labyrinthine plot of revenge against a woman who once spurned her. Each of the last two movies looks like a remake of the previous, drawing white male cops into sexual confusion and deviance while they try in vain to tell murderers from lovers, cops from criminals. In the first and third movies especially, cops learn the futility of even trying.

13. Slavoj Žižek, *The Sublime Object of Ideology* (New York: Verso, 1989), pp. 105–7.

14. See James R. Kincaid, *Erotic Innocence: The Culture of Child Molesting* (Durham, N.C.: Duke University Press, 1998) for a list of embarrassing reasons why adults maintain sentimental views of children.

15. Kwame Anthony Appiah, " 'No Bad Nigger': Blacks as the Ethical Principle in the Movies," in *Media Spectacles*, ed. Marjorie Garber, Jann Matlock, and Rebecca L. Walkowitz (New York: Routledge, 1993).

16. Margaret Cohen, "The *Homme fatal,* the Phallic Father, and the New Man," *Cultural Critique* 23 (1993): 131. See also Cindy Patton, "What Is a Nice Lesbian Like You Doing in a Film Like This?" for another look at *Internal Affairs* and the way it centers its vision of moral justice, not on the Latino male hero or bad white male dirty cops, but instead on a white lesbian who seems to be the only person in the movie who can daily tell right from wrong.

17. Male cops almost always romance their female partners. When they do not, they are already dating or married, of the wrong race (black male cop/white female pairings do not occur until 1998's *U.S. Marshalls*), or physically unable because they are cyborgs or dead (*Dead Heat*). At the extreme of heterosexual aggression, heroes of *Basic Instinct* and *Rush* rape their female colleagues, and the hero of *Blade Runner* appears to be ready to do the same if his civilian lover does not go along. Though no other heroes attack women with his level of force, and the coercion of women generally marks a man as a criminal bound for death, these heroes are simply outliers on a continuum of heterosexual entitlement among cops at work. The exception to the pattern of women romanced is the stalwart hero of *The Silence of the Lambs,* whose disinterest in heterosexuality is justly famous among analysts and fans.

18. *Basic Instinct*'s conclusion vexes many, so I should acknowledge that others might read it differently. The movie's authors, however, claim to intend what I interpret: that Catherine did it all and will do more when she damn well pleases. The foolish, misogynist hero will die screaming before long. I like that.

19. They are played by such actors as Charles Bronson, Nicholas Cage, Robert De Niro, Clint Eastwood, Harrison Ford, Mel Gibson, Gene Hackman, Chuck Norris, Al Pacino, Jason Patrick, Keanu Reeves, Burt Reynolds, Arnold Schwarzenegger, Steven Seagal, Sylvester Stallone, Bruce Willis, and Jean-Claude Van Damme, all brunettes.

20. "Harry doesn't play any favorites," says a white male cop of the title character of *Dirty Harry* (1971). "Harry hates everybody: Limies, micks, hebes, dagos, niggers, honkies, chinks."

"How does he feel about Mexicans?" asks sidekick Chico Gonzalez.

"Ask him."

"Especially spics," says Harry with a wink to his friend.

21. See bell hooks, "Doing It for Daddy," in *Constructing Masculinity,* ed. Maurice Berger, Brian Wallis, and Simon Watson (New York: Routledge, 1995), p. 104. Sometimes reading these analyses makes me wonder whether I and the authors have seen the same movies. The black hero of *Rising Sun* (hero because introduced first, followed to the end of the story, given more

attention to his domestic life, more time on screen, greater skill in combat, etc.) begins to flirt with the white sidekick's girlfriend in the last scene of the movie. Does such flirtation count as "falling in love?" Also, the description of this cop hero as "happily do[ing] as the master orders him, always eager to please," seems odd.

22. David Ehrenstein, "War Business," *Sight and Sound* 3, 10 (1993): 13.

23. Paul S. Cowen, "A Social-Cognitive Approach to Ethnicity in Films," in *Unspeakable Images: Ethnicity and the American Cinema*, ed. Lester D. (Chicago: University of Chicago Press, 1991), p. 373.

24. Ibid., p. 374

25. Ibid., p. 375.

26. Donald Bogle, *Toms, Coons, Mulattoes, Mammies, and Bucks: An Interpretive History of Blacks in American Films* (New York: Continuum, 1991), p. 276.

27. Ibid., p. 281.

28. Ibid., p. 282.

29. Manthia Diawara, "Black Spectatorship: Problems of Identification and Resistance," *Screen* 29, 4 (1988): 71.

30. Ed Guerrero, *Framing Blackness: The African American Image in Film* (Philadelphia: Temple University Press, 1993), p. 126.

31. Bogle, *Toms, Coons, Mulattoes, Mammies, and Bucks*, p. 284.

32. Ibid., p. 285.

33. Constance Penley, "Crackers and Whackers: The White Trashing of Porn," in *White Trash: Race and Class in America*, ed. Matt Wray and Annalee Newitz (New York: Routledge, 1997).

34. The professional-class sidekick mocks the working-class white hero of *Midnight Run:* "Do you know why you have an ulcer? Because you have two forms of expression: silence and rage." The hero seethes in silence.

35. See Susan Jeffords, "The Big Switch: Hollywood Masculinity in the Nineties," in *Film Theory Goes to the Movies,* ed. Jim Collins, Hilary Radner, and Ava Preacher Collins (New York: Routledge, 1993); and Fred Pfeil, *White Guys: Studies in Postmodern Domination and Difference* (New York: Verso, 1995).

Chapter Five

1. *Dances with Wolves* (1990), though more a "sensitive man" western than a cop action movie (and, like many contemporary westerns, more sentimental about the helplessness and moral purity of nonwhite peoples than is cop action), presents the most extreme version of this. The hero so resents the predations on Native Americans of the other white agents of law en-

forcement that he wishes not to be one anymore ("Turned injun, didn't ya," scoffs a prouder soldier). After a violent bonding experience with the tribe of Lakota who have welcomed him into their home, the hero, John, narrates, "I felt a pride I had never felt before. I'd never known who John Dunbar was. Perhaps the name itself had no meaning. But as I heard my Sioux name being called over and over, I knew for the first time who I really was." Later, severely beaten, face covered with blood, he proclaims to his white interrogators his Sioux name as the ultimate defiance. I return to the role of violent martyrdom in contemporary fantasy below.

2. Jacquie Jones notes that *Deep Cover,* with its black male hero, uncovers "the inability, or unwillingness of the law to adequately meet the needs of the [African American] community" and "validates a Black Nationalist agenda." See Jones, "Under the Cover of Blackness," *Black Film Review* 7, 3 (1992): p. 33. Jones argues further that this plotting subverts "the assumptions and very tenets of the mainstream action movie" and effects "a hybridization of cinematic traditions." I argue in the Appendix that all genres mix their elements and that cop action mixes, among other things, blaxploitation (*Shaft, Cleopatra Jones*) and liberal conspiracy theory plots (*Magnum Force, Serpico*). *Deep Cover* was directed by a black man—Bill Duke—and is thus very unusual in that respect of its production (though Kevin Hooks directed *Passenger 57* and *Fled*). In most other respects, however, it strikes me as being just another white-male authored, paranoid, antigovernment, antiracist, antidrug, pro-violence action movie.

3. See Carol J. Clover, *Men, Women, and Chainsaws: Gender and the Modern Horror Film* (Princeton, N.J.: Princeton University Press, 1992).

4. See Paul Smith, *Clint Eastwood: A Cultural Production* (Minneapolis: University of Minnesota Press, 1993), p. 133.

5. These brief appearances, with their explicit political references, are among the few in white-produced film. They occur in non–cop action movies written or produced by Robert Zemeckis and Bob Gale, including *1941,* the *Back to the Future* movies, *Trespass,* and *Forrest Gump,* as well as those directed by Walter Hill, which include *Trespass* and the cop action movies *48 Hours, Another 48 Hours, Extreme Prejudice,* and *Red Heat.*

6. Disagreement arises here, of course. Manthia Diawara, working within a dominance/resistance framework, argues that the black man in *48 Hours* is "punished" afterward by the next fight he gets into, a long bout of fisticuffs with the white hero. See Diawara, "Black Spectatorship: Problems of Identification and Resistance," *Screen* 29, 4 (1988): 71. I see the fight as a stand-off broken up by others before the hero and sidekick can beat each other into unconsciousness. (Diawara holds out the possibility that "resisting spectators" [ibid., 75], by which he means black spectators [ibid., p. 66],

could read such movies differently than he does.) I return to the reading of such *mano a mano* violence as a force of "punishment" or "discipline" in Chapter 7. I analyze it also as a form of erotic fun in which such men come as close to equality as they are going to get in this world.

7. See, for instance, Susan Jeffords, *Hard Bodies: Hollywood Masculinity in the Reagan Era* (New Brunswick, N.J.: Rutgers University Press, 1994), pp. 125, 6.

8. See Andrew Ross, "The Great White Dude," in *Constructing Masculinity,* ed. Maurice Berger, Brian Wallis, and Simon Watson (New York: Routlege, 1995), p. 170.

9. Ibid.

10. See Christopher Ames, "Restoring the Black Man's Lethal Weapon: Race and Sexuality in Contemporary Cop Films," *Journal of Popular Film and Television* 20 (1992): 52–60; David Bogle, *Toms, Cooons, Mulattoes, Mammies, and Bucks: An Interpretive History of Black in American Film* (New York: Continuum, 1991); Paul S. Cowen, "A Social-Cognitive Approach to Ethnicity in Films," Cynthia J. Fuchs, "The Buddy Politic," in *Screening the Male: Exploring Masculinities in Hollywood Cinema,* ed. Steven Cohan and Ina Rae Hark (New York: Routledge, 1993); bell hooks, "Doing it for Daddy," in *Constructing Masculinity,* ed. Berger, Wallis, and Watson; Susan Jeffords, "The Big Switch: Hollywood Masculinity in the Nineties," in *Film Theory Goes to the Movies,* ed. Jim Collins, Hilary Radner, and Ava Preacher Collins (New York: Routledge, 1993), and *Hard Bodies;* Tania Modleski, *Feminism Without Women: Culture and Criticism in a "Postfeminist" Age* (New York: Routledge, 1991); Fred Pfeil, *White Guys: Studies in Postmodern Domination and Difference* (New York: Verso, 1995); Smith, *Clint Eastwood;* Yvonne Tasker, *Spectacular Bodies: Gender, Genre, and the Action Cinema* (New York: Routledge, 1993); and Robyn Wiegman, "Black Bodies/American Commodities: Gender, Race, and the Bourgeois Ideal in Contemporary Film," in *Unspeakable Images,* ed. Friedman, and *American Anatomies: Theorizing Race and Gender* (Durham, N.C.: Duke University Press, 1995).

11. Though I would hardly follow Tasker in arguing that the movie "operates without any explicit reference to racial difference," I see little open racial conflict in *Lethal Weapon,* perhaps in part because producers intended the sidekick role for Nick Nolte, the white actor who plays the heroes of *Extreme Prejudice, Mulholland Falls,* and the *48 Hours* movies, as well as the racist rogue cop of *Q & A.* See Tasker, *Spectacular Bodies,* p. 45.

12. In *Lethal Weapon 4* Chinese slave traders complete the picture of "Lethal Weapon" evil. The race of evil changes, but nonwhites remain the victimized group. Roger certainly identifies with the Chinese as "slaves" ("I'm freeing slaves!" he cries).

13. Tasker, *Spectacular Bodies,* p. 45; Wiegman, *American Anatomies,* pp. 138–40.

14. See hooks, "Doing It for Daddy," p. 105.

15. This moment completes a subplot originating in an earlier scene in which Roger, after chastising Martin for his overkill approach to the job, fails to disarm a criminal and so allows him to endanger both cops. He has to apologize to Martin and says no more about the white hero's paranoid violence. In this later fight, however, Martin fails to stop a criminal and so allows him to threaten Roger's family. Roger takes the lead in blowing this Aryan bad guy away. Though white male heroes take many opportunities to demonstrate their skill at the job, black sidekicks tend to prove their own worth at the end, in part perhaps because they defend their own lives, families, and homes.

Chapter Six

1. The few obviously Jewish men in the genre are mostly lawyers and accountants, and the Jewish women usually their wives. Sometimes they are the butts of humor, as in *Beverly Hills Cop 2.* Rarely are they hurt, though the three exceptions are interesting: The Jewish lawyer in *Innocent Blood* dies in the silly high style of every other vampire in the movie. The death of a hassid in *A Stranger Among Us,* in contrast, counts as a major tragedy and friends mourn him for several long scenes. The nastiest fate met by an apparently Jewish character is that of the lawyer Eli Gould in *Se7en*—forced to hack away a pound of his flesh in the tradition of an anti-Semitic play by a Roman Catholic serial killer. We see his wife grieve in case anyone wonders whether the man was loved. Such rituals of mourning for civilian victims are rare in cop action. These scenes in *Se7en, A Stranger Among Us,* and the funeral for a black kid in *Lethal Weapon 3* are among the few. Thus does cop action find another way to associate familial love with every group but WASP men.

2. *Die Hard* contrast the deaths of an Asian American and a white guy. A brave and dignified Japanese businessman guards his huge corporate fortune and so meets a quick end. His death results in a loud musical chord of shock and the hero's equally shocked expression. Others gasp in horror when they hear the news. On the other hand, a craven white male executive, a coke head and sex harasser, is mocked by criminals and chastised by the hero before he dies. No one grieves.

3. See Robert C. Fuller, *Naming the Antichrist: The History of an American Obsession* (New York: Oxford University, 1995); and Jon Oplinger, *The*

Politics of Demonology: The European Witchcraze and the Mass Production of Deviance (Selinsgrove, Pa.: Susquehanna University Press, 1990).

4. Andrew Delbanco, *The Death of Satan* (New York: Farrar, Straus and Giroux, 1995), p. 182.

5. Ibid., p. 182.

6. See Barbara Ehrenreich, *Fear of Falling: The Inner Life of the Middle Class* (New York: Harper, 1989), p. 253.

7. Ibid., p. 253.

8. See Delbanco, *The Death of Satan*; Alisa Solomon, "The Eternal Queer," *The Village Voice*, April 27, 1993, pp. 29, 34; and Philips Stevens, "The Demonology of Satanism: An Anthropological View," in *The Satanism Scare*, ed. James T. Richardson, Joel Best, and David G. Bromley (New York: Aldine de Gruyter, 1991).

Chapter Seven

1. In 1998's sequel, *Lethal Weapon 4*, all parties end up in the hospital gathered around this sidekick and another young woman (sidekick Roger's daughter) who have just given birth. They celebrate "family!"

2. In the 1976 "dirty" Harry movie *The Enforcer*, sidekick Kate asks Harry about his large weapon, a "great big forty-four. Every other cop in this city is satisfied with a thirty-eight or a three-fifty-seven. What do you have to carry that cannon for?"

"Because I hit what I aim at, that's why," says Harry. "Three-fifty-seven's a good weapon, but I've seen thirty-eights careen off windshields—no good in a city like this."

"I see. So it's for the penetration," says Kate with a meaningful look.

"Does everything have a sexual connotation with you?"

"Only sometimes."

For once, Harry is impressed: "Want to go have a few beers?" he asks, with no apparent (heterosexual) romantic intent. The exchange stands out against most cop action banter, for women rarely interest themselves in the eros of gunplay.

3. The crucified male figure does not show up that often (mostly in Sylvester Stallone and Arnold Schwarzenegger movies), but when it does it makes me think of all of the other sweaty bare-chested male bodies. The brief moments in *Die Hard*, in which a wildman nemesis slams the hero's body spread-eagled onto a wooden frame, and that hero's wife later looks upon his wounds with a hushed "Jesus," certainly point to the fleshly sacrifice of a spurned hero. I would also retitle *Hard to Kill* as *Jesus Kicks Ass*. For a more

general analysis of Jesus on screen, see Peter Malone, *Movie Christs and Antichrists* (New York: Crossroad, 1990).

4. For *Beverly Hills Cop,* see Trey Ellis, "The Gay Subtext in *Beverly Hills Cop,*" *Black Film Review* 3, 2 (1987): 15–17; For *Deep Cover,* see Kendall Thomas, " 'Masculinity,' 'The Rule of Law,' and Other Legal Fictions," in *Constructing Masculinity,* ed. Maurice Berger, Brian Wallis, and Simon Watson (New York: Routledge, 1995). For *Die Hard* see Ann Ardis and Dale M. Bauer, " 'Just the Fax, Ma'am': Male Sentimentality in the *Die Hard* Films," *Arizona Quarterly* 47, 2 (1991): 117–29. For *Falling Down* see Richard Dyer, *White* (New York: Routledge, 1997). For *Lethal Weapon,* see Tania Modleski, *Feminism Without Women: Culture and Criticism* in a "Postfeminist" Age (New York: Routledge, 1991). For *Midnight Run,* see Ina Rae Hark, "Yuppie Critique and the Buddy-Road Movie in the 1980s," in *The Road Movie Book,* ed. Steven Cohan and Ina Rae Hark (New York: Routledge, 1997). For *Sea of Love* and *To Live and Die in L.A.,* see Sharon Willis, *High Contrast* (Durham, N.C.: Duke University Press, 1997). For *Total Recall* see Jonathan Goldberg, "Recalling Totalities: The Mirrored Stages of Arnold Schwarzenegger," *differences* 4, 1 (1992): 172–204.

5. See Alan Bray, *Homosexuality in Renaissance England* (London: Gay Men's Press, 1982); Jonathan Goldberg, ed., *Reclaiming Sodom* (New York: Routledge, 1994); and Michael Warner, "New English Sodom" in *Queering the Renaissance,* Jonathan Goldberg, ed. (Durham, N.C.: Duke University Press, 1994).

6. Eve Kosofsky Sedgwick, *Tendencies* (Durham, N.C.: Duke University Press, 1993), pp. 50, 51.

7. See Eve Kosofsky Sedgwick, *Between Men: English Literature and Male Homosocial Desire* (New York: Columbia University, 1985), p. 89.

8. As I argue further, below, cop action bears down on exchanges among men, not least those of fluid in the heat of combat. *Demolition Man* features the only straight sexual partners to pose sex in terms of "disgusting fluid transfer." In the twenty-first century, the female sidekick informs her paramour that, "the rampant exchange of bodily fluids was one of the major reasons for the downfall of society." She recoils from the idea of kissing and fucking, but then finally changes her mind in part because she is such a try-anything thrill seeker—trying to be one of the boys.

9. Bray, *Homosexuality in Renaissance England,* p. 26.

10. Goldberg "Introduction," in *Reclaiming Sodom,* p. 6.

11. Warner "New English Sodom," p. 331.

12. Eve Kosofsky Sedgwick, *Epistemology of the Closet,* (Berkeley and Los Angeles: University of California Press, 1990), p. 185.

13. See Christopher Newfield, *The Emerson Effect: Individualism and Submission in America* (Chicago: University of Chicago Press, 1996), p. 95.

14. See Tomás Almaguer, "Chicano Men: A Cartography of Homosexual Identity and Behavior," *differences* 3, 2 (1991): 75–100; Ana Maria Alonso and Maria Teresa Koreck, "Silences: 'Hispanics,' AIDS, and Sexual Practices," *differences* 1, 1 (1989): 101–24; Leo Bersani, "Is the Rectum a Grave?" *October* 43 (1987): 197–222; Andrea Dworkin, *Intercourse* (New York: Free Press, 1987); Michel Foucault, *The Use of Pleasure,* trans. Robert Hurley (New York: Vintage, 1985).

15. Bersani, "Is the Rectum a Grave?" p.212.

16. Cops do not compare penises and guns around women, perhaps feeling that such metaphors bear articulation only between men. The single exception comes in a scene in *Excessive Force* in which cop Terry arms his endangered girlfriend. Standing close to her on the street, he says, "I want you to feel something."

The woman objects: "Terry!"

"Feel it."

She is self-conscious. "That boy can see us."

"I want you to take it out, slow. Go on, do it." She does so. "Good girl. Now when I get home tonight, I'm going to teach you how to shoot it." The woman looks appalled by all of this, the cop looks excited.

17. See Bray, *Homosexuality in Renaissance England;* Sedgwick, *Between Men,* p. 89.

18. See Robin Wood, *Hollywood. From Vietnam to Reagan* (New York: Columbia University Press, 1986), p. 293.

19. Modleski, *Feminism Without Women,* p. 145.

20. See Paul Smith, *Clint Eastwood: A Cultural Production,* (Minneapolis: University of Minnesota Press, 1993), p. 185. Pop press reviewers have written the same of criminals in such movies as *Die Hard, The Hard Way,* and *The Last Boy Scout,* though to my frustration none ever tells us why he or she thinks anyone is gay. Smith does this with the early "dirty" Harry movie *The Enforcer* (1976), in which Harry blows away the androgenous male criminals in order to keep the relations among male cops "free of any perverse taint" (ibid., p. 143). Smith also argues, without elaborating, that the teaming of white and black male cops in the killing of a criminal "specifically portrayed as gay" draws upon "the rather painful prevalence of homophobia in black American culture" (ibid., p. 185). Of course, Smith can blame collusion with black homophobia (huh?) only after already deciding with no obvious warrant either that a criminal (in this case from *Beverly Hills Cop*) about whose sex life we know nothing is homosexual, or that somebody (besides Smith) thinks that he is. In any case, I can only think that cops make a lot more sense than this analytic logic.

21. Cynthia J. Fuchs, "The Buddy Politic," in *Screening the Male: Exploring Masculinities in Hollywood Cinema,* ed. Steven Cohan and Ina Rae Hark (New York: Routledge, 1993), p. 196.

22. Ibid., p. 197.

23. Ibid., p. 199.

24. Robyn Wiegman, *American Anatomies: Theorizing Race and Gender,* (Durham, N.C.: Duke University Press, 1995), p. 228 n16.

25. Ibid., p. 141.

26. See Steve Neale, "Masculinity as Spectacle: Reflections on Men and Mainstream Cinema," in *Screening the Male,* ed. Cohan and Hark, p. 16.

27. See Christine Holmlund, "Masculinity as Multiple Masquerade: The 'Mature' Stallone and the Stallone Clone," in *Screening the Male,* ed. Cohn and Hark, 16.

28. See Christopher Ames, "Restoring the Black Man's Lethal Weapon: Race and Sexuality in Contemporary Cop Films," *Journal of Popular Film and Television* 20 (1992): 58; Christian M. Chensvold, "*Speed,* Nietzsche and the American Cultural Palate," *Films in Review* 46, 1/2 (1995): 8–11; Christine Holmlund, "'Cruisin' for a Bruisin': Hollywood's Deadly (Lesbian) Dolls," *Cinema Journal* 34, 1 (1994): 41; Susan Jeffords, *Hard Bodies: Hollywood Masculinity in the Reagan Era* (New Brunswick, N.J.: Rutgers University Press, 1994), p. 155. For helpful exceptions, see Dyer, *White;* Fred Pfeil, *White Guys Studies in Postmodern Domination and Difference* (New York: Verso, 1995); and Steven Shaviro, *The Cinematic Body* (Minneapolis: University of Minnesota Press, 1993).

29. See Michael Paul Rogin, *Ronald Reagan, the Movie* (Berkeley and Los Angeles: University of California Press, 1987), p. 106.

30. Yvonne Tasker, *Spectacular Bodies: Gender, Genre, and the Action Cinema* (New York: Routledge, 1993), p. 90.

31. One could define homophobia in different ways, of course. Writes Lynda Hart of the possibility of displacement in *Basic Instinct:* "I do not think there are *any* lesbians in *Basic Instinct,* which invalidates the claim that the film is homophobic due to its negative portrayals of lesbian/bisexual women. Nevertheless, *Basic Instinct* is surely a homophobic film in the sense that it renders visible the systemic homophobia of masculine heterosexual desire." See Hart, *Fatal Women* (Princeton, N.J.: Princeton University Press, 1994), p. 134. Thus the genre does not so much displace deviance onto those who might be "clearly" homosexual, as invest in the hero's panic over his heterosexual status. I would not label a movie homophobic for rendering visible the workings of masculine heterosexual desire; but I would agree that *Basic Instinct* deals with heterosexual male panic. Thus may the movie become useless to those looking for queer images to celebrate, even while it

says much about straight white guys, their problems, and the fates they might deserve.

32. Chensvold, "*Speed,* Nietzsche," p. 9.

33. D. A. Miller, *The Novel and the Police* (Berkeley and Los Angeles: University of California Press, 1988), p. 147.

34. Carol J. Clover, *Men, Women, and Chainsaws: Gender and the Modern Horror Film* (Princeton, N.J.: Princeton University Press, 1992), p. 225.

35. Richard Dyer, "Action!" *Sight and Sound* 4, 10 (1994): 10.

36. See Michel Foucault, *The History of Sexuality,* Volume 1, *An Introduction,* trans. Robert Hurley (New York: Vintage, 1980).

37. Ibid., p.47.

38. Smith, *Clint Eastwood,* p. 138.

39. See Bersani, "Is the Rectum a Grave?" p. 210. He reviews the work of feminist theorists (Dworkin, *Intercourse;* and Catharine A. MacKinnon, *Toward a Feminist Theory of the State* [Cambridge: Harvard University Press, 1989]) on the links men make between sexual penetration and defilement and then suggests that this rough treatment of "the masculine ideal (an ideal shared—differently—by men and women) of proud subjectivity" (Bersani, "Is the Rectum a Grave?" p. 222) may be exactly what a homophobic society requires before it will relax its collective sphincter. As Dworkin's and MacKinnon's analyses of heterosexual violence make abundantly clear, though, this drive toward masochistic dissolution will probably not work for most women. If we are to solve problems of brutal sexual aggression and most other warfare, then it's men who need to stop worrying and love the experience of being penetrated.

40. Ibid., p. 211.

41. Jack Katz, *Seductions of Crime: Moral and Sensual Attractions in Doing Evil* (New York: Basic Books, 1988).

42. The novel *The Silence of the Lambs* raises the question that nobody asks in cop action: How does the female hero manage her rage? The hero never answers; she just hunts down the serial killer of women and blows him away. Thomas Harris, *The Silence of the Lambs* (New York: St. Martin's, 1988).

43. Pfeil, *White Guys,* p. 66.

44. Ibid. p. 14.

45. See Linda Williams, "Film Body: An Implantation of Perversions," in *Explorations in Film Theory: Selected Essays from Cine-tracts,* ed. Ron Burnett (Bloomington: Indiana University Press, 1991).

46. Miller, *The Novel and the Police.*

47. Linda Williams, *Hardcore: Power, Pleasure and "Frenzy of the Visible,"* (Berkeley and Los Angeles: University of California Press, 1989), p. 72.

48. On porn, see ibid; on melodrama, see Christine Gledhill, ed., *Home*

Is Where the Heart Is: Studies in Melodrama and the Woman's Film (London: British Film Institute, 1987); on horror, see Clover, *Men, Women, and Chainsaws.*

49. The unfortunate characters enter the immediate and sometimes overwhelming presence of physical pain, the aversive sensation that, in Elaine Scarry's words, signals sentience and life. This pain, direct or vicarious, is belief. "The fragility of the human interior and the absolute surrender of that interior . . . does not simply accompany belief . . . is not simply required by belief, but . . . *is itself belief*—the endowing of the most concrete and intimate parts of oneself with an objectified referent." See Scarry, *The Body in Pain* (New York: Oxford University Press, 1985), p. 204. Indeed, the sight of violence to a man's crotch usually draws grimaces and groans from male onlookers. Similar shots line these movies, and the link bears more study than it has so far received. I have felt the difference in the way my body feels after seeing such fights. If researchers into the effect of porn are to be believed, then that genre may have similar effect. Immediately after the fights, and perhaps for quite a while, viewers may simply feel different: meaner, sexier, tougher, smarter, whatever. This is the power of movies.

50. See Jude Davies, "Gender, Ethnicity and Cultural Crisis in *Falling Down* and *Groundhog Day,*" *Screen* 36, 3 (1995): 221.

51. Katz, *Seductions of Crime.*

52. In a consideration of action movie masochism, William Warner observes the tension in *Rambo* movies between overwhelming bureaucratic state systems and the traumatized individual self. See Warner, "Spectacular Action: Rambo and the Popular Pleasures of Pain," in *Cultural Studies,* ed. Lawrence Grossberg, Cary Nelson, and Paula Treichler (New York: Routledge, 1992). *First Blood* and the *Rambo* movies stage masochistic dramas of the punishment of this Oedipal son deprived of liberty and the pursuit of happiness by the stern, deceitful father. That is, the hero suffers mightily at the hands of foreign powers and the U.S. military bureaucrats who exploit and abandon him. Perhaps Rambo feels guilty over losing so much ground to this system—for believing his lying fathers, for ceding his liberties until they are all taken away, for participating in his own ruin. Over the course of the movies he suffers, often enough at his own hand, in some spectacular scenes of physical torture. Finally Rambo bounces back to author the punishment of everyone who crossed him. The different genre produces a different take on white manhood: The main white male criminals get away with their lives in the first two movies (*First Blood* and *Rambo: First Blood Part II*). The third movie does not offer even a duplicitous agent of the government for Rambo to kill or not. The portrayal of villainy and penance thus differs in an important way.

53. Wiegman, *American Anatomies,* pp. 109–10.

54. Pfeil, *White Guys,* p. 28.

55. Indeed, I quibble merely with Pfeil's distinction between 1980s and 1990s fare. He argues that the more recent cop movies reject coherence and even further abdicate breadwinning and *polis*-ruling responsibility. I reject the first view on principle and respond to the second by thinking of "dirty" Harry throwing his badge into the bay in 1971, and *Cruising*'s hero heading off into who-knows-what-sort-of-deviance in 1980. In my view, cops have long ceded contested privileges and responsibilities, as long as they could earn attention while doing so.

56. Newfield reviews reactions to the famously homoerotic work of Walt Whitman, in which, according to his offended reviewers, Whitman's deviance comes across as a "dirty excitability which identifies him as a man of the herd. Like any member of a crowd, Whitman is imbecilic under the pressure of 'strong excitement,' but adopts a false 'superiority' that allows him to disregard established rules and follow his own." See Newfield, *The Emerson Effect*, p. 94. Newfield describes the threat that manly crowds pose to a social order built on hierarchy, in which loyalty to established authority props a patriarchy. "For Freud," Newfield notes, "the ties between members of a group can overwhelm the ties between members and leader, causing the leader to be overthrown" (ibid., p. 113). When they're not busy abusing women and disenfranchised men, manly crowds can also work against traditional order. In cop utopia heroes give up some authority for the alternate privilege of lawless and bloody play that also happens to remind the world of the superiority of their skills.

57. Barbara Ehrenreich, "The Decline of Patriarchy," in *Constructing Masculinity,* ed. Berger, Wallis, and Watson.

Conclusion

1. Paul Smith, *Clint Eastwood: A Cultural Production* (Minneapolis: University of Minnesota Press, 1993) p. 93.

2. Ibid., pp. 103, 107.

3. Susan Jeffords, *Hard Bodies: Hollywood Masculinity in the Reagan Era* (New Brunswick, N.J.: Rutgers University Press, 1994) pp. 62–63.

4. Robert Miklitsch, "*Total Recall:* Production, Revolution, Simulation-Alienation Effect," *Camera Obscura* 32 (1993): 28.

Appendix

1. I used international release as my criterion because it most safely rules out direct-to-video product. But, I have made six exceptions in the cases of

movies that I know to have been given general theatrical release in this country but not internationally (*8 Million Ways to Die,* 1986; *Excessive Force,* 1992; *Jennifer 8,* 1992; *Low Down Dirty Shame,* 1994; and *Showdown in Little Tokyo,* 1991), or that were produced for theatrical release and then snatched up for cable presentation at the last moment (*Extreme Justice,* 1993). All of these movies seem to be well known both among fans and in the literature in ways that their direct-to-video cousins are not.

2. See Stuart Kaminsky, *American Film Genres* (Chicago: Nelson-Hall, 1985); and Robert Reiner, "Keystone to Kojak: The Hollywood Cop," in *Cinema, Politics, and Society in America,* ed. Philip J. Davies and Brian Neve (Manchester: Manchester University Press, 1981), and *The Politics of the Police* (Toronto: University of Toronto, 1992) for useful overviews.

3. Reiner, "Keystone to Kojak," p. 208.

4. Ibid., p. 211.

5. See Kaminsky, *American Film Genres;* Will Wright, *Sixguns and Society: A Structural Study of the Western* (Berkeley and Los Angeles: University of California Press, 1975); John Cawelti, *Adventure, Mystery, and Romance: Formula Stories as Popular Art and Popular Culture* (Chicago: University of Chicago Press, 1976); Joan Copjec, ed., *Shades of Noir* (London: Verso, 1993); Bruce Crowther, *Captured on Film: The Prison Movie* (London: Batsford, 1989); Carol J. Clover, *Men, Women, and Chainsaws: Gender and the Modern Horror Film* (Princeton, N.J.: Princeton University Press, 1992); Stephen C. LeSueur and Dean Rehberger, "*Rocky IV, Rambo II* [*sic*], and the Place of the Individual in Modern American Society," *Journal of American Culture* 11, 2 (1988): 25–33; Elizabeth G. Traube, "Redeeming Images: The Wild Man Comes Home," *Persistence of Vision* 3–4 (1986): 71–94; Nelson George, *Blackface: Reflections on African Americans and the Movies* (New York: Harper Collins, 1994); Ed Guerrero, *Framing Blackness: The African American Image in Film* (Philadelphia: Temple University Press, 1993). Maurice Yacuwar, "The Bug in the Rug: Notes on the Disaster Genre," in *Film Genre Reader,* ed. Barry Keith Grant (Austin: University of Texas Press, 1986).

6. See Fredric Jameson, *Signatures of the Visible* (New York: Routledge, 1990), p. 20.

7. Clover, *Men, Women, and Chainsaws,* p. 11.

8. For analyses see Robin Wood *Hollywood from Vietnam to Reagan,* (New York: Columbia University Press, 1986), p. 222.

9. See Stanford M. Lyman, "Anhedonia: Gender and the Decline of Emotions in American Film, 1930–1988," *Sociological Inquiry* 60, 1 (1990): 3–19.

10. See Cawelti, *Adventure, Mystery, and Romance;* and Wright, *Sixguns and Society.*

11. See Teresa de Lauretis, *Alice Doesn't: Feminism, Semiotics, Cinema* (Bloomington: Indiana University Press, 1984), p. 112; and Jean LaPlanche and Jean-Bertrand Pontalis, "Fantasy and the Origins of Sexuality," in *Formations of Fantasy,* ed. Victor Burgin, James Donald, and Cora Kaplan (New York: Routledge, 1989), p. 19.

12. See Elizabeth Cowie, "Fantasia," in *The Woman in Question,* ed. Parveen Adams and Elizabeth Cowie (Cambridge: MIT Press), p. 163.

13. See Gina Marchetti, "Action-Adventure and Ideology," in *Cultural Politics in Contemporary America,* ed. Ian Angus and Sut Jhally (New York: Routledge, 1989), p. 187.

14. See Wright, *Sixguns and Society,* p. 193.

15. See Michael Ryan and Douglas Kellner, *Camera Politica: The Politics and Ideology of Contemporary Hollywood Film* (Bloomington: Indiana University Press, 1988): p. 94.

16. See Susan Jeffords, *Hard Bodies: Hollywood Masculinity in the Reagan Era* (New Brunswick, N.J.: Rutgers University Press, 1994).

17. Variations on these continual abound, but Raymond Williams and Stuart Hall have influenced many. Williams recommends that we "speak of the 'dominant' and the 'effective', and in these senses of the hegemonic." See Williams, *Marxism and Literature* (Oxford: Oxford University Press, 1977), p. 121. In contrast, "emergent" meanings are "new," substantially alternative or oppositional. Hall carries these ideas forward by defining "*dominant-hegemonic*" as the interpretation that takes the meaning "full and straight" and "decodes in terms of the reference code in which [the object] has been encoded." See Hall, "Encoding/Decoding," in *The Cultural Studies Reader,* ed. Simon During (New York: Routledge, 1993), p. 101. Hall elaborates by defining a "preferred" meaning as one both intended by the object's producers and structured by the means of production. See Hall, "Reflections Upon the Encoding/Decoding Model: An Interview," in *Viewing, Reading, Listening: Audiences and Cultural Reception,* ed. Jon Cruz and Justin Lewis (San Francisco: Westview, 1994), p. 261–62. In contrast, "negotiated" and the more extreme "oppositional" interpretations are those that "make their own ground rules" ("Encoding/Decoding," p. 102) and "decode the message in a *globally* contrary way" (ibid, p. 103). Both Hall ("Reflections," p. 266) and Williams (*Marxism and Literature,* pp. 122–23) warn that in practice people will find these meanings and readings really difficult to distinguish (see n.19 below).

18. See Hall, "Reflections," p. 266.

19. Certainly analysts who want to discuss inequality are going to have to understand how such authoritative "rightness" works. Such study merits interpretative research not offered by the viewing of a movie. For instance,

one could keep track of objections such as "that's stretching it" or "you're just reading that into it" among viewers confronted with various interpretations. But, Hall actually warns against recourse to audience study in articulation of a "preferred reading," on the grounds that audiences cannot be relied upon to "decode" texts in the preferred manner, and in fact are likely to "read against the grain." See Hall, "Reflections," p. 266. The unruly behavior of mass audiences leaves Hall with little use for his "Encoding/Decoding" scheme in his own research (ibid., pp. 272–73).

20. See Janet Staiger, *Interpreting Films: Studies in the Historical Reception of American Cinema* (Princeton, N.J.: Princeton University, 1992), p. 76; and Hall "Reflections," p. 266. One response to the problem of the interpretive circle takes another step along it by analyzing interview transcripts or movie reviews. The reception study approach has the advantage of looking at first-person accounts from a variety of people of what the films might do for them. Of course, this step along a circle of interpretion simply gives us new data to interpret rather than an escape from the circle into some noninterpretive science, whatever that might be. However, some cultural analysts disdain interpretation in favor of such hard science. For an example, see M. Gottdiener, "Hegemony and Mass Culture: A Semiotic Approach," *American Journal of Sociology* 90, 5 (1985): 979–1001.

21. See Tania Modleski, *Feminism Without Women: Culture and Criticism in a "Postfeminist" Age* (New York: Routledge, 1991), p. 44.

22. See Charles Kurzman, "Convincing Sociologists: Values and Interests in the Sociology of Knowledge," in Michael Burowoy et al., *Ethnography Unbound: Power and Resistance in the Modern Metropolis* (Berkeley and Los Angeles: University of California Press, 1991).

23. The "resistant" or "rebel" identity proves popular among politically conscious people. There may well be as many on the political right, loosely defined, who consider themselves to be the embattled resistance to the hegemony of a liberal establishment as there are leftist intellectuals who feel victimized by a conservative status quo. Labels "dominant" and "resistant" thus provide tools in a tug-of-war over the morally potent labels "powerless," "innocent," and "oppressed." In a discussion of standpoint epistemologies, in which theorists and activists prefer ways of knowing on the basis of the putative distance of the knowers from positions of power, Wendy Brown discusses the performance of this political innocence: "Reason . . . drape[s] itself in powerlessness or dispossession: it attacks by differentiating itself from the political-ontological *nature* of what it criticizes, by adopting the stance of reason against power. This desire for knowledge accounts that are innocent of power, that position us outside power, is rooted in the need to make power *answer* to reason/morality and to prohibit demands for accountability in the

opposite direction." See Brown, "Feminist Hesitations, Postmodern Exposures," *differences* 3, 1 (1991): 76. While noting the temptation that morally potent labels of innocence provide, I want to perform my own politically engaged research in another way. Even if the accountability of a researcher were not at stake, though, I still do not understand how it helps fights against, say, white supremacy, misogyny, or homophobia, to accuse those of whose behavior we disapprove of conforming to "dominant" standards of behavior as though the rest of us were not. Neither do I understand how we advance our causes by celebrating movies we enjoy as "resistant" or "subversive" when every action and object resembles *and* resists (differs from) a variety of actions and objects that surround or precede it. Everything conforms to some patterns and deviates from others. Nothing either just conforms or deviates, roots in power or stays aloof, simply dominates or resists (as the inability of theorists to advance usable criteria for these distinctions would seem to indicate). This insight founds the contemporary sociology of deviance, which studies attributions of deviance more than it elaborates them.

24. See Roland Barthes, *S/Z: An Essay,* trans. Richard Miller (New York: Noonday, 1974), p. 10.

25. See, for example, Charles Eckert, "The Anatomy of a Proletarian Film: Warner's *Marked Woman,*" in *Movies and Methods,* vol. 2, ed. Bill Nichols (Berkeley and Los Angeles: University of California Press, 1985): 409.

26. See Christine Holmlund, "Masculinity as Multiple Masquerade: The 'Mature' Stallone and the Stallone Clone," in *Screening the Male: Exploring the Masculinities in Hollywood Cinema,* ed. Steven Cohan and Ina Rae Hark (New York: Routledge, 1993), pp. 221–22.

27. Ibid., p. 225.

28. See Clifford Geertz, *The Interpretation of Cultures* (New York: Basic, 1973): p. 18.

29. See Michael Paul Rogin, *Ronald Reagan, the Movie,* (Berkeley and Los Angeles: University of California Press, 1987), p. 105.

30. Ibid., p. 106; and Guy Debord, *Society of the Spectacle* (New York: Zone, 1990).

31. I also wonder about the limited notion of "history" implicit in the amnesia argument. Presumably, this "history" refers to social relations the analyst thinks important, portrayed in a way an analyst recognizes as "explicit." But, that narrow criterion cannot indicate "history" per se. Historians have directed us to the constructed and contingent nature of all histories, and to the massive changes they undergo. It seems easy to argue that all movies tell stories and so invoke or perform histories of some sort, even if not the ones desired by the analyst. Why condemn others' versions as ahistorical? Why not regard them as products of different politics instead?

32. Geertz, *The Interpretation of Cultures*, p. 9.

33. Ibid., p. 18.

34. Like Yvonne Tasker, I am struck by the number of petty mistakes analysts of cop action make—misnamed production personnel and characters, misquoted dialogue, mistaken plot points, and other errors abound (see Tasker, *Spectacular Bodies: Gender, Genre, and the Action Cinema* [New York: Routledge, 1993], p. 60). Because analyses depend upon the details researchers cite, getting the quotations right seems important. The lack of empirical engagement characteristic of this literature both suggests an unbecoming sense of distance—Tasker calls it "textual contempt"—as though the movies were held at arm's length and produces analyses more constrained by initial suspicions than they really need to be.

35. See Clover, *Men, Women, and Chainsaws*. Clover suggests that "low," exploitation movies, by virtue of their distance from the homogenizing Hollywood machine (resistant as opposed to dominant?), more likely offer coherent moral logic, one issuing as directly as possible from our collective subconscious. I counter that any genre, even the big-budget product of Hollywood studios, can look coherent to one who studies it on a large enough scale. Sociology rests on the faith that crowds produce notable patterns.

Index